The Great
Indoors

The Great Indoors

Eric Broder

GRAY & COMPANY, PUBLISHERS
CLEVELAND

GRAY & COMPANY, PUBLISHERS
1588 E. 40th Street
Cleveland, Ohio 44103
www.grayco.com

ISBN 1-886228-34-5

Printed in the United States of America
10 9 8 7 6 5 4 3 2 1

Contents

Preface
Eric Broder: A Fascinating Case Study

As a fully licensed, trained psychology paraprofessional, I have been following the career of the writer Eric Broder with fascination for 15 years.

I first encountered the writings of Eric Broder in August 1984, when his humor column first appeared in the *Cleveland Edition*. His initial column concerned Broder's fantasies of beating up juvenile delinquents on the rapid transit and being rewarded for his efforts with large amounts of cash.

Amazingly, this piece turned out to be a microcosm of the themes Broder would explore over the next 15 years in his "Great Indoors" column. Again and again, Broder has written about his various fantasies and dreams of glory, few of which involve him leaving the comforts of his home.

As a mental health professional, I have been repeatedly struck by the tone of Broder's work. Whether he's writing about his work, social life, medical and health issues, or sex, Broder has been remarkably consistent in the total cluelessness and often pathetically self-delusional nature of his work. It's a kind of celebration of infantilism.

Note in this collection of columns a recurring reference to himself as "The Sex Machine." This grandiose self-reference is the sign, obviously, of a troubled and insecure sexuality. Additionally, his fantasies of dates with such celebrities as Madonna and Katarina Witt are abundantly clear evidence of Broder's vast and ongoing delusions of grandeur. Certainly men fantasize about attractive female icons, but Broder's public detailing of how these dates with these women "might" go is the ultimate in self-humiliation for the sake of a few laughs. It really is quite astonishing the lengths to which Broder will go to make a complete fool of himself.

In these celebrity fantasies, too, Broder takes pains to point out how little money he spends on these dates—plus his request that these ladies travel to Cleveland, at their own cost, to meet him. I am compelled by Broder's image of himself as a suave ladies' man, yet one who is not only afraid to drive a car but a complete cheapskate to boot.

Broder also spends much time discussing snack foods, such as pretzels and potato chips and his Homeric, obsessive search for the lost snack of his youth, cocktail tacos. One must presume that Broder's emphasis on "comfort foods" symbolizes a desire to return to childhood, home, perhaps even to the womb itself. "The Great Indoors," indeed.

But what I find especially interesting in many of Broder's columns is his technique of giving an imaginary dialogue with the reader where he puts his words into the reader's mouth. Consider such lines as "You ask, 'What about the toe? Tell us about the toe first,'" and "You say, 'You really had a bad experience with that cough syrup.'" Here Broder attempts to present a mutual, conspiratorial imbecility between himself and his readers. What better way to make yourself feel more intelligent than by tapping into the classic "I'm an idiot, you're an idiot" paradigm?

My mental health colleagues and I spend considerable time discussing the meaning of Broder's work. One of these colleagues dismisses Broder as a mere "nitwit" and "jerk-off," saying he writes about himself because he can't think of anything else to write about. I think it goes deeper than that. (I did once make an anonymous phone call to Broder at his office and asked him what he thought his columns meant. His reply: "I dunno . . . they're meant to be funny?" What a cunningly disingenuous response!)

I will continue to study Broder and his mental progression—or, perhaps more accurately, regression—in his "Great Indoors" columns as the years go by. In the meantime, this generous sampling of columns will provide the lay reader with an excellent introduction to this writer who, in his work, presents such a formidable challenge to mental health professionals such as myself.

Deric Droder
Licensed psychology paraprofessional
Cleveland, Ohio, September, 1999

Introduction

The book you are holding is the story of a young, slim, vital person from Cleveland—me. It is a selection of comic pieces from the *Cleveland Edition* and *Cleveland Free Times* that originally appeared in the weekly column "The Great Indoors." Thus the title of the book. But that's not the half of it.

It is also an unauthorized autobiography. It's unauthorized in the sense that though I haven't actually given myself permission to reveal these very private, behind-closed-doors aspects of my life in this book, I feel if it is to be done, it's best that I do it. Because you see, if I don't do it, no one else will. This is the very essence of being unauthorized.

You say, "Why should we read an autobiography of an obscure person who hasn't done anything of enough interest to make anybody care if it's authorized, unauthorized, or even high in fiber? What's the big payoff here?"

Fair question. But here's another one, right back at you: "Why not read it?"

Thousands of Clevelanders have been reading the column "The Great Indoors" since its inception in 1987 for no apparent good reason. No good reason but that it provides spellbinding, tantalizing delight. I suppose spellbinding, tantalizing delight isn't much in the grand scheme of things, nor even heightened sexual appetite and proficiency, which, incidentally, most of my regular readers enjoy. And I suppose spellbinding, tantalizing delight and heightened sexual appetite and proficiency aren't important to most people. In that case I apologize for being wrong about that all these years. But these delighted, sexed-up readers seem pleased, so what can I tell you?

As for the "big payoff," as you so crassly put it, there's none but this: If you read this book carefully and follow its underlying precepts, there's no telling what can happen for you, financially or otherwise. There, I've said it, I can't say any more. I've been instructed by my legal team to not make any specific promises.

All right, here's what I'm saying. Merely look at the subtext of these short comic essays. While on the surface they may appear to be pieces about the life of a slim, vital Cleveland young person, they're far more than that. Far more. And, as the material is unauthorized, nothing will be held back. Nothing! This is strictly no-holds-barred stuff. No one's censoring it, because the only one who could censor it is me, and I'm the one who's writing it. That means you get it all, every filthy thing, every dirty bit of business you can imagine, along with the possible financial advantages you'll get from reading it.

I can't say anything more about that. Legally, I'm on thin ice here.

What I can tell you, however, is that this collection includes a number of columns culled from the go-go, I-got-mine-you-get-yours Reaganomic '80s to the somewhat more demure let's-find-out-what-bioregion-we're-in '90s. This has absolutely nothing to do with these pieces, but try to think of these characteristics of our time as a background to the events described within. Or don't try to think of them. It doesn't matter to me.

My publisher has decided to place these columns in chronological order, which will approximate how people originally encountered them in the *Edition* and the *Free Times*. You may find certain themes repeated through the book.

The theme of the endless, futile, Homeric search for the lost snacks of youth. The theme of raging hypochondria and medical misinformation. The theme of enraged babies and cats. The theme of whining and sniveling at every minor inconvenience. And don't forget the theme of sexual self-delusion. That one's in there big time.

But—imagine I'm emitting a rueful, yet knowing chuckle here — isn't life itself repetitive? Isn't it all so Blondie and Dagwood, with all its rushing off to work, lying on the couch, complaining, eating sandwiches, sleeping? I think so, too. So that covers that.

As to the authenticity of these articles, I can honestly say that all are true, save for the ones in which I'm lying. But I want you to know that even I feel the reality may be a little on the dull side, so that's why I felt compelled to tart some of these stories up. And who really knows what is fact, and what is fiction? Let me put it this way: the ones with appearances by people like Katarina Witt or Bill Clinton are somewhat exaggerated, and the ones where I'm eating something nasty or complaining about being sick are pretty much as-it-happened. Keep that in mind and you won't go off the track.

The Great
Indoors

The *60 Minutes* Nightmare: Mike Wallace Comes After Me

MIKE WALLACE (*in the* 60 Minutes *studio*): The Broder File began with a phone call, made to a *60 Minutes* producer, from an Ohio dentist who told us about a patient of his who is chronically late in making payments for oral surgery performed in 1984. We investigated and discovered that the patient—a 29-year-old Cleveland man named Eric Broder—has indeed been late, sometimes by up to two weeks, with the $25 monthly installments.

We wanted to know: is a simple dental bill the only thing Eric Broder neglects in his life? We went to Cleveland and found out that this was just the tip of the iceberg in *The Broder File*—an epic of personal irresponsibility.

> **"Through videotape, we know where Broder eats, banks, shops, and goes about his daily affairs. (Pause.) And what we found isn't very pretty."**

WALLACE (*walking down Euclid Avenue in downtown Cleveland*): This is downtown Cleveland, where Eric Broder "works." (*He stops by an unmarked brown van.*) Inside this van is a television camera that has followed Broder's activities for the past month. Through videotape, we know where Broder eats, banks, shops, and goes about his daily affairs. (*Pause.*) And what we found isn't very pretty.

WALLACE (*inside a downtown bar and grille, talking to a bartender*): Eric Broder comes here for lunch nearly every day, you're telling me?

BARTENDER: That's right, almost every day.

WALLACE: What does he usually order for lunch?

BARTENDER: Nearly always a cheeseburger and chips.

WALLACE (*incredulously*): A cheeseburger and chips—*potato* chips—every day? No salad?

BARTENDER: Nope. Cheeseburger and chips. He never even eats the sliced tomato on the burger. He just leaves it there.

WALLACE: Have you ever seen him eat any vegetables, or lettuce, or anything even *remotely* nutritious?

BARTENDER: I can't say what he does at home, but I never seen him eat any of those things here.

WALLACE: Do you think that's *healthy*? How would you feel if you ate hamburgers and potato chips every day?

BARTENDER: I'd feel awful. That's just not being responsible to your body.

WALLACE (*craftily*): Does Broder ever have anything to drink with his lunch?

BARTENDER: Sometimes Diet Pepsi. Sometimes water. And sometimes . . . beer.

WALLACE (*squeals*): Beer? Are you telling the truth?

BARTENDER: (*shrugs*): Well.

WALLACE (*calming himself*): Okay. Let me ask you one more thing: does he leave you a tip? Ever?

BARTENDER: Occasionally. Never more than 10 percent.

WALLACE: So you'd say Eric Broder is one cheap customer?

BARTENDER: Well . . .

WALLACE (*driving*): Ten percent is pretty stingy, isn't it? Isn't a proper tip *at least* 15 percent?

BARTENDER: Well, yes, generally. But he dresses so ratty I figure he doesn't have the money.

WALLACE (*back on the street*): But Eric Broder *does* have the money, which we found by looking at his bank accounts. Eric Broder has in his checking account $525, and in his savings nearly one *thousand* dollars. It isn't money that's the problem.

WALLACE (*inside a downtown bookstore, talking to a clerk*): Eric Broder come in here often?

CLERK: Three, four times a week.

WALLACE: He a valued customer? or a browser?

CLERK (*laughs*): Oh, a browser. *The* browser.

WALLACE: Never buys a thing?

CLERK: Hardly ever.

WALLACE: Doesn't that strike you as a little *odd*? I mean, here's a man with a job, with money in his pocket, and he just *looks*?

CLERK: Well, he did buy something last week.

WALLACE: Which was?

CLERK: A *Penthouse*.

WALLACE (*shakes his head*): Could you repeat that?

CLERK: A *Penthouse* magazine.

WALLACE (*in disbelief*): You're telling me he doesn't buy books, but he buys *porn*?

CLERK: It's not my business. I mean, I wouldn't live like that . . . but you know . . . I don't know.

WALLACE (*now standing in front of the Ameritrust downtown office*): *Nobody* seems to know about Eric Broder. This is where Broder banks— one of Cleveland's most respected financial institutions. Employees here tell us of a customer they have who doesn't fill out deposit slips properly, who doesn't have transactions ready for the tellers, who doesn't respond to bank mailings, who doesn't keep scrupulous personal banking records. The customer's name? Eric Broder.

WALLACE (*in front of an apartment building*): This is where Eric Broder lives. We came here last week to interview Broder. (*Pause.*) This is how that interview—which was cut short—went.

WALLACE (*sitting inside Broder's apartment*): This is a nice place.

BRODER: Thank you. What's this all about? (*Eagerly.*) Is someone I know involved in some trouble?

WALLACE (*not wasting time*): There's some people in this town, Mr. Broder, who tell me you don't exactly like to spend money, that you aren't quite all there in your dealings with them, that you're late, that you're, well . . . *irresponsible.*

BRODER: Huh?

WALLACE: May I ask you something, Mr. Broder?

BRODER: Huh?

WALLACE: What'd you have for dinner tonight?

BRODER: Uh . . . Franco-American ravioli and some chips . . . and, uh . . . some milk.

WALLACE: Franco-American ravioli, chips, and milk.

BRODER (*strained heartiness*): It didn't taste good, but there was plenty of it!

WALLACE: Were you wearing those clothes? Those sweatpants? Did you put any shoes on?

BRODER: Huh?

WALLACE: Let me ask you something else. That 1968 Catalina parked behind the building. Your car?

BRODER: Well, yes, I think so . . . I . . .

WALLACE: Is it running?

BRODER: No, I gotta get it jumped.

WALLACE: You gotta get it jumped.

BRODER: Yeah, I . . .

WALLACE: Isn't it true that that car has been sitting in that lot, dead now for five months, completely ignored? You just haven't taken care of it, have you?

BRODER: Well, I was *going* to. I mean, I've been real busy lately, you see, and I haven't had time to . . .

WALLACE: When's the last time you changed your sheets?

BRODER: Now wait a minute!

WALLACE: Two weeks? *Three* weeks?

BRODER: None of your beeswax!

WALLACE: I'm asking you a simple question. *When did you last change your bed sheets?* (*Suddenly a shot of Broder jumping up and rushing toward the camera—then a blank frame.*)

WALLACE (*back in the* 60 Minutes *studio*): At that point in the interview, as you saw, Broder got up and unplugged the camerman's equipment, and then he ordered us out of his apartment. Repeated requests for another interview failed. That's the last we spoke to Eric Broder.

And what about the car that had been sitting dead in that parking lot for five months?

It's still sitting there.

(tick-tick-tick-tick-tick-tick-tick-tick)

Amazing Stories!

I suppose you think that because this column is called "The Great Indoors" its author never goes outside. Just a couch potato who watches TV and eats Smokehouse almonds all night. A shlub who shuffles around the apartment giving himself carpet shocks. A guy to whom nothing happens.

Most of that is right. I do give myself shocks because I don't pick up my feet when I walk. I'm trying to conquer this. I do watch a lot of TV, but that's my job. I cover the waterfront. I admit I lie around on my can quite a bit. However, lots of things happen to me—amazing and exciting things. And they happen indoors.

> **I was conscious of the sound it was making: whizzzzzzz. And then crash, of course. It was an exciting few seconds in my life; perhaps the most exciting.**

I'd like to begin with my most exciting indoor incident. It involves *Irma La Douce* and a roach.

My friend Barbara and I went to the video store one summer evening last year and rented two movies on videodisc, *Irma La Douce* and *A Thousand Clowns*. We watched *A Thousand Clowns*, and enjoyed it very much. It was funny and heartwarming. Thought-provoking, too. It was dynamite entertainment, and I recommend it without reservation.

Anyway, we finished watching that and put on *Irma La Douce*. This movie was directed by Billy Wilder, one of my favorites. It wasn't very good, but it was a handsome production, set in Paris and starring Jack Lemmon and Shirley MacLaine.

I should mention at this juncture that it was brutally hot and humid that night, and I was just wearing shorts. Total vulnerability! Naked human flesh that any vermin would be delighted to chew on! This is important to the story.

So we are watching this movie and having a fine time when we hear a small scuffling sound come from around the TV. We're not children. We know this is a bug or a rat. In this kind of weather you expect them. But you don't like them around, that's for sure.

I instructed our cat, Vince, to flush the animal out and kill it, but she was not interested and went away. I tiptoed over to the TV and peered behind it. There it was: a roach, a good-sized one. I could say it looked up at me and spit, but that would be embellishing an already exciting story.

I clapped my fingers against my palm like a schoolteacher to frighten it out into the open. That didn't work. I stomped my foot. The roach only moved his leg a little. At that point I decided to sit back down and just wait and enjoy the rest of *Irma La Douce*.

We didn't have to wait long. The movie was almost over when the roach came out. We expected him to run off to the side of the room somewhere and disappear. But he didn't. He came charging at us like L.A. Raider defensive lineman Howie Long! I can still hear him galloping across the room: *pittapittapittapitta*. I'd like to say I met him head on, but I squealed and bounded up onto the couch. Barbara moved fast but didn't scream like I did. The roach went under the couch.

We determined that this roach had to go or we'd be hostages to fear. I lifted the couch and there he was, going to the lavatory. Barbara put a plastic cup down on top of him. Caught! But now the hard part. Sliding the top of the container under the bug. I told Barbara that I would do this, since it was my home and thus my bug. She held the couch up, and I carefully started sliding the lid under the roach's legs.

I got him, and carried the cup to the incinerator in the apartment building's back hall. I tried to throw the roach down the incinerator, but he flew back at me and landed with a thud near my feet. I jumped around a little, then raced back into the apartment, locking him out. It was a narrow escape.

That was the roach story. This next one is a little less heroic, but again proves there is as much danger indoors as there is out.

Several years ago, I was to take a car trip up to Northern Michigan. The night before I left, I foolishly drank to excess. I woke up early, and felt keen pain all over my body—and was not at my best mentally, either.

In my little second-floor apartment I had a Carry-Cool air conditioner balanced in the window, held down by the sash. I knew I had to bring the unit in because I would be gone three weeks.

I staggered over to the window and just lifted the sash. Instantly I knew I had made a mistake. I forgot to hold on to the air conditioner.

How can I possibly convey the thrill I felt at that moment, when I knew my air conditioner was falling out of my second-story window? I was conscious of the sound it was making: *whizzzzzzz*. And then *crash*, of course. It was an exciting few seconds in my life; perhaps the most exciting. I really knew I was alive. Though at that particular time I did wish I was dead.

I looked out of the window, and down. There was the air conditioner, all right, lying on the concrete driveway. It was broken. It looked like a cartoon burlesque of a broken thing, springs coming out of it, nuts and bolts scattered. It looked like that then, anyway. I rushed outside, gathered it up, and put it by the trash.

That was it for the air conditioner.

These are just a few stories from the indoor world of adventure. I could think of plenty more, like when the Great Blizzard of '78 shattered my storm window when I had the flu. But I think I've made my point.

3/26/87

California, Here I Come

It was a crazy moment. I don't usually go off half-cocked, but I made a decision and as a result will end up in sexy hot Los Angeles, California, for three days.

No, I'm not kidding. I bought my tickets already and I'm booked on an airplane. The deed is done. My friend out there has been begging me to come visit her, and I couldn't because I had no money. I still have no money, but I have a credit card so I'm going. I'll go out there and see all the nutsies, what do I care. It won't rub off.

I get to see the ocean; that's good. I'm going to swim and take great gulps out of it. I'll show them what Cleveland dudes are made of!

I never go anywhere and was disappointed that the travel agent didn't make a big deal over the fact that I was going out to the Coast. She didn't say "Cool! Do it!" She buried her nose in the Apollo computer and found me a deal. Her mumbling style was infectious, and I was afraid she misheard my destination and my name. But when I got the computer itinerary print-out it said Los Angeles and my name was right. It showed I was actually going to go to Los Angeles. No turning back! Non-refundable!

I'm wondering what it's going to be like out there. All I know of California is what I see on TV.

It's warm, I know that. There are palm trees instead of real ones. Everybody is relaxed, physically fit, and involved in some kind of organized crime. They wear big billowy shorts with flowers on them and go surfing. Everybody looks older than they really are because of the sun. Rich people let their homes burn down to the ground in brush fires, and they sit in hot tubs and drink carbonated water.

Adults skate along city thoroughfares in Venice, this I know. They don't work, just zip along and listen to the radio. Most of the young guys are handsome but dumb, so they just skate around. The weather never changes, so there are a lot of mass murders, and a lot of religious cults, too. Everybody's very insecure and looks to all kinds of odd stuff to lead them through life.

One thing's going to be awesome. I'll be on the same turf as movie stars. When my friend drives me down Sunset and Wilshire and streets of this nature, I'll know that people like Raymond Burr and Mamie Van Doren did the same thing. Driving to the studio for the day's shooting! Maybe, too, on the freeway I'll see young singles jump from one car to another based on license plates; that's how some people meet in California. They put information about themselves on the license plates and pick each other up on the road. Strange but true. They have to because there are no decent bars in Los Angeles County. People don't drink out there because it makes them logy, and they can't take that.

I get to see the ocean; that's good. I'm going to swim and take great gulps out of it. I'll show them what Cleveland dudes are made of! I'm also going to eat at a restaurant in Malibu and look out over the Pacific. Eating in Malibu is something one only dreams about, but I'm going to do it. It will be different from the Flats, a change of scenery. That's what flying out to the Coast is all about. Plus shopping. I have nothing I want to buy, but I'll look around. It's a great way to kill a couple of hours in California.

It's too bad about Hollywood, a place I always wanted to tour. I'm not going near the studios, with all that male prostitution nonsense going on there. I can skip that whole area. You don't have to see *everything*. I'm a wholesome person from Cleveland, and that's not for me, all the killing and drug-taking.

Well, I know I'm going to have a good time out there. I'm sure some of the scenery will be interesting, and there will be lots to do between meals. The malls should be very good. There should be loads of movies to see if it's too hot and muggy for comfort. Maybe a good rain will wash away the smog before I get there. The time will fly, and I'll be back home in front of the TV before I know it.

5/7/87

A Fabulous Trip

You know how some people are unflappable? I'm not one of them. I'm very flappable. I'm flapping all over the place thanks to incidents that occurred during my sexy hot trip to Southern California, which turned out to be a one-day jaunt to the teeming and ever-busy Chicago O'Hare airport and back again to Cleveland, which I was trying to get out of for a fun, relaxing trip to sexy hot Southern California, if you follow me so far.

I had scheduled a trip to Los Angeles, to stay four nights and three full days. This was a rare and exciting thing for me, not to mention expensive.

I had scheduled a trip to Los Angeles, to stay four nights and three full days. This was a rare and exciting thing for me, not to mention expensive. I left my home early on May 20, hopping on the rapid. The ride to the airport was fine; indeed, it was the best part of the trip. I gazed at the glum scenery and felt a wave of affectionate condescension. "I'm going to be on the beach of the *Pacific Ocean* tomorrow," I thought, "and these people are going to be grousing around on Triskett Road, which is too bad. Heh, Heh."

I got to the airport and was informed my flight would leave an hour late. No problemo! I had a long layover in Chicago anyway. I boarded the plane, and noted that these babies were beginning to look more and more like buses every day. The flight was uneventful, which is usually best. We did have to wait several minutes for another plane to clear our gate, but I had time to kill, so I smiled pleasantly at the old woman sitting next to me and said, "Oh well, I've got three hours here anyway." And she laughed oddly and said something I didn't quite catch. She seemed nervous, but I thought she might have been that way from flying. Now I think she was experiencing "bad vibes." She was a smart woman.

I am a semi-aware person, and I knew Chicago's O'Hare Airport was a hub and busy. But when I got off that airplane I wasn't prepared for the incredible, teeming horde of people there. I know this sounds naïve, but I was truly shocked. This place made a Browns game at the Stadium look like a day at the suburban library. And here was the joker in the deck: there had been thunderstorms that morning, and flights were being delayed. Everything was backed up. I was getting a very real sense of hysteria from the people around me. I thought, "They'll iron this out, I'll be delayed a few hours, I'll just go a little later to a swinging cantina in Southern California with my friend." I still had two hours, so I waited near the TV monitors to find out where my gate was and when I'd be departing.

I waited, read the *Tribune*, twiddled my thumbs. There was always a mass of people around the monitors, peering anxiously up at them, blocking the aisles. I checked for my gate every 15 minutes or so, and time began to run short. Finally, I looked up and next to my flight number I saw the word *canceled*.

Being an infrequent traveler, my first reaction to this was disbelief, then an interior wail. "What am I gonna do? *What am I gonna do?*" Another fellow was in the same boat, and we went to the next gate with another flight to L.A. The besieged agent at the gate told a young soldier that there was a waiting list of 160 people for the flight, which was due to leave in 20 minutes. I did not see this as a hopeful sign.

You must remember that there were thousands of people with my problem or variations thereof (missed connections, ruinous delays) and the confusion was epidemic. The customer service counter was like a prayer meeting: 500 howling travelers and an agent trying to calm them with a microphone and a suave, Continental accent. I tottered around aimlessly for a while, close to despair. There were masses of angry people at every conceivable source of information. I finally followed the Continental-accented agent's advice and called reservations on a free phone.

All flights to L.A. were standby for the rest of the day, the woman said, and here is where I really didn't know what to do. I couldn't see waiting around in that madhouse for a flight that might never materialize, so I decided to go home, an 8 p.m. flight back to Cleveland. That was five hours away, but it was better than staying over and cutting my trip in half with all the travel time.

Now I had to fetch my luggage and call my friend, whose phone number I had conveniently forgotten to bring. I talked to a fellow who assured me that they'd find my bag and put it by the claims office, and I thought that item was handled. "You might want to get a Coke or some coffee," he said. "This might take 30 or 40 minutes." I spent that time tracking down my friend's office number, calling her with the news, and getting my ticket back to Cleveland. I messed around at the ticket counter with a refund form just to get my name in the system, and listened to other tales of woe. Everyone, to coin a phrase, was getting screwed.

I went back down to baggage claim, and as you well know didn't see my bag. I put in another claim. "Relax," the beach boy agent said. "The claim is in. The bag will be by the window." There were many other "relaxed" people there, each with a worse story than the last. I waited in the lounge a few yards from the claim area, and kept checking. Three hours later, at 7 p.m., one hour before my flight was to leave for Cleveland, I went back to the office and waited for the beach boy agent again. He punched in my name and claim number and said, "Yup, we sent your bag on to L.A." I felt a strange kind of perverse joy, grinned, and said, "Ya did, huh?!" He said "Sorry about that," and I started laughing.

Anyway, I didn't have to worry about carting around my clothes, and I awaited my flight back home. It boarded an hour and a half late, and we sat on the runway for another two hours waiting for the pilots to arrive, a new one on me. Then we waited for a new crew, then for clearance. The 8 P.M. flight left Chicago at midnight and arrived at Cleveland at 2 A.M.

One good thing. In the spirit of the Great Indoors, not once did I set foot outside during my entire trip to Southern California.

5/28/87

Reincarnation

Every time you turn around Shirley MacLaine is on TV, making jokes about reincarnation. Like, "That's the best time I've had in 5,000 years." Her books on the subject have been phenomenal bestsellers, so a lot of people must be intrigued by the theory of the soul traveling from one generation to another, landing in a new body. Some believe it can settle in any living thing, say a cat or an artichoke. I guess I'd rather ship my soul over to a bug when I croak than do nothing, though I'm not sure.

Shirley MacLaine was a big shot in a previous life—an Egyptian princess or something. If I had lived in Ancient Egypt I'd have been a pyramid slave, and a complainer. "It's hot, my back is killing me already." But when Moses came to set me free I would have complained about him, too.

In any life I'd have been an indoorsy guy, because that's the way my soul is.

In any life I'd have been an indoorsy guy, because that's the way my soul is. If you go way back, I'd be the fellow lying in the cave, staring at the wall drawings in an early precursor to TV viewing. Waiting millions of years for *The Honeymooners* and Dick Van Dyke. I'd be waiting through the Middle Ages, the Renaissance, the Reformation. I'm not sure if I'd be an artisan or just a slob. These were a murky couple of eras. I would have survived the Plague because I was out of town. I have a dim picture in my mind of pigs and chickens, a small village, and five daughters. No, wait, that's *Fiddler on the Roof*. I don't know what my soul was doing then, frankly.

More recent eras could be easier to pin down. I might have been among the early Virginia settlers, and if I was, I had gout. (I have it today.) A guy named Isaiah Putnam hobbling down the streets of Jamestown, irascibly caning stray dogs and small children along the way. I'd have fought with Washington's army against the British, but without much distinction, working supply in well-heated cabins. I honestly don't see my soul doing much in the years between 1780 and 1820. I was probably blacksmithing or something. I might have died of smallpox somewhere in there.

For some reason I feel I served in Lincoln's wartime Cabinet, but I might think that because my brother wrote a major biography of Lincoln for his fifth grade class and left a lot of Lincoln stuff lying around our house. If I did, I was a good-natured Cabinet member who horsed around at presidential balls and was considered a lightweight.

In the late 19th century I'd have been a guy in New York City, a garment worker who worried a lot. I would have gotten ahead in the business and become something of a dandy. I might even have been the "Collar Stay King," and married a solid woman named Esther and had a son named Gibbon and a daughter named Elsa, plus a dog named Duke who'd roam around our New Jersey estate.

The body that carried around my soul before me, maybe it belonged to a hood that got gunned down in 1955, the year of my birth. He would have been a sensitive guy but one who knew too much and was about to testify in front of a grand jury. I remember this: when I was born, I kept hearing the words, "No Johnny! No!" Just kidding. I don't remember anything like that. Would have been a great story to tell Shirley MacLaine, though.

Well, one thing is certain. My soul's inside me now, and if it's going anywhere, it's not taking me with it. I'm just its shell. In the next life, I just hope it makes more money.

6/25/87

Shortstop Julius Frankel

As I watched the Indians play the Yankees on TV the other day, my mind began to wander. I was thinking: what if, one day this season, the manager of the team, Doc Edwards, took shortstop Julio Franco out of the lineup and replaced him with a retired 79-year-old jeweler named Julius Frankel?

For this to be possible, one event must take place. The owners of the team, the Jacobs, would have to go a little funny in the head. They would have to come down to the locker room with Julius Frankel in tow, introduce the elderly retiree to Edwards, and announce that he would replace Franco.

> **What if manager Doc Edwards took shortstop Julio Franco out of the lineup and replaced him with a retired 79-year-old jeweler named Julius Frankel?**

"His name is just like Franco's," Dave Jacobs would say. "And he's a friend of the family."

"It's a great thrill, believe me," Frankel would say. "I'll do the best I can to replace Julio, through his are big shoes to fill, I know."

Doc Edwards would begin to protest, but Jacobs would cut him off.

"This is what we want," Jacobs would say. "He's a nice old gentleman and deserves the opportunity."

From wire reports, Sept. 8: *In a move that shocked and dismayed 7,300 Indians fans at Cleveland Stadium yesterday, manager Doc Edwards started 79-year-old Julius Frankel at shortstop in place of regular Julio Franco. The Tribe dropped the game to the Seattle Mariners 28–4, due in large part to Frankel's inept batting and defense. The former jeweler committed 19 errors and struck out four times. Seattle batters deliberately hit the ball to the elderly shortstop, running up the score.*

When asked about the bizarre move, Edwards said, "The boss told me to."

The Jacobs brothers, owners of the Indians, could not be reached for comment.

As I envision the situation, Frankel would be an amiable sort who is philosophical about his terrible play. Balls would zip by him at the plate, and after every strikeout he would shrug and say, "Not the end of the world by a long shot." Fans would be enraged at first, screaming obscenities at him. He'd wave happily at them and call out, "I'm having a marvelous time! It's a dream come true!"

After a time the other ballplayers would learn to play around Frankel, whom they'd begin to care for and learn to look up to as sort of a senior spokesman and confidante.

Outfielder Mel Hall: "The man is very wise and has seen some things. He made me settle down a little, which I do appreciate."

Pitcher Scotty Bailes: "Now I go out to the mound with a fatalistic attitude that Julie taught me, and it's improved my game 100%."

Infielder Brook Jacoby: "I don't mind fielding Julie's balls, because he always thanks me so nicely. Also, it's improved my range."

Outfielder Cory Snyder: "Mr. Frankel taught me that striking out is no crime. So when I do, I don't worry about it; and I do it less. He's the greatest."

Outfielder Joe Carter: "Well, he's just The Man, isn't he?"

From wire reports, Sept. 23: *Indians shortstop Julius Frankel won a standing ovation from a crowd of 58,000 at Cleveland Stadium yesterday. The 79-year-old Tribesman finally made contact with the ball in his 56th time at bat, sending a weak dribbler three feet foul down the first base line. He then struck out, prompting another ovation.*

Frankel said after the game: "These crazies. They'd cheer anything. But you might notice I have a tear in my eye." The fan favorite then brushed by reporters and left the locker room.

At the end of the season, Frankel would retire, after five weeks of a dizzying baseball career. Frankel's final batting average would be .000; his fielding average the same. But it wouldn't have affected the team's position in the standings, anyway.

"Let me say one thing," Julius Frankel would say at his big farewell party at the Stadium. "On the field, I didn't set the world on fire. I know this. At bat, I whiffed an awful lot. Alright, alright, every time! You don't let a guy forget, huh? Well, this is all good-natured fun, but I do want to thank the Jacobs boys for giving me the opportunity to play a little ball, and all the wonderful players who caught all the ground balls hit my way and didn't holler when I struck out, and of course the fans, who I guess will put up with anything with this Indians team. You're all beautiful and I love you and good-bye."

And then Julio Franco would get his shortstop job back for the 1988 season.

8/11/87

Dawgs

I was eating a delicious London Broil at Nighttown the other evening when it became clear I would not be able to finish. I asked the waitress for a doggie bag, and to my surprise she brought me just that. A real, old-fashioned 1954-vintage grease-proof doggie bag, with superb drawings of grinning dogs on it and a little song too, "Oh where, oh where have your leftovers gone/Oh where, oh where can they be?/If you've had all you can possibly eat/Please bring the rest home to me!!" Now that's good. I gazed upon this item fondly for a bit, then came to the sober realization that almost all the dogs I ever knew were not like the dogs on the bag.

> **I felt very sorry for Chrissie, the dog that struggled up the stairs fueled only by Alpha Bits and her own determination.**

The dogs I knew didn't pant and grin and jump for joy. They were troubled or oddballs or both. Our family hasn't owned a dog since 1961, because we went through some bad times with them. One dog, Happy, was a misfit, unable to get along with anyone or anything. The next, Jimmy, was run down soon after we got him. The final dog, a Weimaraner named Spook, bit my brother's friend, Tommy, opening a series of doors in the house to get at him. The premeditated nature of this act forced my parents to give Spook away. We've been a cat family since. My sister living in Washington has a dog, but he jumps through closed windows. No one else wants to take a chance.

It was more interesting to observe neighbors' and friends' dogs. Both our next-door neighbors had dogs, and it was like night and day comparing them. On one side there was a collie named Laddie, who I swear was more intelligent than some of the kids I knew. This dog dripped dignity. He was owned by a distinguished German doctor, and when I'd see them walking together I'd think, "That dog likes classical music as much as the doctor does." And that gave me a thrill.

On the other side, however, there were Tony, Pokey, and Violet.

Well, first there was Tony, a nervous little pug who had asthma and a
certain fondness for kids' legs, if you catch my drift. He wasn't bad and
neither was Pokey, a nondescript mixed-breed who seemed about as
average as a dog can get. But Violet . . .

Violet was put out early in the morning every day, and the neighbors' driveway, where she was leashed, was right below my bedroom
window. She was a little black dog with a real big mouth. I have never
before or since heard a dog yap so ceaselessly as Baby Violet did. She
emitted a piercing "Ike" sound, and she went with it. It was unbeliev-
able. She never shut up. Now and then our neighbor would poke his
head out the back door and say "Violet! No!" but that only kept her
quiet for as long as it took him to get his head back into the house. I
would lie in bed gnashing my teeth, listening to Violet every morning.

My friends' dogs were all a little bit off, too. I felt sorry for most of
them. One had a goiter and slobbered. He was nice, but I didn't really
want to deal with him. Another was a St. Bernard named Sam who I
had a healthy respect for. I feared him. While not a violent animal, he
seemed easily offended. I never tried to pet him or even look at him.
He also seemed to know I was a jerk, leading his young master down an
unsavory path, and he looked at me weird. Really.

I should also mention Chrissie, the arthritic dog that ate Alpha Bits
instead of conventional dog food. I felt very sorry for Chrissie, the dog
that struggled up the stairs fueled only by Alpha Bits and her own
determination.

Those were the only dogs I ever really knew. To me dogs are
poignant animals that make me feel slightly guilty, but maybe I've just
been associating with the wrong ones. I like them and I like how people like them, but I'd hate to think of a dog of mine crashing through
a closed window.

9/24/87

Automotive Desire

Would somebody give me a new automobile for Christmas? I would like a Toyota Camry with automatic transmission, AM-FM cassette, air conditioning, and cruise control. Just like my friend Joe the psychiatrist's car. He tells me you don't have to take care of Toyotas for the first three years—just change the oil a few times.

I don't have a car now. I even got made fun of because of this on the radio by WWWE yapper John Krist while he interviewed me. He called me skinny, too. A skinny guy with no car exposed over 50,000 watts! They haven't asked me back, either. No one's squealing for the return appearance of Mr. Small Potatoes on 3WE. Well, let me tell the decision-makers at 3WE something. I may not have a car, and I may be too thin, but there are plenty of people out there who dig the slender look and don't have hang-ups about cars. I mean, they have cars, but they don't have anything against svelte folk who don't have them. Don't alienate a demographic here. You don't know who you're offending by calling me skinny without a car.

> The steering wheel crumbled off in my hands, and there were thousands of dead bees under the dash, evidence of years of hard time in a trailer park in Pontiac, Michigan.

Sure I'd like a car. Why do you think I asked for a Camry? I've only owned one car in my whole life, a 1968 Pontiac Catalina given to me by my Grandma in 1983, and that ended up getting towed to the junkyard. I didn't know how to take care of it, and didn't want to, frankly. From the day I got it I wished it would go away. The steering wheel crumbled off in my hands, and there were thousands of dead bees under the dash, evidence of years of hard time in a trailer park in Pontiac, Michigan. I drove it for a while, but it just fell apart on me. It had no defrosting action. The needle on the speedometer went up to 120 and fluttered and chirped as I drive down residential streets. The interior smelled oily and flammable. Oh, it was a loser. I suppose a car guy could have reconstructed it and made a boss ride of it. I don't know. It's of the earth now.

But a Camry—I would ease that baby out into the traffic with a suave grin. "I'm in my Camry now!" A little wave. Not like my first driving experience, when I slammed my mother's 442 into the bushes. The folks thought I was going to drive into the kitchen. I was 14, and this made quite an impression. I didn't like the idea of internal combustion either, and I began the long, fruitless wait for electrical cars. But if you don't have to take care of a Camry for three years—well, that's all right, then. Camry mechanics are classy, I'll bet, like George Sanders or Clifton Webb. No "Where's your distriburator wires at?" with Camry guys. "The part is indeed here, sir, if you care to wait in the library." A drop of sherry in the oak-lined study waiting for my car. "The automobile is poised and ready now for your inspection, sir." Treated like a duke with my high-priced ride! They wouldn't need to know the car was given to me.

I wouldn't drive my Camry into a tree, like I did with my sister's Le Mans. (The passenger door wouldn't open thanks to the huge dent I put in the side, and I took it to a big guy who hit it with a sledgehammer. This was not the sort of bodywork my sister expected me to get done on it. The door opened, though.) I wouldn't forget that I drove it and leave it overnight in a bar parking lot, as I did with my mother's car. I would be dignified and cordial to other drivers. I'd play classical music on the tape player. I'd glide along the thoroughfare. It would be beautiful. I just don't want to pay for it, that's all.

In the meantime I'll hop on the rapid and bum rides. One thing I won't do is gain 40 pounds and swing my big ass into a Bonneville like they'd have me do at 3WE. They ask too much.

12/10/87

Beloved Christmas Memories

When I was six years old, I was asked by my parents to do an imitation of President John F. Kennedy in front of the Christmas tree for their friends, many of whom had been drinking cocktails. I had a little mop of brown hair like the president's, and I could approximate his Boston accent. So I stood in front of the tree, wearing my Dr. Dentons, and piped, "Ahsk not what your country can do for you, ahsk what you can do for your country," and "Let me . . . ah . . . say this about that." Everyone roared with delight. For months afterward I was known as "Little JFK" around the house.

That's about the cutest Christmas anecdote I can come up with. I have four brothers and sisters, but I didn't notice any cute stuff they did at Christmas. I was too busy rooting around the bottom of the tree like a piglet looking for my presents. I examined each one carefully, estimating value. It was not very attractive. I should have been caroling. I should have been singing "The Little Drummer Boy" at the school assembly. But I wasn't.

I have four brothers and sisters, but I didn't notice any cute stuff they did at Christmas. I was too busy rooting around the bottom of the tree like a piglet looking for my presents.

I don't feel guilty about it. Most of the kids I knew weren't caroling either. It's not that I wouldn't have caroled if asked; I just didn't want to be considered a pill by volunteering. Christmas music is beautiful, but I decided to let Bing and Johnny Mathis do it. I did the JFK shtick, didn't I?

I did have to dance around the elementary school gym to the "Sleigh Bells" song. We children put our arms around one another and danced at the Christmas assembly. I pretended to be uncoordinated so they'd put me in the clodhopper line at the back of the gym where no one could see me. Sleigh bell dancing was undignified, a cousin to the square dance. Of course once the line got moving I began to enjoy it. And I was dancing with those clumsy oafs who stumbled all over themselves, when I could have been showcased with the graceful kids! I learned a valuable lesson, though it didn't really hold. I still act dumb to get out of stuff.

But to me Christmas has always primarily meant presents. As a little boy I secretly felt it was far, far better to receive than to give. It's terrible and it's shameful. Even today, when I Christmas shop, I'm thinking about what I want. I give it much more thought than what my family and friends might enjoy. I know where this attitude will land me—in a lonely efficiency apartment, ignored, despised, with a malfunctioning 13-inch black-and-white TV my only friend. That's what happens to Christmas cruds.

And it happens to Christmas snoops. I was searching the attic for unwrapped presents just before Christmas one year, and I found one clearly meant for me. It was a *Mr. Ed* board game in which the talking horse had to reach some goal or destination, though I can't remember what. I told our babysitter Stella that I saw it, and she gave me a tongue lashing: "Now you won't be surprised on Christmas morning. I hope you're happy. Your parents went to a lot of trouble getting you that game." What a sneaky little turd! This was one of the worst Christmas memories of my childhood, which, looking back on it, wasn't exactly Dickensian but was dramatic in its own way.

I think of treasured gifts on Christmas Day: a toy Sinclair multilevel gas station with little cars you rolled up and down the ramps. An Aurora racing car set. A Mattel Vac-U-Form, with which you could make smelly plastic toys that were non-toxic (as I didn't die after chewing on them). A Danny O'Day ventriloquist dummy. The soundtrack to *The Wizard of Oz*, an incredibly beloved present. "If I were King of the Forrrrest!" The most asked-for present throughout elementary school: a chemistry set. Some of these science kits even included a dead frog to dissect. The immortal Lionel train. Books, records, puzzles, games, models, balls, mitts, bikes.

Oh, we were lucky.

12/17/87

What to Do for Your Valentine

It's terrible to get a valentine from your dentist, particularly if it's the only one you get. The lone valentine on the mantle: "Best Wishes for a Happy Valentine's Day. Dr. Paul Grau and associates." Or maybe it would be next to the valentine from your insurance company. Thank goodness I'm not lonely. That would send me right over the edge.

I'm not much of a giver of valentines myself. I don't like shopping for greeting cards of any kind, except maybe for the "Far Side" line. When I worked in bookstores, I'd watch people shop for cards. They had a big time of it, too, some of them. They'd stand by the racks and open every card and run a gamut of emotions. What a spectacle. A few would stop by the counter and ask me to call when we got any "new cards" in. Fat chance! Today, being a mature individual, I would consider performing that sort of service, but in those days I wasn't about to make any calls about greeting cards. I had *machismo* then. I didn't do cards.

Rite-Aid shavers. A nice pack of gum. Small things. One of these gifts every six weeks or so will make all the difference in your relationship.

I have a hangover from those years today. Like most people who are too lazy to buy cards and send them off, I say that it shows far more care and concern to make your own. True. But am I cutting out paper hearts and pasting them onto construction paper? No. I usually wait and see what my girlfriend does first, then try to match it. If I get a card, I then rush to the drugstore and look for one for her. By the time I get around to it, all of the decent cards are gone, and what's left are glossy religious-looking photographs that cost $1.75. Those are too weird even for me, so I run over to Revco for some bargain chocolate-covered cherries or maybe an economy-sized Whitman Sampler. And I know she probably spent an hour by the card rack, thoughtfully picking out the perfect valentine. Like those nerds I use to watch in the bookstores. What a huge circle this life is.

Cards are shallow substitutes for the real thing, anyway. Romance, that is. Every day should be Valentine's Day for you and your sweetheart. When you're together, say something kind: "You're looking a little less rat-like today." Their beady red eyes will tear up and they'll thank you. A hug and a kiss. Or tell them they smell "superfine." Pat them on the back. Rub their feet. Feed them individual Grape-Nuts like they do on TV. Go to Revco and buy them one of those 39-cent moisturizer samples, just for the fun of it. (They're usually in a bin near the check-out.) How about some batteries from Radio Shack? They've got a deal on those now. Some Rite-Aid shavers. A nice pack of gum. Small things. One of these gifts every six weeks or so will make all the difference in your relationship.

If you don't feel like spending that much money, here's another thing to do. Stop complaining for a little while! What a precious gift that can be. Just once don't complain about how her fingers look funny opening a bag of chips or pressing the buttons on the car radio. Just once don't comment on those noises he makes as he chews, the tongue-against-the-gum noises that nobody else makes. Let her whistle through her teeth if she wants. Let him make his foolish pornographic jokes and call your Junior League meetings "hen conventions." What's the big deal? You'd rather be alone?

Speaking of loneliness and symbols of that emotion, what about those dental valentines? How do they do them? Does the photographer tell the hygienists where to stand in the group shot, or does the dentist? "No, Carol I want you over here." What goes on with these people?

2/11/88

Human Baseball Failings

A nice new Rawlings baseball glove, a Dave Winfield model, black, with an Edge-U-Cated heel and a good strong webbing, is what I bought last week in these days of a little extra cash. It replaces the Mickey Mantle model that I got in 1966, a glove that I never properly broke in anyway. Already the Dave Winfield feels better. I walk around the living room wearing the glove, pounding the palm, sticking it under the cushion of the chair and sitting on it to make it flat and professional. Smarter than when I was 11, when I told my brother to drive over the Mickey Mantle with the car. It didn't do the job. The glove was always wide open.

I was becoming what I hated most: Vic Morrow in *The Bad News Bears*.

My friend Barbara and I played catch the same day. I discovered disturbing things about myself. I discovered I shouldn't be a Little League coach. I was cruelly mocking some of her throwing and catching attempts. Imagine doing that to an impressionable child. I cursed her when I nicked a fingernail going after a sizzling grounder she rolled at me. How could I blame her for my own uncoordination? But I did. I was becoming what I hated most: Vic Morrow in *The Bad News Bears*. The win-at-any-cost Little League coach. The very sort of zealot that kept me off softball teams— big mouths burning with competitive fire, guys who couldn't take a joke or appreciate an inept play. I'm not talking about intentional, beer-induced slapstick on the diamond, either. Just human baseball failings.

When I was in Little League I rode the bench. I'm the first who ought to be compassionate. Our team was coached by a man named Mr. Jenkins, who placed his two towheaded kids, Ronald and Randall, at the glamour positions, pitcher and shortstop. Shades of the Ripkens over in Baltimore (though the old man was recently fired as manager). They were good, though, like the Ripken boys. The name of the team was the Polaris, plural already, no extra "s" needed.

I was the right fielder, and I got perhaps six minutes playing time the entire season. Mr. Jenkins wasn't crazy. I couldn't hit or field with any confidence at that point in my career, and he did want to win. I did holler "go Ronald" and "go Randall" from the bench, but I wasn't sucking up to Mr. Jenkins for playing time. I had been out there in right field, and I didn't want to go back.

I had just one chance in right field. It was a fly ball that turned me around a few times before I figured out where it was going, which was over my head. I chased it down, aware that it was going for extra bases, but I didn't know the ball was going to get tangled in the spokes of some kid's bicycle! The kid was walking the bike across the field, and the ball actually got caught in the wheel. Imagine the chagrin of an 11-year-old whose first opportunity in the field is screwed up in this manner. I yelled at the kid, "We're playing baseball! This is baseball!" I couldn't get my fingers around the ball. Finally I got a throw off to the cut-off man, but the bases had long been cleared. A homer. It was terrible.

I had two chances at the plate. The first time I stepped out in front of a pitch and got hit. The second I managed to hit a weak liner to the shortstop. That was it for Little League.

Thank God for softball, invented for those of us who can't hit a regulation baseball, or field it, either. It's easier to go after that big moon of a ball. I became a stellar center fielder in softball, part of the famous "vacuum cleaner outfield." That's what my friend in left field and I called ourselves anyway. Not many balls got past us. These games were fun and not taken too seriously, but seriously enough. Who wants to get yelled at by some psycho-competitor, yet who wants to play softball in a drunken stupor? I avoided organized softball, because I didn't sense there was a middle ground. Plus those damn beer commercials on TV depicting games—I wish I could figure out how they make every activity seem so unappealing. Maybe because I see some people acting like the people on the commercials, with weird unnatural heartiness. It gives me the willies.

I'm just going to play catch this summer with specially selected people and catch high fly balls they throw at me and field hot grounders. Fundamentals and hand-eye coordination will be worked on. I'll behave myself and be concerned only with my own play, and my Dave Winfield mitt and I will stand out in the sun.

4/28/88

Horny

Let's everybody put our little fingers in our ears and feel around in there. Do you feel a bone sticking out? I do. At the age of 32, I'm growing an antler. Some people worry about hair growing in their ears or their noses. Compared to growing an antler, these concerns seem petty, don't they? I'm talking perspective here. Think about me when you're troubled by nose hairs, think about me in the supermarket weeping quietly as I knock products over with my horn or my antler or what have you. *Look, Mommy, the man has an antler! I know, Jimmy, shh . . .* Of course, that's the worst case scenario.

> **Think about me in the supermarket weeping quietly as I knock products over with my antler.**

I think a lot about worst case scenarios. They rarely come true, so they're an odd comfort. For example, I think about the Rock and Roll Hall of Fame. You may know that a few other cities are not sitting quietly by and accepting that Cleveland is the designated site for the Rock Hall of Fame and Museum. San Francisco and Memphis want it, too, and they're not giving up. There's no way of knowing what's going to happen with this thing.

Now here's the worst case scenario. Both San Francisco and Memphis get big fancy museums, chocked to the gills with pop, rhythm and blues, and rock memorabilia, with frequent guest appearances by Mick Jagger, Bob Dylan, Tina Turner, and Aretha Franklin, and all Cleveland has are a couple of bulletin boards on display in the lobby of the National City Bank Building with some signed photos of people like Eric Carmen, Michael Stanley, the Outsiders, and Don Webster. This is what people fear most.

Some people fear we *will* get the Hall of Fame, attracting bikers from Oakland roaring into town to see the Steppenwolf "Born to be Wild" show; or earnest folkies thronging around the Bob Dylan "Times They Are A-Changin'" display; or ratty Grateful Dead heads filling the air with dope smoke at the "Sugar, Magnolia" exhibit; or— worst case yet—this Hall of Fame will be heavy on Heavy Metal.

Actually, what I fear most isn't the pitiful bank display or the hippie/greaser/biker invasion. It's that we get leftovers from the other museums. We'd end up with the Garfield Monument instead of the

Jefferson Memorial, if you catch my drift. We'd get Elvis's pencil box instead of his first guitar. James Brown's fourth-string cape. A blanket from a hotel room that Keith Moon *didn't* trash. Live performances by Bo Donaldson and the Heywoods or Toni Tenille. Special appearances by Gary Lewis, John Sebastian, Mac Davis, and Helen Reddy. A cut-out B-side Rock and Roll Hall of Fame and Museum.

I might as well admit something to you. I honestly don't fear anything when it comes to the Rock and Roll Hall of Fame compared to this antler business. Perspective again. I can envision the worst case scenario with the Hall of Fame, and I can envision it with this bone growing out of my ear, and frankly the Hall of Fame has to take a back seat to the bone. I mean, Cleveland will live on, Hall of Fame or no Hall of Fame. There are more serious problems facing this city. Terrible things can and will happen, and to be selfish about it, my being transformed into a rhino or a goat or an elk is a hell of a lot more cause for concern than if Dion and the Belmonts get inducted into some Rock Hall of Fame or if Michael Jackson donates a glove or a pair of socks. Now I'm no more self-absorbed than your average single 32-year-old man, but Number One is, after all, Number One. Walk a mile in my shoes. Did you put your finger in your ear? Did you feel firm, normal ear flesh? Yes, you did. That's one worry you don't have. Your life may be filled with heartache, you may be broke, you may be ill. But I got the antler.

This is what I mean by perspective.

5/5/88

Happy Teeth

A friend writes: "On your next visit to our office you'll notice some very positive additions that we've made for your protection against infection . . . each staff member and I will now be wearing latex gloves, masks, and eye protection when treating you."

That's the only piece of mail I got yesterday. If you guessed that it was from my dentist, you were right. I have an excellent dentist. His name is Huck Finn. Yes it is. You might say he's riding a "raft" on a "Big River" of satisfied dental patients. And I'm one of them.

I do feel bad, though, that my dentist and his assistants are going to be wearing masks. I assume they will for everybody. Wouldn't it be terrible if that letter was intended just for me? "Carol, send this guy a letter telling him we're going to wear masks, gloves, and goggles when he's in the chair. Tell him it's for *his* protection so he doesn't complain. I'm not going to risk my life chipping away at his filthy tartar." I'm sure it's not. Still, I'm going to miss looking up at the faces, chins, and nostrils.

On the other hand, who can blame them if they're tired of being hit by flying bits of tooth

> The last thing Dr. Courtney said to me, a few weeks before he died, was, "Will you brush every night? Honest?" Who would have thought a dental covenant could carry such weight?

decay? That's the reality of it. They've put up with it far too long already. Dentists and dental assistants are people, too. They're the nation's mouthworkers and deserve respect. A hearty "Fine Job!" to our dentists and dental assistants.

You'll find no cheap jokes here about dentists. I've never minded any of my trips to the dentist. As small children we went to a dentist who had a playroom with an aquarium. I associate my childhood dental care with tropical fish, along with the magazines *Highlights*, *Jack'n'Jill*, and *Humpty Dumpty*. My dentist never hurt me. While never squealing excitedly about a trip to the dentist, I always got into the car without a word of complaint. I'd merely think to myself, "Well, now I'm going to the dentist."

Our family switched dentists, to the crusty old Dr. Courtney, when I was 13. Dr. Courtney was a dental grandfather to me. The last thing he said to me, a few weeks before he died, was, "Will you brush every night? Honest?" I'm not saying this was the last thing he ever said to anyone, of course, but it was to me. I promised him I would. It's as sacred a promise as I've made to anyone. Who would have thought a dental covenant could carry such weight in a person's life? But it has.

I didn't even mind orthodontia. The orthodontist, Dr. Morse Ruggles Newcombe, was another older guy. I'd stare at the name "Ruggles" on his diploma as he tightened my braces. What a noise that tightening made. Squeezing metal around your teeth. That grossed me out so I liked it a little. He put rubber bands in my mouth that snapped whenever I opened too wide. It was no bother, though.

This is beginning to sound like I enjoy dental work—maybe even like a sicko, like the Bill Murray character in *Little Shop of Horrors*. Not so. I didn't like getting all four of my wisdom teeth removed at once. You'd have to be a sicko to like that! I had local anesthetic and could hear the teeth being pulled out of the jaw. Cra-a-ack! It wasn't painful, but it was pretty tiring to me as well as to the dentist. He earned his pay that afternoon. The worst part of the business was the weird painkiller he prescribed. It made me dream of terrorists in Michigan. Plus I feared the dread "dry socket," which your dictionary will tell you is a "painful inflammatory infection of the bone and tissues at the site of an extracted tooth." Dry socket teased me a little during my post-surgical period. I had a taste of it, and that was plenty.

That was the worst of it in my dental history. Now my dentist is going to wear protective gear while working on me. I'm not offended. Sure it's a little impersonal, and that latex feels disgusting in your mouth, but it's better than an infection. Time marches on, in dentistry as in life.

5/12/88

Mr. Dough-Re-Mi

This weekend we shall return to the Garden of Earthly Delights for some good dime store fries. I am speaking of Severance Mall and the Woolworth's snack bar located therein. My friend Barbara and I go to Severance every single weekend, and eat fries at Woolworth's like teenagers. There's nothing like fries alone, with salt and ketchup. And there's nothing like having a little extra cash to throw around at the mall.

A little extra cash. The four most beautiful words in the English language. I've got it, and I'm going to spend it. *Hello, you at the Aramis counter! I've got a little cash today, I just might buy some astringent!* Those sales people can see it on my face. The happy consumer. The acquisitive American. They're ready to sell, I'm ready to buy, and another transaction will help to keep this big train we call Capitalism rolling down the track. No wonder I'm smiling and ready with a saucy quip for the salesperson. Mr. Dough-Re-Mi is here and going to grease the wheel at Higbee's, with a celebratory air. Not like the old days, certainly.

A little extra cash. The four most beautiful words in the English language.

In the old days, I'd skulk through the mall. No money. I'd sniff and poke and ogle with no intention of buying. I wrote about this once and aroused the ire of the employees of Al Berger, Jeweler, of Beachwood Place, in a blistering letter to the editor. They read my piece and wrote that I was a "pompous ass" in the "lower percentile of intelligence," and that I engaged in "neurotic babbling." Well, now I have money and have raised myself above these characterizations. Money has ennobled me. No longer a time waster, I can now walk into Al Berger, Jeweler, of Beachwood Place and buy a ring if I wanted one. Which I don't.

So I spend it elsewhere. I go into a shopper's trance at the book and record stores. I want to buy things twice. My habit is to look into the Nick Lowe section in the record store, but I've already bought his latest album, and there's nothing new that could possibly have been added. I look anyway, in a trance. I look for copies of books I've already got. I want to buy them over again, to relive the moment. The pathology of shopping. Buying for the sake of buying. I mean, I wanted to buy the Original Cast recording of *Kiss Me, Kate* twice because I enjoyed it so much. Is this crazy?

Most of the time, though, I'm gleeful in the mall. I like to watch people enjoying themselves spending money. I really got choked up over this the other day at Severance Mall. I was standing in line at the Money Station bank machine, and behind me was a black family, a Chinese family, and a white family. They were all chatting away. Brotherhood at the mall! I wanted to burst into song, but I couldn't think of anything appropriate at the moment. (Later we thought of "We Are the World" and "I'd Like to Teach the World to Sing.") It was sheer American dynamite.

My favorite thing, though—the best—is walking around the department stores. I love to see the displays and the interior decorating. The floor is so shiny. There are lots of colors and everything's new. I *really* like the women in the nice clothes. Mr. Shallow. But I do. And I like the mannequins as well. And I like the TVs and the typewriters and the stereo systems, and the gourmet shop that each store has, and the BarcaLoungers that I test-sit, and the pianos. I like the men's accessories, the ladies' lingerie, the housewares, and the notions. I like the escalators. I like going up, and I like going down. I like to think about spending money on small-ticket items, like cotton shirts on sale. Last weekend I bought a comforter with ducks on it, ducks in a glade surrounded by pussywillows. I got it home and it looked terrible on my bed, like an old man's smelly bedspread. But I returned it with no problem at the department store and started fresh with a dandy white number they gave me in exchange. I was only temporarily soured! That's why department stores are great.

The curious thing about all this is the dime store fries element. With this little extra money I got I could have a fine lunch. But all I want are 75-cent Woolworth fries. They taste particularly delicious to me these days when I'm flush with cash.

5/19/88

My Advice to J. D. Salinger

Got a call from J. D. Salinger the other night. Right in the middle of a great rerun of *Cheers*, dammit.

"Yes, Jerry, what can I do you for," I said, one eye on the TV. Sam and Diane were really going at it, and I was missing it.

"How you doing?" said Jerry.

"I'm kind of busy right now, Jerry, so if you could just tell me what you want, I'd be obliged."

"Well . . . you know they got that book out on me now? It makes me look bad. And they put my picture in *Time* a couple of weeks ago and I looked *terrible*. And they think my lawsuit against the author of this book on me will *thwart* biographers in the future, and that makes me look like a *fascist*, you know? And I'm not. You *know* I'm not! I just want to be left alone. You know that, don't you?"

> "What's your idea, Jerry?" Rats! He was going to make me miss the beginning of M*A*S*H*.

"Huh? . . . I'm sorry, Jerry, I was watching something. What was that last part?"

"I just want to be left alone. Why can't they leave me alone?"

"Because you're a very famous writer, Jerry, and they're interested in you," I said. It was like talking to a child.

"*Sure* they're interested, but how come they have to send their crummy photographers out to snap me buying groceries? What's the big deal? How's a picture of me buying groceries going to help *anyone*? Stupid goddam morons!"

"Now take it easy, Holden . . . *oops*. I mean Jerry," I said, getting in a little dig.

"I guess I deserved that," Jerry said humbly.

"Yeah, yeah."

"Leave it to you to bring me down to earth."

"We all need it once in a while, Jerry."

"Though I hate it when you bring up that lousy character."

I rolled my eyes. Here we go again.

"It's a great character, Jerry, and a great book. *Catcher in the Rye* has been in print for 35 years and is on the required reading list of nearly every high school in the country. It's sold tens of millions of copies and considered to be *the* classic novel of adolescence in American literature and will live on for all time in the hearts of its readers."

"For all time?"

"For all time, Jerry."

He was quiet for a moment and then said, "I don't believe you."

I sighed. "Jerry, just what *is* the point of this call?"

"Well . . . all this *stuff* they're saying . . . it's *embarrassing*. They say I've got a superiority complex, that I want to be a *saint*, and all that crap . . . I had an idea and I wanted your advice on it."

"What's your idea, Jerry?" Rats! He was going to make me miss the beginning of *M*A*S*H**.

"I thought maybe I should go on all the talks—like Donahue, Winfrey, Carson, even Larry *King*, for cripe's sakes—and tell my side of this story. Listen to the psychology of it. I figure if I go on all the talk shows, just babble on about myself, everybody will see how *boring* I really am, and then they'll just leave me alone. What do you think?"

"I dunno. That could backfire, Jerry."

"How?"

"Well . . . they'll probably take everything you say, analyze it to hell-and-gone into some kind of 'significance' that's got nothing to do with anything and nail you on something you never even meant in the first place."

"Wow." Jerry was thoughtful. "You could be right about that."

"In other words, keep 'em guessing, Jerry," I said. "That's my advice to you."

"Boy, I will," he said. "That's a good idea."

"All set then, Jerry?"

"Yeah . . . so what are you up to?" he asked, which sounded like a prelude to a very long conversation, which was exactly what I didn't want. So I made a few clicking noises, told him I had a call waiting, and hung up. Because he could go on, and I had a *M*A*S*H** to watch.

5/26/88

Party! Party!

Party! Party! I think we'll have a party. We haven't had one for some time. I'm going to haul out the disco whistle and the dip dish, spray a little Fantastik on the lava lamp, and try to find my aloha shirt, the one I wore in Daytona Beach in 1973. I've got to get my *Belafonte Live at Carnegie Hall* album back from a buddy I lent it to in 1978. Wait. He moved to Denver six years ago. What the hey, I'll buy it again. This is a party we're talking about.

I went to a great party a few weeks ago. The people (a bunch of Cleveland Heights Yuppies) were friendly and drank and spoke freely. Not only that, the floor in the living room collapsed. I was in the kitchen and heard a loud noise and a collective gasp. Boom! The floor had fallen in. Nobody seemed too concerned, though they were surprised. I feel if a party can continue after an incident like this, it's a good party.

> There'll be plenty of Busch beer for everyone. If people want better-quality beer, they're free to bring it.

Ours will be good, too. My sister and I will throw it. She's a Cleveland cop and will invite her friends from the force; I'll invite my flaky artist and writer friends. There'll be a meeting of the minds. Maybe. Actually, I think cops get along better with flakes than with upstanding citizens, like lawyers. (There are plenty of flaky cops.) Cops *don't* get along with smartass college kids at parties, though. We had a party with that mix 10 years ago. You could cut the mutual distrust with a knife. I remember one of my liberal longhaired college smartass friends saying under his breath, "It looks like a cop convention in here." My friends were afraid the cops were going to bust them for smoking dope. But the cops weren't there to work. They were there to look at the college girls, who were afraid that the cops were there to bust them. It didn't make for a fun party, all in all.

Not to worry this time around. I don't hang around druggies anymore, so there'll be no chance of embarrassing party arrests. No cocaine nonsense at our shindig! There'll be plenty of Busch beer for everyone. Or Mountain Dew or Squirt, or Wink, the sassy one from Canada Dry. (Are Squirt and Wink still around? Is Hillbilly Juice currently available?) If people want better-quality beer, they're free to bring it. Any guest who wants to haul over some good Molson beer is okay in my book. Your genial host is happy to drink it. Let the lower-class chumps drink the Busch. Whoops, I didn't say that. At our party everybody drinks their favorite cocktail or beverage. This is Cleveland, America, U.S. of A.

We'll have plenty of mouthwatering food, chock full of essential vitamins and some that aren't so essential. There will be plenty of cheese-and-cracker-type vitamins, with your Kraft Extra Sharp Cheddar and your Monterey Jack and Brick cheeses. Plus you have your quality Premium saltines, maybe some Brit water biscuits and rye and/or sesame toasteds. No Ritz. Ritz only goes with deviled ham, and we're not made of money. We'll get some Tostitos, and if someone wants to bring some guacamole dip that's okay. The food is, as they say, handled.

Of course, I'll wear my aloha shirt and my khakis. I'm going for the Montgomery Clift look in *From Here to Eternity*. Festive, but potentially soulful. I'll take it easy on the firewater. Last party we threw, I believe it was in 1980, I exposed myself not once but twice to my friend's date. And I'm not that kind of guy. Really, I've never thought that the proper kind of behavior at a party. Think of the next-morning guilt over these witless shenanigans. Not this time. I'm going to pace myself, and maybe dance a little to sweat it out. I'll blow that disco whistle—*fweep*—and put on "Hollywood Swinging" by Kool and the Gang. Yes, we'll "tear the roof off the sucker," and "Agent Double-O-Soul" (me) will glide back and forth on the dance floor.

This will be good. I can feel it. The weather's getting hot and nasty, people are tense, it's party time all over town. I don't know when we'll have it but we'll have it. It's written in the stars. Get ready.

6/2/88

In Dreams

Before I discovered Nature's sleeping pills, I drank beer so I wouldn't toss and turn at night. I'm one of those people who can't stand tossing and turning, who actually fear it. You can't rely on alcohol, though, to smooth your way into dreamland. One, you'll be hung over in the morning. Two, your rest will not have been *healthful* and *natural*. Three, you won't even get into dreamland on brews. Just a wet, heavy sleep.

However, on Nature's sleeping pills (500 mg of L-Tryptophan, an essential amino acid found in warm milk, which is why warm milk is often used to induce drowsiness) you'll dream like crazy. And I mean crazy. In the last dream I had after taking L-Tryptophan, killers with earrings and knives were in my bedroom saying, "Where's the records at?" At first I thought they meant records as in files, information, data. But they were after my record albums. I was stuck in my bed, helpless. In my dreams my bed is an active force, holding me in or flipping me or catapulting me into a wall. Since I'm actually *in* my bed, I'm not sure it's a dream, either, making it a double bummer.

> In the last dream I had after taking L-Tryptophan, killers with earrings and knives were in my bedroom saying, "Where's the records at?"

You may well ask, "What's so good about a pill that makes you dream about killers or rogue beds?" I will answer by saying that terrifying fantasy asleep is better than fruitless anxiety awake. My dreams are more of the frustrating variety than the scary, anyway. I have a lot of the famous "heavy legs" dreams, where you're trying to get somewhere and your legs seem to weigh a thousand pounds and you can barely move. Everyone has those, right? You're running uphill in a losing cause. Basic symbolism. You don't have to be Carl Jung to figure it out.

I still have nerdy school dreams, too, where I panic about a test I forget about or haven't prepared for. In one dream, I was required to take a final in a class I had forgotten I was enrolled in. I hadn't gone to any of the classes or read any of the assigned texts. This might be a realistic situation for some people, but for me it was literally a nightmare. Then I even got lost in the school hallways. What a dink. I sure got caught with my pants down in that one.

Speaking of pants down, I often dream I'm naked or underdressed, which must mean something. I'm never happy being that way in my dreams, except if I'm with a lovely lady, you know what I'm sayin'. To me, nudity is vulnerability, as I imagine it is to most people. More basic symbolism. I'm usually naked on a road, with those old heavy legs and cars coming at me. I remember thinking to myself in one of these heavy-legs-on-the-road dreams, "I'll be glad to wake up out of this one."

Waking up can sometimes be worse. Once I dreamed someone's dainty fingers were dancing lightly on the top of my hand, and I woke up to find a roach walking around on my wrist. I enjoyed that, all right. Worse, when I was little I'd dream I was peeing, and sure enough . . . I'm happy those days are gone. Nowadays only noises like knocking or scratching transfer from dream to wakefulness, and these are usually cat-induced. I don't suppose you actually dream about scratching or knocking; you just hear them and think you're dreaming them, but they're really only waking you up from your dream. Anyway, then I have to get out of bed and take care of the cat, because she can drive me nuts with her noises. I am glad it's her and not some wacko knocking and scratching outside the bedroom door, which is what I momentarily think in my drowsy state.

I just like falling immediately to sleep and slipping off into neutral dreams that leave a few sustaining images in the morning. My good dreams are wispy and float out of my consciousness quickly; I can never remember them. I can remember bad dreams and erotic dreams with equal vividness. Go figure. Give me the pleasant, elusive dreams that leave the barely perceptible aftertaste. That's bedtime at its best.

6/9/88

Note: Nature's sleeping pills, L-Tryptophan, have since been pulled from the market.

Bank Shots

Another question I'm very seldom asked is, "Who is your financial planner?" No one is clamoring for a look at my stock portfolio either. I've got five shares that earn me $6.25 every three months. The people at General Motors must laugh when they send me that quarterly check, or maybe their cashier wearing the green visor complains about it. "Do we really have to waste postage on this guy?" The small investor scorned and ridiculed. Par for the course.

To answer the (unasked) question: I am my own financial planner. From checking to savings and back again, I handle it. I deposit, withdraw, and make balance inquiries. And that about does it. Those are the finances. Oh, I did open a Certificate of Deposit a few months ago. It's a six-month deal with an initial investment of $500. When I opened it, I had dreams of outrageous accrued interest at the end of the period, like $215. No. It'll be about 30 bucks. When they say 6% they mean 6%. Would Donald Trump put up with that? Well, that's why he's where he is and why I am where I am.

> I was paying a phone bill, and the clerk noticed I hadn't made any long-distance calls. "You don't have a whole lot of friends, do you?" he said, chuckling oddly.

Like you, I do most of my banking with my bank card at the machine. I have a blue card and a green card. I'm glad, because my bank has crabby tellers, and at every branch. They were never happy to help me. They sighed and stamped my deposit tickets and listlessly informed me of my balances. When they were done they looked off into the distance as if to dismiss me. Once I stood in line waiting for a teller, and one of them appeared to be unoccupied. I walked up to her window and asked if she was open, and she snapped, "I'm busy right now!" All I did was ask! Put your little sign up if you're busy! I hotfooted it back into line, though.

I did have one interesting teller at my bank. I was paying a phone bill, and he noticed I hadn't made any long-distance calls. "You don't have a whole lot of friends, do you?" he said, chuckling oddly. I liked that better than the usual indifference. I don't think he lasted long at the job, because I never saw him again.

I love the machines. My fingers fly over the keys. My transactions are a blur of beeps and on-screen instructions. If the machine could talk it would tell me to slow down, I'm burning up the microchips. A few of the machines do talk; the one at Pavilion Mall is British sounding, a little like Greer Garson. (Using Greer Garson is an important step forward in banking, but they need to follow this thing through. Put Joey Heatherton's voice in one of the machines to give us male transactors a much-needed banking thrill. Men grinning at the Money Station. Other bank machine voices to consider: Julio Iglesias, Johnny Cash, John Houseman, Joan Rivers.)

When the machine eats the card, it's a nightmare trying to get it back. Eating your card is a punishment the bank has devised when you try to deposit a bad check or when you fool around too much with the machine. I lost a card once in a freak accident, and I still had a hard time getting it back. I used a machine during a thunderstorm, and while I was making a transaction there was a bolt of lightning, and the machine blinked and gulped down the card. It had nothing to do with me. When I called the bank they refused to believe the card-eating was an act of God and not my personal misuse of bank privileges. Even when the truth came out, it took them several weeks to send the card back.

The bank assumed the worst in the matter of my student loan as well. I had taken out a loan of $5,000 with one bank, and, unbeknownst to me, they transferred my loan (along with all their other student loans) to another bank. Then a hard woman calls me up out of the blue and scolds me for not getting in touch with the new bank to arrange payment. I coldly told her I was not informed of the transfer, thus throwing her charge of irresponsibility back in her face. They kill you with interest, and they want you to show up at their door with a checkbook in your hand simpering in gratitude. I've made 52 payments on the loan since 1984, and the payment book is still of epic thickness.

There's another thing Donald Trump wouldn't put up with.

7/7/88

Audio Madness

Don't come after me thinking you can knock me down and take my money because of what I'm about to tell you. I'm not rich, but I did something that maybe you think rich people do. I bought a compact disc player. I bought the cheapest one I could find. I got one that plays one CD at a time and doesn't do much else. I'm not walking around with hundreds of dollars in my pocket, so don't waste your time. The only reason that I can afford a CD player is that I don't have a car. Get it straight right now. I'm not your man.

I bought the CD player at one of those appliance stores that advertise on the back pages of sections of the newspapers. A Midsummer Madness Sale. It cost $150. The salesman was named Eddie. His hair was plastered down with margarine and he had a little mustache. He didn't have much use for me when he saw that I wasn't going to be buying any three- or six-year warranties on the player, warranties that cost nearly half of the player itself. Of the three-month warranty the player included for free, Eddie sneered, "I'll tell ya, ninety days isn't a whole long time." He was sullen about this small-potatoes deal in the first place, and my refusal of extra warranties really seemed to sour him. This was the crabbiest salesman to whom I ever gave $150.

The plastic box was so pretty. I wanted to chew on it, as I do with most attractive plastic products.

No matter. I had a CD player, and the fun part, shopping for CDs, was about to start. When I saw my first CD I was a gone goose. This was one shiny object. The disc was a brilliant silver with a mirrored finish, and the plastic box was so pretty. I wanted to chew on it, as I do with most attractive plastic products. I wanted to hear the vaunted, pristine sound, too—almost as much as I wanted to bite the package. Sure, I'd heard CDs in record stores, but what would they sound like on my 15-year-old system?

I had a half-hour in the music store before it closed to choose my first CDs. I was rushed! My heart was beating a mile a minute, and I was so agitated I made the salesman in the music store nervous himself. I was darting from section to section in search of the perfect inaugural CDs. I settled on Chopin favorites by Vladimir Horowitz and some

1902 recordings by Enrico Caruso. I had some vague thoughts of listening to Caruso while eating mounds of spaghetti, like they did in *The Godfather, Part II*. More importantly, I wanted to hear how Horowitz sounded tickling the ivories on this new technology.

When I did put on the Horowitz, the sound was so good I couldn't believe it. The piano notes floated out of the speaker as if he were plunking away in the next room. Come on in to my room, Vladimir, and take a bow! It was dynamite. I knew this was going to send me off on a buying frenzy.

The next day I spent 50 bucks on compact discs, on the Rolling Stones and other "happening" sounds. The sad thing is that 50 bucks doesn't go a hell of a long way when it comes to compact discs, so you have to very carefully select what you buy. You can't have any dogs in your CD collection. I spent hours in music stores agonizing over the selection. Should I buy a bunch of classical, or would I just be doing that to make myself look good? "Ayy, lookit the smart guy, buyin' dat load a classic music!" I had to think: *what would I listen to on a daily basis?* That was the crucial question. My conclusion was that, as with my other formats (records, tapes), I listened to rock as I groomed and did laundry and listened to the highbrow stuff as I read.

I could get all kinds of discs. I could get the cheapo classical discs— the ones that run $6.99—because I wouldn't know the difference between the hot orchestras and the crummy ones anyway. And I can listen to "Paint It Black" and "Out of Time" by the Stones as I put my pants away in my drawer, and "Cool for Cats" by Squeeze as I stick my pillow in its nice clean case on laundry day, and *Billy the Kid* by Aaron Copland and *Rhapsody in Blue* by Gershwin as I page through some mags. And it'll sound so good.

7/28/88

Into the Woods

I'm outta here. I'm going to spend some time in the woods and commune with nature. I've had it. I've had it with the heat and work and the Cleveland Indians. I've had it with the lousy TV and hearing that *Big* is the best movie of the summer. I'm sick of looking out over crummy old Euclid Avenue from the office window, and I'm sick of crummy lunches. I'm sick of riding on the rapid with lunatics who bark like dogs. I'm sick of smelling the kitty litter box in our dining room, and I'm sick of looking at my bathroom ceiling with the paint peeling from water leakage from the apartment upstairs. I'm sick of sweating on the sofa. It's time to say yes to Michigan.

> **I soon switched from worms to plastic lures. Then I switched from fishing to not fishing.**

We have a place in the woods. We're lucky. I feel sorry for people who don't. Our family started going to this place 60 years ago. It's a little town in Northern Michigan called Charlevoix. Hemingway country. He fished and hunted up there in his youth. I hunt up there, too, but only for bugs in the house. I don't fish, because I don't eat fish. I like the idea of fishing, though. When I was a boy I used to fish off a dock with my older brother. He showed me how to bait the hook, but I soon switched from worms to plastic lures. Then I switched from fishing to not fishing. I enjoyed the sitting around aspect of fishing, but the slime factor had no appeal for me. I won't touch fish and I won't eat them. Except for Chicken of the Sea or Bumble Bee or Star Kist. Tuna is more like chicken or ham than fish, anyway. Put a little Worcestershire sauce and lemon and mayo in tuna, and you can forget it had been squirming around in the hold of some boat. Don't ask me about salmon, though, I don't know a thing about it. You can eat it if you want. I don't want any.

Maybe I'll play a little golf up there. I'll play the 9-hole municipal course. No, I won't. I haven't played in 15 years, and I probably won't this summer, either. I learned how to play golf from the pro at the course when I was 13. I was under pressure from the folks to keep busy, and I had to pretend that this thrice-weekly, hour-long golf lesson was a dominating summer activity, a substitute for the camp I had complained bitterly about going to. My parents were desperate to find something that I would be interested in that would get me out of the house. I probably didn't spend more than six hours a week on the golf course, but I tried to make my parents believe I was *thinking* about playing golf all the time, thus taking some of the heat off. I was satisfied to lay on my butt the whole summer, in other words, but I had to make them think I wasn't. It was hard work.

I wasn't a shut-in, however. I had solitary pleasures. I liked cutting weeds around the house with a scythe, which was easy and another excellent way to keep my parents off my back. Don't think I didn't stretch that out, either. I'd wander around with that scythe for hours, cutting and shuffling, shuffling and cutting. Everyone else in Charlevoix was sailing or waterskiing, but I was slashing at weeds. That's the life I chose for myself. It gave me time to reflect on things. Most of the time I reflected on why the hell I was messing with tall weeds when everybody else seemed to be having fun. I was afraid of looking like a fool while trying to have fun, so I did things by myself. I wasn't angry enough to be truly alienated. I knew it was my own fault. You might say I was passively alienated. So I cut weeds.

After all this cutting, though, I did learn to love the woods. The woods in Northern Michigan are filled with cedar, spruce, and pine, and they look and smell great. They're filled with rabbits and raccoons, and these animals jump around on our driveway. The rabbits do, anyway. The raccoons chew on our garbage. There are snakes and deer and porcupines and foxes, plenty of chipmunks, and don't forget the birds. At night the stars fill the sky. The lake laps gently on the rocky shore. That soft rustling from the woods might be a deer moving shyly and gracefully, looking for plants to nibble on, or it might be one of those raccoons gnawing on an empty frozen dinner box he dragged from our garbage. It doesn't matter to me. I like it all. See you later!

8/11/88

Secret Squirrels

Man, why do these people send me these funky catalogs? What mailing list am I on? It must be that video I ordered last year from Publisher's Central Bureau, *The Best of Caballero Films Vol. 8*. One lousy skin flick and I'm in the Spicy Adventure computer files. One lapse of taste and I'm getting Gordon Liddy's junk mail.

The latest catalog I've received is from Life Force Technologies Ltd., out of Aspen, Colorado. On the cover is a leather-clad killer bimbo holding a "Night Penetrator" hand-held night vision viewer—"the dark holds no secrets from the Night Penetrator"—that costs eight grand, and wearing a lethal Tekna dive knife strapped to her upper arm. She's no Laura Ashley or Ann Taylor, I'll tell you that. After scanning the rest of the catalog to find naked pictures of her (there weren't any), I settled into examining the fine products the Life Force folks were selling.

> **One lousy skin flick and I'm in the Spicy Adventure computer files. One lapse of taste and I'm getting Gordon Liddy's junk mail.**

The first thing that caught my eye was the Stress Analyzer, a little device you hide under your desk to measure your adversary's stress level. It analyzes the voice, which under pressure sends out micro-tremors that this thing converts into numerical digits you can see on the LED read-out. The higher the number, the higher the level of stress. I'm not sure what you're supposed to do when the numbers get way up there. Scream suddenly, then move in for the kill? I don't know. I'm not sure of the advantage of knowing another person's nervousness level. Maybe he'll get so nervous when he discovers you've been secretly analyzing his stress he'll shoot your ass.

I'd rather try something a little safer, like the Voice Camouflage, which will "Change Your voice Into an Intimidating Threat" by turning it into a deep growl. Except I'd use it to call my paper boy to frighten him into delivering my *Plain Dealer* on time. Nothing else has worked. Children may use it, too, says the catalog, for a feeling of security while home alone. Ten-year-olds growling "Mommy and Daddy aren't here." Plus you can touch a button and add the sound of a terrier's yip or the "deep-throated" bark of a Great Dane. Hell, why not a lion's roar? I'd rig it up so if anyone called, the theme to *Jaws* would play as they waited for me to come to the phone. *Mess with this guy and he'll eat you alive.* That's the idea I'd try to get across.

If this stuff doesn't do anything for you, Life Force Technologies offers other nasty little gadgets and dirty tricks. "Think of the many ways you could use the Super Ear Mini-Stethoscope system," says the catalog, next to a photo of a guy pressing the device against a wall and listening to the conversation in the next room through an earphone. The ad copy says you can use it to "detect clocks" in luggage. Uh-huh. How about Expose, the X-Ray Spray? You spray this junk on a piece of mail and you don't have to open it—it turns paper translucent for 30–60 seconds. Just long enough for a peek. Even their non-sneaky stuff is for tough guys. A lambskin attache: perfect for the kind of wolves who'd order spy cameras and secret tape recorders.

Well, maybe I should order some of these items. Then perhaps I could be like the Vice President of Product Development for Life Force, Doug Casey. I mean, the man has even discovered the secret to eternal youth. He did this by adding the personal Radical Shield to his daily regimen. The Personal Radical Shield is an "ultra-high potency, natural antioxidant which bonds with, and eliminates, free radicals in the body. These molecules speed the aging process and inhibit DNA production. It's simply common sense that eliminating free radicals from the body will slow down aging," says Doug in his introductory letter on page two of the catalog. He doesn't look so good in his picture, but at least he won't look good for a very long time with his Personal Radical Shield, which is available, by the way, for only 37 bucks for a 28-day supply.

Yeah, I should order some. Then I can get out of this minnow pond and start swimming with the sharks.

11/17/88

Prescription: Meat

My doctor tells me I must get fat. That's his prescription for what ails me. He told me to eat everything in sight. "Wish I had *your* diet," people say.

And for some it would be a good one. I have to eat a lot of eggs and meat. A James Garner diet. Of course, he just had a triple bypass, but I'm not worried about that. I'm just not that interested in eggs and meat. Listen to this. I'm supposed to eat two ounces of meat, two servings of bread, and a cup of lowfat milk before I go to bed. We're talking about a sandwich made with three slices of bologna or olive loaf, or a big pile of chip-chopped ham. It doesn't appeal to me. I'm not Dagwood Bumstead. I'm only a mild carnivore. And I'm supposed to eat a big meat sandwich as a postscript to an already meat-filled day.

> You can eat just so much meat. Then it begins to gross you out. You begin to think about what it used to be.

You can eat just so much meat. Then it begins to gross you out. You begin to think about what it used to be. I do, anyway. And since I'm no cook, I don't have the ability to present the meat to make me forget that it had been walking in a meadow a few days earlier. It always looks like raw meat to me. Red and gray, and, at its worst, like a horror movie's special effects. I'm in that phase now, probably because I'm *supposed* to eat it. If I was on a vegetarian diet, meat would appear thick, savory, and delicious to me. Now, no amount of Hamburger Helper or Sloppy Joe mix would make hamburger look good.

Eggs aren't much better. It will not do you well to think too closely on those gentlemen. If eggs aren't cooked right they're like any other squishy, runny things you wouldn't dream of eating. And I tell you, I can't stand seeing those little red deals in an uncooked egg yolk. You know what I'm talking about. That's part of the doc's prescription too. I had no problem with them before I knew I had to eat them. Now it seems an act of savagery.

I might as well face facts. I'm too lazy to learn how to cook an attractive, appetizing meal. Of course my eggs and meat are going to look disgusting. I haven't bothered to learn how to dress them up. I scramble the eggs and stick the hamburger on a Finast or Heritage

House bun. Big deal. Who *would* like that every day? I've never prepared a roast or grilled some nice chops. Never arranged the carrots, celery, and spuds around the meat, or browned it, or squirted it with its natural juices. That's the ticket. That's how you cook. But at the end of the day, I'm too tired to even prepare my famous Potato Stir, a tasty mixture of Fleischmann's Margarine, sliced potatoes (chunked if you're strapped for time), and a little subtle sprinkle of the dehydrated onions and brown powder of Lipton's Onion Soup Mix, which gives it a nice MSG flavor. In a microwave age, why should I bother with my Potato Stir when Armour will do the work for me with Le Menu? Seven to nine minutes and you've got sirloin tips, O'Brien potatoes, and vegetable medley steaming and ready. And not bad, either. About on the airline food level—maybe a notch below.

So instead of regular meat and vegetables I eat convenience foods. Safe foods from the earth, like pretzels. The aforementioned frozen and microwave foods. I don't feel that they provide the genuine calories the doctor recommends, though. Some of the stuff I eat, like the pretzels and the crackers and the cheese cubes, go right through me and have no nutritional effect except leaving deposits of salt to mess me up later. (I do try to get my fiber going, though, by shredding a Triscuit cracker with my front teeth before swallowing it, and this makes it work just like Shredded Wheat.) I'd rather have the salt, though, than the potential gross-out of the meat and eggs. I'm not feeling these days like eating anything named Henny, Bossy, or Porky.

12/1/88

A Few Odd Resolutions

1. Probably the first thing I'm going to do for the New Year is change into a nice guy. It's high time, too. I've been operating at around 20–35% niceness the past several years, and I'd like to get up to at least 50% by the end of '89. The first step is to be more compassionate of the constant failings of my co-workers, family, and friends. For example, when somebody tells me their troubles or voices a real concern to me, I either a) walk away in boredom, b) interrupt and ask how my hair looks, c) roll my eyes, or d) pretend to cry, throwing in a few bogus "boo hoo, boo hoo"s. This year I'm going to be Mr. Nice Guy. I'm going to listen and nod right along.

My only worry is that people looking up into my sixth-floor window will not see the trampoline and assume I'm engaged in a leaping-style perversion.

2. Along with niceness, I'm going to bring fitness into my life. My friend gave me a small trampoline—a "personal" trampoline, you might say—and I'm going to literally bounce right into the New Year. Hopping up and down is terrific exercise and I vow to do so three times a week. My only worry is that people looking up into my sixth-floor window will not see the trampoline on the floor—just my body bobbing in and out of view—and will assume I'm engaged in a leaping-style perversion. Plus, what if this activity makes me jumpier than I already am? I'm not kidding. Maybe I'd better take it easy.

3. Another thing people mention to me as a fault is that I don't smile. That's true. I smile very seldom. I'm often accused of solemnity. I'll try to change that this year, but I don't know if I can. When I do smile my eyes are mirthless, leading to a ghastly effect, like the grin on a human skull or the look of a snarling dog. I'm going to fix that (somehow) and start walking around with a spring in my step and song in my heart. If I don't get hit by a number 32 bus crossing Euclid first.

4. I'm going to watch better TV this year. Every day I come home from work, switch on the news (which is okay), but then kill an hour watching reruns of *The Untouchables* on Channel 55. *The Untouchables*

had its day, but that day is gone. I can't keep reliving the glory. It's one of those shows you latch onto, though, like *M*A*S*H** or *Cheers*, and commit to memory. I don't watch many primetime shows, except an occasional *L.A. Law*, *Tattingers*, or *thirtysomething*. I'm morbidly fascinated by *thirtysomething* and the characters that do nothing other than relentlessly talk about themselves in a moist-eyed and humorless way. Or they talk about themselves in a self-deprecating way that's oddly unsympathetic. I can't figure out why I hate these people (with a few exceptions) so much. Anyway, there's better people to watch, and I'm going to watch them this year.

5. Not that I'm going to be sitting inside all year. Not me. No one appreciates the Indoors more than I, but you have to get out once in a while. As a matter of fact, if I'm not Indoors you'll definitely find me Outdoors, to paraphrase Frank Burns from *M*A*S*H**. And this coming year I'm going to run around outside and breathe hard and appreciate all the plants and animals. Once I saw a crow, a squirrel, and a cat sitting on somebody's lawn—*all at the same time*. And I witnessed this unusual occurrence of nature all because I was outside. So that's where you'll find me once in a while.

All in all, 1989 is going to be a dynamite year with niceness, moderate bounding, grinning, quality TV, and natural wonders. I hope you have the same.

12/29/88

A Message from Pleasantville

Hello! I'm writing to you from Pleasantville, New York, home of the *Reader's Digest*. I'm not physically in Pleasantville, but my heart—and a lot of my money—is there. Because I'm rapidly becoming a member of the *Reader's Digest* family, and there's no turning back once you cross that line into *Reader's Digest* territory. Once the *Reader's Digest* has you it tenaciously but *pleasantly* holds on.

I knew I was finished when I received my first *Reader's Digest* Condensed Book the other day. I could never have consciously ordered a *Reader's Digest* Condensed Book. A swinging guy like me doesn't have a shelf full of *Reader's Digest* Condensed Books in his living room, with their triple-titled spines and their cheap, lightweight paper. Grandma keeps these books, not finger-popping urbanites who read *Spy*. But there it was in my mailbox. Three books in one volume, with 1937-style magazine illustrations peppered throughout. And they're going to keep coming every two months until I say "Stop," which I'm slightly afraid to do.

> **A swinging guy like me doesn't have a shelf full of *Reader's Digest* Condensed Books in his living room.**

This is all my own fault. I teased the *Reader's Digest*, which is to say I made the decision to subscribe. But you don't just subscribe to the *Reader's Digest*. They didn't build a media empire on simple subscriptions where they send you 12 issues and politely ask you to renew when it runs out. I was told I made a commitment for two years in a note that seemed to be written by a nice but potentially disapproving elderly woman who makes her home in Pleasantville. And now the *Reader's Digest*s are piling up. You can't throw the boogers out, either. I can't anyway, and I'm not sure why.

It's probably because the magazine looks like a book, chock-full of items that may be useful in the future, like October '88's "Hospital Handbook" and "The Smart Way to Car Shop." What if I threw October '88 away and then suddenly landed in the hospital, or decided to buy a car? Or November '88's "How to Argue with Your Boss." December's "Problem Solving Made Easier." January '89's "How to Beat a Bad Mood." How do I know I won't need these tips? You can throw away other magazines with self-help articles, but not *Reader's*

Digest, with its handy front-cover table of contents that is like an index of helpfulness. It would be sinful to throw a reference away, wouldn't it? These *Reader's Digest* people are shrewd.

They don't neglect the lighter fare either, like "Paradise on the Palate: Pickles" (October '88), "Let's Give Salt a Fair Shake" (November '88), "What Our Fingernails Reveal" (also November), "How to Swat a Fly" (June '88), and "The Wackiest Thing I Ever Heard" (October '88). Not to mention "Humor in Uniform," "Life in These United States," "Campus Comedy," and "Laughter, the Best Medicine," all the chuckle-inducing staples, dumb jokes taken from life, Pleasantville laffs. No filthy talk, no dirty stuff. Sam Kinison wouldn't make it in the *Digest*. We *Digest* readers wouldn't dream of listening to Sam Kinison.

See? I'm thinking like a *Digest*-er already. Phrases are beginning to run through my mind like "A Simple Gift of Blood," "ABCs of Courage," and "Where Joy Abounds." The famous "Drama in Real Life." That one won't go away any time soon. These folks will make any circle square. I know I'm being brainwashed. And I'm getting it every month without fail, and sometimes I think twice a month the stubby little journal is being stuck in my mailbox with its "God Bless Irving Berlin" articles written by Ronald Reagan and "Disney's Five Ways to Make Dreams Come True" and "The Dog Who Knew Better" and "My Father's Greatest Gift" and all the rest of it. I know I'll keep getting it, too, because I don't think you can un-subscribe to the *Reader's Digest*. They're far too powerful in Pleasantville.

2/16/89

Cheeping and Squeaking

What do you do when you're alone? If it's anything like what I do, you should be ashamed of yourself.

Not that I do dirty stuff. At least no more dirty stuff than your average broken-down single guy in his early thirties does. Yes, I do have a few magazines. I don't even refer to them anymore. Tawdry, revolting publications . . . they disgust me. I don't know what I was thinking of when I bought them. *Cheri, Velvet, Club, High Society,* and all the rest of them. I hardly remember their names. That section of the magazine rack is strictly off limits these days. I was on a mini pornography kick then. Can I help it? I was young. It was 1986, the Reagan era of *laissez-faire,* and I took full advantage. I keep the magazines in the bottom of my pants drawer as a reminder. *These are from the days when you were a fool! Don't return to those days!* I think as I look through them.

> I imitate mice, chipmunks, squirrels, and the Bangles' Susanna Hoffs when I'm alone. I cheep and squeak and make animal noises and sing in a high voice.

No, I'm not slobbering over pictures of Amber Lynn or Kitten Natividad anymore. I get my ya-ya's out in a different way today. I imitate mice, chipmunks, squirrels, and the Bangles' Susanna Hoffs when I'm alone. I cheep and squeak and make animal noises and sing in a high voice.

Now there's nothing wrong with cheeping and squeaking once in a while when you're fooling around at home with nobody watching. Even Secretary of State James Baker lets out a squeak now and then when he's by himself, and he's a no-nonsense guy. But I go way overboard. It's getting to the saturation point, where all my noises are animal noises. I'm turning into a cartoon character. I partially blame the Bee Gees for this. Remember their Saturday Night Fever music, when they sang like mice let loose in a disco? You know—"Stayin Alive" and "You Should Be Dancing," songs like that. I've been chirping those tunes to myself for well on a decade. I've always had rodent-like sounds running through my head. Now they're coming out.

For instance, I have a Bangles record with some very catchy tunes on it, sung by Susanna Hoffs. Susanna Hoffs sounds like one of the chipmunks of Alvin and the Chipmunks. Not any particular one, not specifically Alvin, Simon, or Theodore, but like a generic chipmunk who didn't make it into the group. I find myself imitating her helium-like voice in front of the mirror, to the point where I frighten myself. What the hell am I doing! I'm standing there, in front of the mirror, wasting precious moments of my life with this nonsense. Then I run into the bathroom in shame.

But as they say on TV, you can run, but you can't hide from yourself. If I'm not trying to imitate Susanna Hoffs I'm aggravating squirrels with my impressions of them when I walk outside the apartment building. When I see a squirrel I feel a need to make squirrel noises, snapping my teeth together rapidly to simulate nut-cracking and using my tongue and gums to create chewing sounds. They stand on their hind legs looking at me, their tiny brown eyes filled with hate. And who can blame them?

That's nothing compared to how I talk to the cat. I don't just make nauseating baby talk to the cat, though I do do that. I sing to her and do a call-and-response with her when she meows. She doesn't meow often, but when she does she means business. She doesn't need to hear my meows whenever she cries for her food or when she does that mysterious howling by the litter box. It would be like if every time your dog barked you barked back. And I make up songs about feeding her, which must be extremely vexing to her because when I sing to her about feeding her it's precisely the time she wants to be fed. It's in that cartoon character voice, too, that flattens her ears every time she hears it.

My largest fear in this matter is that I'll be caught in the act. I mean, I'd know how to respond if someone caught me with a *Club* or a *Velvet*. But what do you say when someone catches you squeaking?

3/30/89

Hello, I Must Be Going

When you're leaving, I'm not going to hug you, cry, and whisper "I'm no good at good-byes," like they do on TV. I'm very good at good-byes. From me you'll get a wave and a simple "So long" with maybe a *ciao*, *sayonara*, or *vaya con Dios* thrown in. No, I'm usually glad to see you leave so I can go about my business, which is usually not much, but it is mine. And though I enjoy being with people, being by myself involves a lot less strain. So . . . bye! See you later! I'll call you! Take care!

No, for me it's the hellos that are hard. When I first meet someone, I'm supposed to shake hands and say my name. My name doesn't seem like it would be hard to pronounce, but it is. People think I say "Art" or "Ed" or "Mark." I'm embarrassed when older guys in suits stick out their hands and say "How are you doing, Art?" I think they want my name to be Art or Ed, good business names. On the other hand, some women hear my name as "Derek," which con-

> I want my actions to say, "If you try to hug me, I'm not guaranteeing I won't loosen a few of your teeth with my chin on the approach."

jures up the image of a British stud in a tuxedo, *à la* Tom Jones. I feel terrible correcting them, because it was my mushmouth that led to the confusion. No one knows what to make of the name "Eric," either. It's not identifiable with anything. If my name was "Webster," people could say "Like Webster Slaughter, right?" They don't do that with "Eric." No one has the slightest bit of fun with "Eric."

I can't remember other people's names, either. That kind of information flies immediately out the windows of my mind. I can remember your face, your problems, your idiosyncrasies, your hopes, your dreams, your desires, but I probably can't remember your name. Many people mistake my embarrassment for unfriendliness when I pass by them and give them a stiff "Hey, how you doing?" I'm ashamed that I can't remember the name, and so I look pained. Sometimes I don't even say "Hey, how you doing?" when I think of all that could go wrong in mid-greeting. To compensate I try to smile, but I never get a full one out, because I'm not sure what I'm supposed to be doing and so it comes out more like a grimace. In other words, when I pass most people they either think I'm hostile or that I've got appendicitis or a spastic colon. I'm far from being a hail-thee-fellow-well-met.

And when I get to know people better, then I have to worry about hugging them. I don't believe in hugging outside of the family, though I will make certain exceptions. But generally, hugging makes me uncomfortable. I couldn't go on the Oscar or Grammy awards cere-monies with all that hugging. You can't tell me that all those people know each other well enough to embrace. Why the hell should I hug Bette Midler or Carole Bayer Sager? It's no different in Cleveland. There's lots of people around here who believe you should hug friends or even acquaintances.

I try to avoid this. I put on an exaggerated uncoordinated act when I run into people to make them think I'm all knees and elbows, so they won't want to hug me. I'm not saying I jump around and frighten peo-ple—I'm more subtle. I just try to look slightly off. I want my actions to say, "If you try to hug me, I'm not guaranteeing I won't loosen a few of your teeth with my chin on the approach. I also might jab you in a tender spot. But I'm willing to hug if you feel we absolutely have to." Most people leave me alone when I give off these vibes. I can spot oth-ers who use the same strategy to avoid hugging, and I feel a special kin-ship with them. We look at each other in relief, knowing that neither of us are huggers and we can stop fretting, at least for the moment. But we both know that there's always going to be somebody who's going to want to hug in the future, so there's always going to be something to dread.

Yes, good-byes are easy and the rest is hard. So good-bye.

5/3/89

You're Fired

I thought I would do some freelance writing and make a little extra cash. I intended to work several hours a day and write articles to make the people howl with excitement.

I didn't, of course. With so much free time in the day there was no way I could get anything done. I couldn't get anything done in the morning, because I had to take an hour-and-a-half walk. When I returned from the walk it was 11:30, and I spent a half-hour thinking about lunch, a half-hour eating, and a half-hour digesting. I couldn't get anything done in the afternoon, because I spent the afternoons in research, which meant reading magazines and watching TV. By 3:30, I had to think about taking my nap, a siesta lasting from 4 to 5 p.m. And when I awoke from my nap it was almost time for the TV news report, which I

Instead of making literary history I was messing around in dry goods.

prepared for by reading more magazines and wandering around the apartment. And, of course, after 6 p.m. is evening, a time for relaxation. So very little got written.

Another problem was that I couldn't think of anything good to write about when I did think about it. My best idea was a story about Zsa Zsa Gabor, on trial for smacking a Beverly Hills police officer. My theory was that the police officer mistook her for her sister, Eva Gabor, and had made an ill-advised comment about Eva's TV show, *Green Acres*, not knowing that references to *Green Acres* enraged Zsa Zsa, who flew into fits at the mere mention of this CBS situation comedy that kept Eva, not Zsa Zsa, in the public eye. But that's as far as I got with it.

Another idea I was temporarily excited about was a story concerning a fellow running for mayor of Cleveland who held his own left buttock as he campaigned, this representing his political trademark, like JFK twisting his suit button. Then the buttock-holding candidate lost in the primary, far behind Ralph Perk, Jr. I felt this was a good idea but maybe not saleable.

This was the trouble with most of my freelance writing ideas. They weren't practical. I spent a lot of time thinking about one idea I knew couldn't pan out, but I kept thinking about it anyway instead of getting down to real work. It was after I saw a TV commercial with the Pillsbury Doughboy, a revolutionary spot wherein the Doughboy is lying on a chaise lounge asleep or perhaps dozing. Usually, as you know, the Doughboy is poked in the stomach by a human finger and chuckles delightedly. This time, the hand that usually gives him the poke has mercy and covers him with a blanket. When I saw this commercial I took all sorts of notes and paced the room with all kinds of thoughts about the Doughboy and if he really liked being poked. It was a big waste of time. You don't make any money with ideas like that.

More troublesome than the bad ideas, though, was the lack of discipline. Writers are supposed to sit down and write no matter what, which is what I told myself, boss to employee. As an employee I only half-listened to this, smoking a cigarette, watching the clock, impatiently waiting to punch out so I could go home and take that nap we discussed earlier. Or I'd go on missions to Revco that were really just evasions of responsibility. I spent far more time at Revco looking at Shaving Needs than I did working. I compared Barbasol to Edge when I should have been whipping that Gabor piece into shape. I hung around the Duracell display instead of banging out those dynamite stories that would turn American literature upside down, set it on its ear, redefine it. Instead of making literary history I was messing around in dry goods.

I began to see that this was not the formula for success. I decided to take a good hard look at myself. This yawning fellow was not on the fast track to financial freedom with all the napping, crummy story ideas, and trips to Revco. So I said to myself, "I'm afraid your services are no longer needed here. Thank you and best of luck in the future."

10/26/89

Job Hunting: Boring or Stupid?

I don't know of anything in life worse than job hunting. Death, maybe. Junior high. Waiting around in the auto title bureau. But for long-range frustration you can't beat job hunting. It's humiliating, dull, stressful, and frightening, and the end result—landing a job—isn't so hot either.

I had to look for work during the past several months. Pickings were slim. Each Sunday I looked in the classified "Help Wanted" section of the newspaper for a position. I looked under "E" for Editor. There were usually a few editor jobs around, but for rocks and minerals magazines. I couldn't apply for a job writing and editing articles about rocks and minerals. There were jobs for chemical editors, as well. I can't feign interest in that stuff. I know someone's got to do it, and not every rocks and minerals editor grew up dreaming of this kind of life. "When I grow up I wanna be an editor at *Cobalt Age*." Few of your schoolroom youngsters say this. I sure didn't. You didn't see me at the school science fair, either. I can't figure out carbonation; how could I write about zinc or bismuth?

"When I grow up I wanna be an editor at *Cobalt Age*." Few of your schoolroom youngsters say this.

The classifieds never had listings for the things I really wanted to do or was good at. There weren't any help wanted ads for Whiners or TV Watchers or Steady Snackers or Mall Walkers. Wouldn't it be great to sit around all day at home and eat and watch the tube and then bill somebody for it? But it's not going to happen. It's one of the tragedies of this life that we are seldom paid for the things at which we truly excel.

Well, as they say, the good jobs usually aren't in the classifieds anyway. You have to network. That's big fun, too. I enjoyed calling busy people and saying I'd like to come in to talk with them about their work. They know what you're up to. You're looking to come in and beg like a dog for work, take up their lunch hour or their fooling-around time, all under the guise of an "informational interview." The only information I needed in one of those interviews was if any jobs were open. Once I found that out I got the hell out of there.

My problem is I hate bothering people; I hate asking them for anything. I'm not one of those people who feel they're doing an employer a big favor by working for them, though those people generally get ahead, damn it. I'm not pathetically grateful when I'm hired, either, because then you're really asking for it. (They'll give you all the grunt work.) I do well when I'm in, but I find it hard to ask to get in. You know what I mean?

I get flustered when I have to talk to people about my possible employment at their business. Usually silver-tongued and nimblewitted, I change into a Baby Huey–type character when I'm job hunting. I can't hide my nervousness when I make phone calls. Once I said "Duh . . . duhh" to some guy I was talking to about a job. Or I'd have a rare time when I would eloquently describe my skills and qualifications to a potential employer and then forget to mention that I wanted a job. Usually, though, the first thing I say is "Duhhh, I'm looking for a job, actually" which never has worked either.

With all that, it's often true that when job interviews or queries go badly it's just as well you don't get the job. When I first got out of school I was desperately looking for work and answered an ad from Mutual of New York for a marketing position, better known as selling insurance. I imagined myself making lots of money in marketing and even having fun doing it. I pinned all my hopes on this because I had nothing else going.

The interviewer liked me, mostly because I didn't appear to be a total numbskull, though I did feel he himself was a serious dweeb. He gave me a sales aptitude test, scored on a range from 1 to 18. "Don't worry," he told me. "Everyone gets above a 9, and that's all we're looking for."

I told the truth on the test. When it asked how I would respond to a person declining to buy insurance from me, I marked (c.) Give up and go away. When it asked what was my favorite activity I marked (c.) Sitting by myself. Like that. The interviewer called me later in the week and told me I scored a 4. He sounded mad. "Thanks for your interest in Mutual of New York," he said and hung up on me.

Now that I think of it, maybe job hunting could be worse. I might have done well on that test.

11/2/89

King Kong vs. Patty Duke

The other evening I pulled a buttock muscle while watching cable TV. What happened was that I had shifted slightly on the sofa and the muscle went, causing me considerable pain the rest of the night and giving me a pronounced limp well into the next day. It may well be that the slippers I had on were ones I wasn't used to wearing and had caused the injury, but who can tell about these things? I tried to work the pull out with the small $3.99 Pollenex electric massager I got on sale at the May Company, but it didn't work. I was just glad I had cable TV to get me through this trial, to distract me from the pain.

Believe me, I love having cable. I would be living a lie if I pretended I didn't.

I've had cable for several months now. It was installed in May in what I'll always remember as a heartwarming scene. A guy named Keith put it in, and he and I had a friendly chat as he did. We joked about the wires going through the cabinet there in the living room, and although the conversation wasn't too scintillating, I thought to myself, "Here are a couple of American guys, up until now total strangers, talking about wires and cables and electrical stuff in a free and easy way." A couple of American guys. It made me feel good. Plus the cat was sitting contentedly nearby, watching us, to round out this inspirational tableau.

Not only did I feel good about the American-ness of my cable installation, I was excited about the new world of TV programming I was about to experience. After Keith left, I ran the gamut of the new channels. I couldn't believe it. All these great old shows were on, like *Father Knows Best*, *Make Room for Daddy*, *Car 54*, *Where Are You?*, and *The Donna Reed Show*, and they were on all the time. You can always catch a glimpse of Andy, the Beaver, Jed and Granny, Lucy and Desi, Hazel, Samantha and Darrin, Perry Mason, Hoss and Little Joe, Bugs Bunny. And the movies! TNT and American Movie Classics run them all day, and with TBS, USA, Lifetime, the Family Network, and the rest of them pitching in, there's always something decent on.

That's the trouble. I had always scorned those who zapped through the channels with their remote, never settling on one thing. I felt I had a moral superiority in this admittedly minor area of life. Once I had decided on a show, I stuck to it.

But once I got cable, I became a channel zapper too. What can I say? It was my first remote. There's no sense sitting through a muffler commercial in the middle of *Two Guys from Milwaukee* when you can press a button and see Paula Abdul dance and squeak her way through a song on VH-1. I enjoyed the novelty of channel zapping for the first few weeks, wallowing in what I thought was viewing freedom. But it soon became the slavery that my instincts had told me it would be.

Everyone with cable has felt it. You sit there, remote in hand, flashing from one idiotic show to another, becoming increasingly nervous and irritated, getting that boredom pain in your urinary tract. Nowadays I turn the TV off when I get to this point (at least most of the time I do). I turned the corner on this problem several weeks ago when I was switching from the movie *King Kong* to *The Patty Duke Show*. I went back and forth, King Kong to Patty Duke, Patty Duke to King Kong, until I almost went into a trance. I had to throw the remote down, get up off the couch, and walk it off. I swore: Never again.

I also discovered that 99% of the old shows I was excited about at first were really pretty dismal. I was sure that I'd be watching *The Donna Reed Show* all the time for its nostalgia and suburban American Dream value. I couldn't even sit through one episode, it was so foolish. I realized that I couldn't stand Carl Betz. I'd gone through my whole life thinking that Carl Betz was cool, and it took ten minutes of cable TV to change my mind. And this wasn't my only disillusionment with old black-and-white sitcoms. The only one I'll sit through any more is *The Dick Van Dyke Show*—or maybe *The Many Loves of Dobie Gillis*, if they ever bring it back. *The Honeymooners* and *You'll Never Get Rich*, too. The rest they should just bury in the sitcom graveyard.

But believe me, I love having cable. I would be living a lie if I pretended I didn't. There's always something for me. Right now I'm in a phase where all I watch are documentaries on Hitler. If you have cable you can see all you want on Hitler and Nazis and World War II. Last Sunday I watched a show called *The Fatal Attraction of Adolf Hitler* and then one called *Hitler: The Whole Story*. Four hours of Hitler. I like getting worked up about Hitler, though, granted, there's not much I can do about him now. But it's good to have the extra opportunity to watch educational stuff that cable gives you.

Yeah, I love having cable. There's so much of it.

11/30/89

A Cheap Uncle

My question is this: Why should I spend my valuable time shopping for Christmas presents for my nieces and nephews, who are scattered throughout the county and who I rarely see, and who, when I do see them, act weird? I'm not saying my nieces and nephews are creeps or psychos, or that they flick lit cigarettes at me when they see me (their median age is about six), but they don't act too respectful when their uncle's around. When I see them they break off into little groups and make faces at me. Maybe they're not making faces at me, but they're definitely doing something disrespectful with their faces. And for this they want presents every year?

But squirt guns can run into money, and they can be (and have been) used against me. Maybe I'll just send them legal pads.

(I should add that there's one nephew, out of Washington, D.C., who treats me with respect. He's about two years old, and I can carry him around or jab him with my finger and he doesn't care. He just looks at me with his mouth hanging open, which is the way I should be treated.)

Most of these children live in the state of Washington, a world of canoes and bikes. They're not indoorsy kids, though sometimes I suspect they'd like to be. There's not much I can teach them about camping or survival tactics; their dad is good at that. But they should come to me when they have TV questions. "You want to know about E. G. Marshall, Jon? Come here and sit down. I'll tell you a few things." "What's that, Willie and young Tom? A question about Karen Valentine? Well, why don't we take a look at the book here." You know, uncle stuff.

Perhaps I should blame their parents. And why not? Someone's to blame for this situation. My sister has these five kids and a full-time job, but that doesn't mean she shouldn't be teaching the children to treat their uncle with respect. It should be part of their daily routine, thinking about their uncle in Cleveland and being grateful that he knows so much about TV and '60s pop songs and Robert DeNiro movies. Granted, my sister does send me their drawings, but these are usually a depiction of somebody eating a booger cookie or a dinosaur crushing a cow. This is respect?

And what would I get them for Christmas even if they did treat me right? My niece in New York City goes through toys like a buzzsaw. I can imagine how my toys would be dealt with in the sophisticated Big Apple. "Oh how marvelous, a package from Cleveland!"—flung carelessly into the corner of the room, to be opened later after the live entertainment has left. What are you supposed to buy for a hot-tempered eight-year-old in New York, anyway? She'd tear the head off a Care Bear or a Cabbage Patch doll.

It's easier with the kids in Washington State. They're mostly boys, except for one girl, Emily (she's a twin named after my twin sister, but her twin brother is named Edward, not Eric, another insult I'm not about to forget), and I can always get them squirt guns. Whenever I see them they seem to be holding squirt guns, so I know they like them. But squirt guns can run into money, and they can be (and have been) used against me. Maybe I'll just send them legal pads. I'll send the whole family a package of six. Each child and adult will receive one legal pad apiece. With the twins Edward and Emily splitting one. Those two are small, anyway. They won't know the difference.

I don't like being this way. I don't believe in family grudges or melodramatic statements like, "I have no nieces or nephews!" But how else can I feel? Have I been offered a choice? Get this. When I call my sister long distance and one of my nephews answers the phone, it's never "This is certainly an honor, Uncle Eric!" or "Please tell me another of your famous stories, Uncle Eric!" It's always "Uh, hi," and I hear the phone clatter on the kitchen counter and I have to wait. Is that outrageous? Is that disrespect or isn't it? Should that kind of behavior be rewarded with lavish gifts? You should treat your uncle with respect, then maybe you'll get the nice presents.

12/14/89

Momentous Events of 1989

The Balance of Power Shifts in Eastern Europe—Big doings, indeed, with the communists going down for the count and democracy kayoing the Berlin Wall and vaulting over the rubble to freedom, so to speak.

I Finally Get Some Decent Pants—The ongoing tragedy of my bad luck in pants-buying finally ends in December when I pick up some beauties at the May Company on sale for $29.95 each. These all-cotton Levi Dockers don't billow out at the waist like the other Dockers I've bought; they're flattering to my figure and require only minimum care. Plus they look fabulous with a blue or gray sportcoat. A new era begins.

Is it Mother Nature . . . or Father Time? That's the critical question in the matter of my eyebrows.

Glasnost Marches On—Mikhail Gorbachev pushes the Soviet Union toward a new age in internal and external relations as the world holds its breath.

I Find a Shampoo That I Like—And high time, too. 1989 marked my very first purchase of Thrive shampoo, which is specifically designed for us fellows with thinning hair. Thrive builds up protein in my hair follicles, strengthens the ever-jeopardized dainty strands of top hair, and puffs out my coiffure to a Liberace-like fullness that excites comment at home and in the workplace. Thrive has also stymied my hairline's backward advance and put off for at least a few years the necessary purchase of the rainbow-colored Afro toupee that I plan to wear in my old age and that Northern Michigan lounge entertainer Al Breezy wears in his wonderful organ act that has thrilled literally hundreds.

The United States Invades Panama—Confusion reigns in Panama as U.S. troops attempt to overthrow strongman Manuel Noriega's regime.

I Discover That My Totes Spell V-A-L-U-E—To be candid, I didn't get my Totes ankle-length rubbers in 1989, but the fact is that they have kept my feet warm and dry throughout the year and have taught me a valuable lesson: a quality product will pay for itself in time, and if you only spend four dollars for a pair of rubbers they'll fall apart on you one day; the momentary satisfaction you had in finding a bargain in footwear will shatter into disillusionment.

George Bush Takes the Reins of Power—The Reagan Administration ends as George Bush brings his wait-and-see attitude and commendable organization skills to the White House.

Michael's Thermos Continues to Not Explode—1989 was also noteworthy in that my friend Michael's thermos, filled with coffee in 1984 and stuck in the back seat of his car, still hasn't been opened in five years and still hasn't exploded.

The White Administration Heralds a New Era in Cleveland Politics—Mike White defeats George Forbes in the bitter mayoral race of '89 as the city anxiously awaits White's assumption of office and his crucial decisions in the appointments of a new police chief and safety director.

Mother Nature Messes with My Eyebrows—Is it Mother Nature . . . or Father Time? That's the critical question in the matter of my eyebrows, which seem to be growing out of control and threaten to take over the upper regions of my face. (I actually have to comb them.) Is this aging, or is it a genuine phenomenon? It's difficult to say. What about this new harvest of nostril hairs, as well? I suspect the new year will answer many of these nagging questions.

The Jacobs Brothers are Granted Millions of Dollars in Tax Abatement—The Society Center development gets the "Big OK" from City Council—but at what cost down the line?

I Don't Feel Good After Dinner—1989 saw a troubling trend in my not feeling good after dinner. I won't go into details—I don't like to talk about such things—but suffice it to say I will be working in the upcoming year on improving my diet, being at one with my body, and making sure I keep lifting my dumbbells so my arms don't get all feeble and decrepit.

I Get Cable TV—This, of course, was the landmark event of 1989.

12/22/89

Browns Notes

It was certainly very nice to see the Browns beat the Oilers for the AFC Central Division championship. That was a typical Browns game, full of love and hate. At the end of the game, there was love. During the game, there was hate. When Clay Matthews tossed that lateral over to the Oilers, I remarked, "You dumb M - - - - - f - - - - -! You m - - - - - - f - - - - - - beach boy, you think this is a f - - - ing volleyball game, you stupid sonuva b - - - -! M - - - - - f - - - - - a - - -, g - - - s - - -!" At the end of the game, there was love. "Good old Clay, he's like a boy on a sandlot out there, isn't he? Good old Clay, from good old USC."

> **They've got a shot at the Big One. Stranger things have happened. And you know where I'm going to watch their playoff game(s)? Yes. In the finest living room on earth.**

I like the Browns because they're easy to talk about. I know that hundreds of thousands of Clevelanders were saying the exact same thing as I was when Clay Matthews lateraled, at the exact same time, and that they also good-naturedly forgot the whole thing when we won. People who don't understand why football fans are football fans don't understand the bond between fans who think and say the same things during and following a game. The difference between people in their response to the game is so small that it's a great equalizer. And when you listen to ex-coaches and players on TV, they don't sound any smarter than an average fan. Even a "genius" like Bill Walsh routinely says stuff like "The Bengals better get going if they expect to win this game." It isn't too complicated.

Growing up following the Browns has been satisfying. They've always been competitive; it's a fluke when they have a losing season. I don't think I've missed more than three games in 20 years because of this. I liked Leroy Kelly, Bill Glass, Milt Morin, Ben Davis, Erich Barnes, Walter Johnson, Jack Gregory, and Paul Warfield from the late '60s into the '70s. I liked the Kardiac Kids: Brian Sipe, Reggie Rucker, Thom Darden, Calvin Hill, Dave Logan, Mike and Greg Pruitt. But I like the current Browns best—Bernie and Ozzie, Webstar, Eric Metcalf, Kevin Mack, Good old Clay, Frank Minnifield, Michael Dean, Big Daddy. They've got a shot at the Big One. Stranger things have happened. And you know where I'm going to watch their playoff game(s)? Yes. In the finest living room on earth.

I usually watch the games with my friend Barbara and/or my psychologist buddy ("I heal sick minds") Joe. Barbara sits up close to the TV, rocking, and pitches forward or falls backward depending on the game action. Joe and I sit on the sofa, he on the left (or right, as you approach the viewing area) and I on the right (or left, see above). We both sit up straight, in our gameday posture. We don't drink during the game and don't get too emotional. Joe, being a psychologist, is highly controlled, and I, not wanting to look crazy to a trained professional, keep quiet except at really bad plays. Then I say in a high whine, "M-----f-----, g---a---, s---." Joe looks the same at good plays and at bad, except at the good ones he murmurs "alright" or "not bad" if he's really excited. In other words, we're no fun to watch a football game with.

I used to go to quite a few games down at the Stadium. When I went with my father, I'd sit quietly and not swear at all, even at the really bad stuff, except maybe for a mild "s---." When I went with my buddies, I drank like a fish and babbled like an idiot. On one Monday night game against Pittsburgh several years ago, my friend's wife made us up a huge Coleman jug filled with Bloody Marys, which, when I saw it, I thought we'd never be able to finish. However, we'd polished it off while we were still on Martin Luther King Drive on the way down to the Stadium. Then we drank beer at our seats, gibbering and raving during the whole game, except I don't remember the second half. All I remember of that night was sprinting to the bathrooms at Burke Lakefront Airport after the game.

The past few years it hadn't been fun going to the Stadium for Browns games, because the group of guys with season tickets sitting next to us kept making us get up and down while they recycled their Genesee. They drank big tubs of beer, ejected the liquid, then drank more tubs. As soon as one sat down, another wanted to be let out. (They were sitting in the middle of the row.) The game became a backdrop to their trips to the lavatory. It's not easy getting up, either, when you're all bundled up and holding binoculars, a thermos, and a program. Our dirty looks were lost on them, as they weren't catching subtleties. They were nice guys, but they went to the bathroom a lot.

Great Indoors playoff predictions: Browns beat Buffalo. Broncos beat Browns.

1/4/90

The Great Indoors: The Movie

I happen to be negotiating with a Hollywood producer who wants the rights to my story. His name is Harv, and he produced *Batman* and *Fatal Attraction*. Either he produced them or he saw them, I don't remember exactly, but he says all he needs is a small advance to get my story out to the "right people." (That's Hollywood talk for prospective stars and directors.) So I'm going to front him the five thousand bucks he asked for to get the ball rolling, and away we'll go.

Harv says he's thinking Tom Cruise to play me. Cruise is an okay choice, but he'd have to tone it down a little. I see him overplaying the TV-watching scenes, tossing the remote control from hand to hand and prancing around for a simple channel-changing sequence. Hey, doll, let the action speak for itself! The audience wants to see authentic indoor stuff, a real guy making real choices. Frankly, Kevin Costner could pull these scenes off better than Cruise. You believe in Kevin Costner changing channels; you know why he's doing it. Plus he looks good in slippers. Harv's really going to have to talk me out of Costner.

> **Tom Cruise is an okay choice, but he'd have to tone it down a little. I see him overplaying the TV-watching scenes.**

And Costner has that lived-in look I think is crucial to the role. He has a world-weariness that can be very effective in the mail-opening scenes. The part of the movie where Johnny Hombre (that will be my name) receives his Publisher's Clearinghouse Sweepstakes entry will be pivotal. Costner can capture Johnny's feelings with a shrug and a wry smile. Or the *Reader's Digest* scene—that's going to take a certain delicacy. Johnny's torment over his seemingly unending subscription to the stubby monthly is of paramount importance in understanding his character.

The extended episode when Johnny Hombre joins that Columbia House Record and Tape Club will be a test of the actor, too. Costner—or whoever plays me—has to suggest the revealing vacillation of a man who can't decide which 11 tapes he wants for a penny. Is this a part of his life where he should take risks? Or is this a time to stock up on old reliables? The record club sequence has to be played just right, because it is a metaphor for Johnny Hombre's life.

Johnny's relationship with his cat is likewise revealing. They have a love-hate interplay that culminates in the cat's biting Johnny's wrists and hands and kicking him with her rear legs as Johnny sits on the sofa trying to watch TV. You have to build to this sequence so it will shock the audience with its power. (It should come soon after scenes of Johnny cleaning his room, for maximum contrast, and thus impact.) Johnny finally putting the cat on the floor should be a moment of supreme sympathy; it has great tearjerking potential, like the end of *Born Free*.

The movie should be an accumulation of episodes: Johnny receiving recorded sales messages on his answering machine; Johnny vacuuming; Johnny standing by the microwave waiting for his frozen burrito to cook; Johnny's troubled relationship with the Triple-A; Johnny's fruitless search for an extension cord. The success of the film depends on Costner acting these episodes *with drama yet realism*. The audience has to believe in Costner as Johnny Hombre. And not only as Johnny awake, but as Johnny asleep. Costner has to be just as convincing in the nap scenes as in the bedtime scenes.

Though the movie will be mostly about me, the supporting cast is tremendously important. I see Daryl Hannah as my girlfriend—a woman who can't quite get to the bottom of Johnny Hombre, but she'll be damned if she quits trying. Also in the cast will be Melanie Griffith as a long-suffering video store clerk who's secretly in love with Johnny and his excellent taste in movie rentals. Meg Ryan's a possibility, too, as Johnny's spunky co-worker who is secretly in love with him.

I'm very excited about this project. Harv tells me he's going to put a package together as soon as I give him his advance. I see a major smash on the horizon. Watch for it at a theater near you.

2/15/90

Why I Am Not a Mercenary

Don't ask me to be a mercenary or soldier-of-fortune. Though I might seem an ideal candidate to go on covert operations in El Salvador, Nicaragua, or the Middle East, my response to you would have to be a firm "I'll pass." Let me detail my reasons for this and finally put this mercenary business to rest.

Mercenaries don't weep on top of horses. Frequently, mercenaries are required to ride horses, and my experience with horses has not been good. When I was six and attending Red Raider Camp here in Cleveland, I was put on top of a filly or mustang or stallion, I don't know what it was, but that booger wouldn't move. As the other kids' horses ambled down the trail mine kept his head down and ate. As they moved out of sight I said "Come on, Lady . . . Red . . . Fury . . . " I couldn't remember the name. I kicked the horse with my sneakers and flopped the reins up and down, but we were still sitting there when the other kids returned from their ride, and I was weeping. Mercenaries can't do this.

> I'm not sure of the availability of Honey Maid grahams (which I consider to be a painless, even pleasant way to fill my fiber needs) in places such as Tripoli or Managua.

Contact lens care suffers in the field. As a soft lens wearer, it's imperative I keep my lenses clean, which does take some effort.

SQUAD LEADER: Let's move! What the f--- are you doing?!

ME: (waiting for the disinfection cycle to complete): You try wearing soft lenses without thoroughly cleaning and disinfecting them first. You get a nice little protein buildup, and I don't need that, thank you very much.

This body of mine isn't getting any younger. I can't ride on the undercarriage of speeding trucks or outrun explosions like I used to. These days, I climb two flights of stairs and my thighs kill me. I don't know if I could handle a dozen guerrillas anymore. And this little bit of self-doubt isn't good for a mercenary.

I'm a climate control kind of guy. One thing I can't stand is being hot. It makes me irritable. Mercenaries have to be even-tempered, but El Salvador's climate would test me severely.

SQUAD LEADER: Come on! Let's move! Let's move!

ME: Oh, keep your shirt on.

SQUAD LEADER: What the f--- did you say? I'll cut your d--- n--- off, you son of a b---!

ME: I'm sorry. I'm just hot.

I'm a little blade-shy since cutting my thumb two weeks ago. I'm not sure that I could be as effective against knives and razors as I'd like anymore. Two weeks ago I cut my thumb badly on a tuna can lid, and missed an entire segment of *60 Minutes* trying to stop the bleeding. As I applied pressure to the wound I thought wearily, "This isn't fun for me anymore." That's no attitude for a mercenary to take.

Can you guarantee me my oat bran and honey grahams in the world's hot spots? I try to get as much fiber in my diet as I can, and I'm not sure of the availability of Honey Maid grahams (which I consider to be a painless, even pleasant way to fill my fiber needs) or oat bran cereals (or muffins) in places such as Tripoli or Managua. Guarantee me ready access to sources of fiber and I'll consider going on your mission. You can't? *Well, then neither can I!*

My experience with firearms is limited. The only time I ever shot off a gun was in my sister's basement in Washington in 1978. My brother-in-law set up a tree stump for me to shoot at, and handed me his shotgun. I sat in a chair, fired, and the recoil knocked the chair and me back a foot, and the blast blew out the single light bulb hanging from the ceiling. And my sister yelled at us for firing a shotgun in the house. Mercenaries should have more experience with firearms than this.

2/22/90

My Right Foot

My question is, how can I go on this vacation I've been thinking of taking with a mortified small toe plus my problem with sleeplessness? You ask, "What about the toe? What's the matter with it?" You say, "Let's hear about the toe first before going on with the other stuff."

Well, all right. The toe first, then the sleeplessness, then the vacation plans.

You know how you step on your baby toe with the one next to it as you walk? Even if you don't know, believe me, it happens. And when things aren't going right, that adjacent toe can flatten out the bottom of the baby toe, creating a horny ridge, a ridge so sharp it could cut paper. You could shave with it, honest. That's what I'm facing right now. A toe that has turned into a weapon, a total instrument of pain; a toe that has

> I found it quite fascinating how the Toe Cap resembled a big Russian fur cap, and how it made my toe look like Lara in *Dr. Zhivago*.

turned against its master: specifically, the host foot, and generally, me.

You say, "That's terrible! How can a person live with a condition like that? How can a person walk while he's stepping on his own toes?" Well, I won't claim that it's easy. Each step brings a new experience in pain, a fresh rush of discomfort.

"Bad," you say? There's more. I also have to contend with the insensitivity of others. When I brought my Dr. Scholl's Toe Cap into the office the other day and slipped the foam cushioning cover over my toe, I thought, naturally, others would be interested in seeing this. I, for one, had never seen a Toe Cap at work, and I found it quite fascinating how the Toe Cap resembled a big Russian fur cap, and how it made my toe look like Lara in *Dr. Zhivago*. But when I showed my capped toe to the boss he displayed no reaction. That hurt even more than the toe itself. Slapped down, I hobbled back to my desk.

Now prepare yourself for a real shock. I mentioned my problem with sleeplessness. Among the reasons I have trouble sleeping are the leg tingles I get at night. These tingles are much like the needles and pins you get when your leg falls asleep. But imagine having these tingles and not being able to get rid of them. You feel like you're being tickled all night. I try shaking my leg and even waving it around in the air, but when the tingle is in there, it's really socked in. There's no getting away from it. You say, "That is shocking." Imagine a human being putting up with such torment, forced to shake his leg like a dog so he can sleep. But the worst—and this is what I can't believe—is that this is a whole different leg than the one with the sharp toe! This is an entirely separate problem! I'll wait a moment as you absorb the full force of this statement.

Mix all this together, if you can, and add to it that I'm trying to make vacation plans. I need a break from routine, too. I want to see the world, just like everybody else. There are places I want to see, cultures I'd like to observe, peoples from different societies to talk to. But how can I think about taking a trip to Tokyo or Nepal with my toe and leg so up in the air? How do I know that the sight of my crested toe won't send sensitive peoples of other nations into fits of murmuring and prayer? Not that I can realistically afford to go where people fall down in prayer. At most, I might be able to swing a trip to Detroit or Windsor, Ontario. Even so, can I be sure that Michigan has the facilities to cope with toe-or-leg-related emergencies? What if I lost my Toe Cap in Canada? These are the things I have to think about.

"Whew," you say. "We thought we had problems."

3/22/90

Walking and Dogs

For a while there I thought I'd bounce my way to fitness, but the second time I jumped on my mini-trampoline a spring broke, making a *doinn-ng* sound. I got off the thing immediately. The next spring that broke could be the killer. I didn't want to be found lying dead in my bedroom with a broken-through mini-trampoline around my ankles. I decided then there's no sense risking my life on a trampoline when I could get the same beneficial effects by taking a vigorous walk after dinner. (We athletes call this sort of decision-making process "cross-training.")

> "If it doesn't bother them, how come when you give some dogs the finger they bark even more furiously?"

On my vigorous walks, I listen to the Realistic Stereo-Mate personal cassette player I picked up at Radio Shack. (I got it, too, without the usual Radio Shack nonsense where they ask your name and address even for the most piddling purchase. Next time they ask, I'm going to point to my cash on the counter and say, "Andrew Jackson, Abraham Lincoln, and George Washington are the only names you need to know.") The Stereo-Mate entertains me and thus makes the walks go faster.

On the first few walks I took, I listened to a documentary about World War II. I'm a history nerd, and this stuff never fails to stir me. When I heard the recording of CBS's Bob Trout announcing the Japanese surrender—"This, ladies and gentlemen, is the end of the Second World War! The united nations, on land, on the sea, to the four corners of the earth, are united and victorious!"—I pumped my fist and said "Yes!" It was exciting. There I was, walking down a suburban Cleveland street with earphones on, and the Japanese surrendered. How could I have wasted my time bouncing with all this going on?

I also listened to a tape called *TeeVee Toons: The Commercials*, a collection of recorded TV commercials from the '50s, '60s, and '70s like Cracker Jack ("Waddya want when ya gotta have something"), Good-n-Plenty (Choo-Choo Charlie), Polaroid Swinger ("Meet the Swinger, Polaroid Swinger"), Coca-Cola ("Things go better with Coke" and "I'd Like to Teach the World to Sing"), Nestle's Quik (sung by the dog Farfel), Bosco, Mr. Clean, Ajax ("Ajax *boom boom*, the blue dot cleanser"), Salem ("You can take Salem out of the country, but you can't take the country out of Salem"), and about 40 more.

There's nothing like walking along to the bouncy tootling of Rice Krispies' "Snap! what a happy sound/Snap is the happiest sound I've found" or the groovy mid-'60s lady singing "Come alive, come alive/This is the Pepsi Generation." Or Edie Adams singing about Muriel cigars. Or Noxzema Shave Cream's "Take it off . . . take it all off." The Gillette March ("You'll look sharp . . . you'll feel sharp") nearly got me moving at a canter. The only really bad commercial was for Dippity Do, with the man and woman chanting "Dippity Do! Holds and holds! Dippity Do! Dippity Do! DIPPITY DO!" I felt sorry for the man, who sounded like he'd be more comfortable talking about tires gripping the road than hollering the name of some women's hair gook—and for me, who had to look nervously around to make sure this junk wasn't escaping out of my earholes into the fresh night air. Beyond that, listening to my *TeeVee Toons* was big fun.

There is, however, a darker side to walking. Every night when I walk, there's always some wisenheimer dog that barks at me from behind a fence or from inside a house. As a matter of course, I give these barking dogs the finger. You might say, "Why bother? What do they care?" My response to that is, "If it doesn't bother them, how come when you give some dogs the finger they bark even more furiously?"

I've been working on a theory about this. My theory is that many times a dog will look away from you for that split second while you're winding up to flip them the bird. And when they look back, all they see is your hand in the air, finger extended, and their tiny minds register something like, "Hey, this guy's throwing me a treat!" And they get all excited, because dogs are always on the make for food. So it isn't outrage at being shot the bird, but simply the thought that a Liv-A-Snap or a pork chop is flying their way that causes these dogs to bark so much. And while I'm at it, let me tell these dog owners something. You should feed your mutts enough, so they don't bother solid-citizen types like me who want to walk and listen to their *TeeVee Toons* in peace, and maybe then they won't think that they're getting a treat when in reality all they're getting is the bird. Then everybody'll be happier.

4/5/90

Nightmare on *60 Minutes*, Part II

MIKE WALLACE *(in the* 60 Minutes *studio):* Five years ago, *60 Minutes* broadcast a story about a Cleveland man that generated more mail than any story in our history. The story of Eric Broder shocked and sickened many of you—and did you let us know it! You also let us know that you were curious as to what happened to Broder. *60 Minutes* went to Cleveland recently, where we sat in Broder's apartment and talked with Broder about where he's been with his life—and where's he's going.

WALLACE: I've got to ask you, Eric—why did you want to talk with us again? The last time we were here, in 1985, you jumped at the cameraman and tried to wrestle the film out of the camera.

BRODER *(jovially):* He certainly got the better of me there, Mike! No, seriously, Mike, I wanted to set the record straight on some things that were said, particularly about my laundry and my diet. I think your viewers got an unfair picture of my lifestyle, and I wanted to . . .

WALLACE: Wait a minute, wait a minute. Hold on a second. Most of what was said was said by you. You're the one who said you ate Franco-American ravioli and potato chips for dinner . . .

> "The story of Eric Broder shocked and sickened many of you—and did you let us know it! You also let us know that you were curious as to what happened to Broder."

BRODER: Yes, but Mike, you made it sound like that was all I ate for dinner, when in reality all that happened there was that you caught me on a bad night. I didn't get a chance to say that I frequently have nutritious snacks, Mike. Like an apple or a banana, you know?

WALLACE: I don't know. Are you asking me?

BRODER: No, I mean I definitely have nutritious snacks, Mike. I think what you're failing to see here—and I think you're missing the forest for the trees—is that I eat lots more than Chef Boy-Ar-Dee or Franco-American stuff and potato chips. I mean, I like potato chips—and let's not kid ourselves, who doesn't, Mike? But that's not all I eat. I eat lowfat stuff high in fiber, bran, you know, bran. You made it sound like all I eat is canned food or cheeseburgers and beer, and that's not the case. Certainly not the case at all.

WALLACE: Come on. There's more to this than what you eat and you know it.

BRODER: Well . . .

WALLACE: How about the pornography?

BRODER: Porn . . . *ography?*

WALLACE (*holding up magazines and showing them, one by one*): *Velvet. High Society. Club. Cheri. Celebrity Skin* . . .

BRODER: You got those out of my pants drawer!

WALLACE: But they're yours.

BRODER: I bought those four years ago! I don't use 'em anymore!

WALLACE: You don't use them anymore. What does that mean?

BRODER (*chuckling nervously and looking imploringly at the cameraman*): Heh, heh heh heh . . .

WALLACE: Don't look at him. He's not going to help you.

BRODER (*determined to get off the defensive*): I'm not looking for help, Mike. I thought maybe he was a man of the world, a—

WALLACE (*incredulous*): You think having these magazines makes you a *man of the world?* Come on, Eric. That's kind of pathetic, isn't it?

BRODER: No, I don't think I'm a man of the *world,* per *se,* but these magazines, if you would note this, Mike, all of them are at least four years old, and I didn't even know I had them anymore. You know, I thought I gave them to the guys in the garage in this building. Their names are Bobby, Lou, and Tony. You ought to check with them. I mean, if I still have them, it's certainly nothing I know about. But I'm really going to look into it. I appreciate you bringing it to my attention. I'm going to make a note of it right now . . . (*writes in a notebook*), I'm going to investigate this, Mike, you can be sure about that.

WALLACE: All you did was make a couple of tic-tac-toe signs in that notebook.

BRODER (*grabbing the notebook and hiding it in his lap*): I did not! I made notes about the skin mags!

WALLACE (*resignedly*): All right. Let's move on. You're in a relationship right now, aren't you?

BRODER: Yes I am, Mike, and with a very lucky young lady. (*Frowns, not sure the answer came out as intended.*)

WALLACE: She seems to think she's not so lucky. Quote: "We rarely go anywhere. I go over to his apartment and we watch videos or *Bewitched* and *Donna Reed* reruns. And that's about all we do."

BRODER: Mike, I think what we have to understand here—and I what I meant to say was that I think I'm very lucky, let's get that straight—is that we're working here within a very limited time frame, and the whole relationship as is contains within itself elements—

WALLACE: Let me quote you something else she said, "I've tried to get him to go out to someplace new, but all he wants to do is go to record stores or out to eat lunch or dinner. Which usually I pay for. I drive him to the mall on weekends, and he hollers out the car window and makes noises. I get so embarrassed sometimes." Unquote. I'm not sure I understand this. You holler out of the car window? What do you holler?

BRODER: Mike, I don't holler out of any car window. Obviously this woman has her own agenda, and I won't comment on it. I mean, if she's saying I yell stuff at people or runners on the street, things of this nature, or you know, squirrels and birds . . . I mean . . . yelling things out of a car window, well, obviously I don't know anything about that. Listen, I think I've said enough. I think you just better leave. (*Folds his arms and stares stonily ahead.*)

WALLACE (*back in the* 60 Minutes *studio*): And that was the end of the interview. We tried to get Broder to comment further, but he refused. When we asked if we could come talk to him at a later date, he refused. He told us he didn't want to have anything more to do with us, or with *60 Minutes.*

(tick-tick-tick-tick-tick-tick)

4/12/90

Me and the Champ

When people have car trouble I have a good laugh to myself. Today our music writer is standing around the office forlornly, waiting for someone to help him jump his car battery. "I'd like to help, Pete," I say. "But I don't have my car down here today." This is a half-truth. It's true that my car isn't downtown, but it's not true that I'd like to help. The last time I tried to jump a car, in 1983, the cables jumped out of my hands and started a small fire in a nearby pile of leaves. My philosophy is, you leave car batteries alone, they'll leave you alone. Electrocution or a faceful of battery acid is a mighty high price to pay for helping Pete.

> My car strategy? Let the car be. Don't drive it around, don't touch it even, and it won't give you any problems. It'll last for years.

And that's my entire car strategy. Let the car be. Don't drive it around, don't touch it even, and it won't give you any problems. It'll last for years. I plan on keeping my Plymouth Champ around for a long time. It's a 1982 model that cost $900. I've had it a year now, and I've driven it maybe 10 times. I've got one thin key for it, and that's all it needs. It's got an AM radio and a fan and a sensitive braking and acceleration system—it's sensitive to you slamming your foot down on the pedals to get any kind of results. It drives like a dream, if your dreams shake and are noisy.

The first few weeks I had the Champ (which is basically a Mitsubishi-made Dodge Colt with a different name; they don't make them anymore, so don't go looking for a new one) I was tender with it. I took it to a parking lot and sprayed the vinyl interior and wiped it down. I looked at the engine, keeping my distance from the battery, of course. I emptied the ashtray of the cigarette butts from the previous owner and by hand picked up all those whirlybird things that fall off trees that were on the floor. I opened the rear hatchback and checked the spare. It was flat. I closed the hatchback quickly, in the faint hope that I really didn't see this or that maybe when I looked again it would be inflated.

Then I drove the Champ around the neighborhood trying to look like an experienced driver, imagining I was a big ham-fisted guy whose hand dwarfed the steering wheel, and who had driven several thousand miles in his day and had seen everything there was to see on the road. I wanted my expression to say, "Yeah, I've driven everything from Cutlass Cieras to Toyota Land Cruisers to Chevy Blazers and even Peterbilt trucks, but this is the baby I've settled on. This is my Champ." I was only able to sustain this hard-driving illusion for a few minutes, though, and soon I was back to being a nervous guy in a sub-compact.

After a month I took the Champ to a Procare to get its oil changed and to fix the interior light that kept flashing and beeping. I wanted the guys at Procare—all named Mike—to think I was an old hand at auto maintenance so I tried to act sour and taciturn. The Mikes were so friendly my facade quickly melted, and I ended up confessing to them that I hardly ever drove and knew nothing about cars. I don't think they charged me extra, though.

I also took the Champ in for the Emission Test at a Sunoco on Cedar. I wanted to seem like a casual Joe who was used to taking cars in for Emission Tests so I said to the mechanic, "While you're doing that I'm going to go across the street to Nighttown for a cold drink." He looked at me strangely and said, "If you like." What the hell did he care what I did! I was just another toad in for an Emission Test and here I was telling him my life story! That's what I was thinking over my drink until I settled down and realized he was probably a nice guy who just wasn't used to people telling him their plans as their cars were being given the Emission Test. When I got back to Sunoco I was heartily friendly to him in my new spirit of understanding, and he looked at me strangely again.

After those two maintenance episodes I pretty much put the Champ away, lending it to my sister when she didn't want to drive her Thunderbird in nasty weather or if she wanted a car she could leave a week or so in the airport parking lot when she flew out of town. I drive it once in a while to kick out the jams a little but that's all. I also look for other Champs on the road and give them a raised fist when I see them. Most of them are ramshackle affairs that look like they're head-ed for housepainting jobs. And I saw one crumbling away on the street that had bumper stickers that read "Would you believe this SUCKER runs" and "Warning: This car explodes on impact." Beyond this, though, I don't have much to do with the Champ.

5/2/90

Up in Michigan

I don't think anyone's really interested in hearing about my recent vacation up in Northern Michigan. Oh, all right.

It takes about seven and a half hours to drive up to the resort areas of Northern Michigan. This is Hemingway country, filled with lakes, birch, fir, and pine. I drove up there with my girlfriend Barbara, borrowing my sister's deluxe, air-conditioned Thunderbird. I let Barbara drive the whole way to give her the experience of handling a luxury automobile. I kept the trip from getting dull by giving Barbara bulletins every half hour on how I was feeling, as I had a trace of that virus that's been going around. I like to let people know how I'm feeling at all times so that when I fade out they know the cause is organic and not that I'm not lazy or, worse, psycho. I consider lots of people lazy or psycho, but I sure don't want them thinking that about me.

> I let Barbara drive the whole way to give her the experience of handling a luxury automobile.

There's not much to say about the first few days of our vacation, because on the second day it started to snow and sleet. I hadn't expected to get a tan up north, but I didn't think it would be snowing in the middle of May, either. We went to a town called Petoskey on this cold day and looked in gift shops. Since we were there off-season, the merchants were bored and thus extra talkative. One guy tried to sell us plastic playing cards that you could wash and then powder, bringing them back to their original luster. I couldn't believe the guy was talking about washing and powdering playing cards. Another guy in a game store was in a near state of ecstasy describing Deluxe Scrabble. "Once you put the letter tiles on the fitted squares, they're there to stay. No slipping or sliding around. And they're really high quality tiles, really nice," he said. He very nearly got misty-eyed. We bought the game because he obviously felt so strongly about it.

On the way back from Petoskey, we stopped at a roadside park along the Lake Michigan shore. We stood on the rocky shore and gazed out over the lake. I would have thought about questions of mortality at this juncture, but it was too nippy. Plus there was a fish corpse on the rocks that had two rear ends. It was either a mutant fish (there's a nuclear power plant near Petoskey), or it was two fish, one within the other, though of approximately the same size. One of the fish had tried to eat the other, apparently causing a double fatality. That's a hard lesson in nature for you, though I'm not sure how you can apply it to everyday life. Just don't eat stuff that's too big for you, I guess is the main thing.

The highlight of the vacation was our trip to picturesque Mackinac Island. We crossed the huge Mackinac Bridge that joins the two peninsulas of Michigan, and we talked about how it would feel to fall off the top of the bridge into the straits below, and the thought of it made my crotch ache. (I'm sorry, but that's where I ached, and I can't start sugarcoating things now. If you ache in other parts of your body as you think of falling off a suspension bridge, write and let me know. I promise to publish it. In the meantime, I have to continue telling the truth, no matter how shocking.)

Anyway, Mackinac Island was beautiful. No cars are permitted on the island, so people get around on bikes, horses, or horse-drawn carriages. We walked up to the famous Grand Hotel (the world's largest summer hotel) and had a drink in the Audubon Room, which probably looks exactly the same as it did in 1939, except for the TV. We stood on the hotel's great porch and looked out over the lake and the Mackinac Bridge in the background. It was satisfying on two levels—the experience itself and also getting it over with, so we could say we did it and not have to think about it anymore. Then we roamed the 19th-century streets of the island, stepping around road apples the horses dropped, taking pictures, and acting like a couple of tourists, which is what we were, after all.

That's basically it. The rest of our three days up north we ate in restaurants or walked around. Thanks to the virus I mentioned earlier, I had woozy moments, none coming at a worse time than when a convict almost attacked me in a McDonald's in Milan, Michigan, on the drive back to Cleveland. Milan is the home of a federal correctional facility, and this tough-looking guy in blue jeans and a blue work shirt came into the McDonald's, gave me a look, and went into the bathroom. He might have very easily been a con, and here I was with a touch of the flu, so weak a small turtle could have nudged me over and disabled me. Nothing actually happened—the con came out of the bathroom and drove right off—but it was a potentially explosive situation I defused with a fierce pose that was a complete bluff. I'm glad he didn't call it, because one punch would have laid me out cold.

Aside from this potential bad moment in Milan, our vacation trip was great. Thanks for asking.

5/24/90

The Great Insomnia Battle

I went for the heavy thread count when I bought my fitted sheet at Higbee's last week. I needed a sheet that I didn't have to break in, a sheet so buttery soft it might have been manufactured by Land O'Lakes or Chiffon. So I got the highest thread count I could find—230 per inch—threw that bad boy in the washer and dryer, put it on my mattress, and prayed I wouldn't squiggle around in agony on it for three hours like on that 180-count, $7.50 dog of a new sheet I'd used the past two nights. I thought I could handle a 180-count, and in my younger, grittier days I could. But my body is a sensitive instrument now, and it's not going to put up with low thread counts anymore.

I'm desperate. *I can't sleep, can't sleep, can't sleep*, like that poor guy on the TV commercial several years back. It's just a phase, but it's driving me crazy. That's why I'm buying the fancy sheets—I need all the help I can get. I use to drink myself into a mini-coma every night, but that's no good, is it? Then I took the infamous L-Tryptophan amino acid pills, recently pulled from the drug store shelves because it gave some people a terrible blood disease. I also recommended L-Tryptophan to my friends, so they all could get blood disease and whisper to me from their hospital beds, "You told me to take those pills." Now I don't use anything, except for the three cigarettes I smoke (the only ones I have all day) in the bathroom before I hit the sack. The cigarettes make me nauseated and dizzy, which helps me conk out quicker. Or so I believe. I can't tell you how stupid I think this is, but I keep doing it anyway.

The old classic insomnia-beater of reading before retiring hasn't been working so well for me, either. My troubles actually began while I was reading *Death of a President*, by William Manchester, the minute-by-minute account of JFK's assassination. I couldn't sleep after reading about this stuff, though it's a little late to be worried about it now. I read about Lee Harvey Oswald sitting in front of the TV, going mad. It didn't take much to send him around the bend. How much would it take to send me? I go ape over ridiculous things like when my girlfriend, *unbeknownst to me*, refrigerated the corned beef I had deliberately wanted left at room temperature for sandwich purposes. I get so worked up by trivialities that I'm afraid when I'm really stressed out they're going to have to call out the SWAT team, and Channel 8 will have pictures of me handcuffed and being pushed into a police car without a shirt on, like those other crazy guys.

You might say, "Hey, stop reading that book!" Well, I did. I switched to a theatrical autobiography by Moss Hart that was guaranteed not to disturb, but I still can't sleep. After a half-hour of reading about this playwright's experiences at summer camp, I go to bed. I know it's too early, but I'm so bored of the waking life that I want to sleep. I'm also anxious to tackle the insomnia, which is precisely the wrong attitude to have. Insomnia isn't something you get geared up to overcome. You don't want to be up; you want to be down. But I come out wanting to kick insomnia's ass, and so it kicks mine.

I lie there—hapless as Elmer Fudd—wide awake, songs running through my head, on occasion flopping like a seal or waving my tingly leg around. I'm not worrying about anything specific—like when I couldn't sleep the night before the Browns played Denver in the AFC Championship game, and I knew they were going to lose, and I worried about how miserable I was going to be—except not being able to sleep. I get up and walk around the bed, arranging and rearranging it, like a phantom. I'm blind as a bat, and walking around my room in the dark at 3 A.M. is spooky. My bed looks like it's floating, and I feel like I'm floating, too, because I can't see my feet. Night of the living dead! Finally I do fall asleep, but I can never pinpoint just when I go down. It seems while I'm flipping and flopping that I'm only going to get an hour's sleep, but I probably get four. To be honest, I don't really feel any worse getting four hours instead of seven, but I hate to think insomnia's beating me this way.

I am going to kick its ass *tonight.*

6/14/90

Toot, Toot, Tootie, Good-Bye

I cry my eyes out every day thinking of life without Tootie. Tootie, my sister's cat, will be moving out of the apartment when my sister gets married in a few weeks. The place is going to seem empty without Tootie mooching around in it.

All kinds of things will remind me of Tootie when she's gone. The corner of the dining room where her litter box is now will be mere space. It's going to take me a while to get used to a dining room that smells like a dining room and not a used litter box. I won't see Tootie's head sticking out of the hole in the litter box cover, her eyes shining, her ears alert to possible dangers, as she goes to the lavatory. And I won't see her walking around in circles near the box when she's done, either. I don't know why she does this, but I'm sure she has a good reason. No more of that when Tootie leaves.

There'll be no more of Tootie's affection. People think cats are cold. Not Tootie. She'll jump up and sit with you, even if you're a stranger. She'll want to be near you even if for some unfathomable reason you don't like cats. Tootie still likes my psychologist buddy ("I heal sick minds") Joe, though the nicest thing he's ever said to her was "Get the f--- away from me, cat." Tootie recognizes that some persons are deficient in the humanity/compassion/intellect department and that's why they don't like cats, but she understands and forgives. She believes in second and third chances for chuckle-headed numskulls no matter what. She stands up to insults like a celebrity at a roast. Her good nature triumphs over small minds.

Not that Tootie's a saint. Far from it. She has moments of irritability, manifested in her sudden unprovoked bouts of biting and kicking. Tootie and I will be sitting peacefully on the couch watching TV when an unexpected notion or thought will make her mad, and she'll commence biting and kicking me, which in turn incites me to blow on her head, which makes her even madder. She'll jump down off the couch and sit at my feet staring at me, quivering in vexation. Then she'll come flying at me when she thinks I'm not looking and clamp down on my arm with her sharp teeth. I know when she's really mad because she's breathing heavily like some people do when they're enraged. I probably shouldn't try to honk her off, but after all, she started it. She comes back around to being friendly again in a few minutes anyway, licking me with her huge, Gene Simmons–like tongue, which, I swear, is almost as big as her head and which they ought to put on TV somehow.

Tootie also eats breakfast with me on the weekends. Every Saturday and Sunday I fix up a bowl of corn flakes and bring along to the table that week's *Sporting News* or *Sports Illustrated*. Tootie is sitting on the table at my place every time, without fail. Then, when I attempt to eat and read, she squirms on my publication, making it very difficult for me. I push her away, but she keeps wriggling back. She's having such a big time I don't have the heart to dump her on the floor. Yet I pay the penalty doubly when I find a couple of her hairs floating in the milk in my cereal. I try to keep her away from the bowl, but she manages to shake in a few hairs anyway. I don't mind. I just pick them out. They don't affect the milk anyway.

I won't see Tootie's head sticking out of the hole in the litter box cover, her eyes shining, her ears alert to possible dangers, as she goes to the lavatory.

I don't mind, either, when she shakes her ear gook out and it lands on my arm. Let me clarify this. Tootie has an ear infection (currently being treated with drops and the use of Q-Tips), but for a while she'd shake her head, and gook would come flying out of her ear and land on my arm. It wouldn't land anywhere else. She could be across the room shaking her head, and a second later I'd look at my arm and there the ear gunk would be. You might find this disgusting. Well, so did I. But then I thought about it. What if a baby of mine—a fruit of my loins, so to speak—shook its ear gook on me? Would I be so queasy? What kind of dad would I be if I recoiled at every function of nature? Well the same with Tootie. That settled that.

These have been just a few reasons why I'm going to miss Tootie. There are more, but I can't go on. Thanks for (*choke*) listening.

6/28/90

My Hot Date with Ivana Trump!

I figured I'd waited long enough after the split. If I wanted to go out with Ivana Trump, now was the time to ask.

I called Trump Tower. "Is Ivana there?"

"Who's calling, please?" asked the operator.

I told the operator my name. She said "Just a minute." I heard her holler, "Mrs. Trump! You've got a long distance call from Cleveland!" I sat and waited. Then the operator yelled, "Mrs. Trump! It's *long distance!*" Finally I got Ivana on the phone. I had my speech ready.

"Hello, Ivana. You don't know me, but I live in Cleveland, and I heard you and Donald were getting a divorce. I hope you don't mind me asking, but I was wondering, would you like to go out with me? We could go to dinner or something. You know, if you felt like it."

Ivana didn't say anything right off. But after a moment she said, "Sure. Vy not?"

Here was the hard part. I said, "Great! But I was wondering . . . would you mind coming to Cleveland? I know it's inconvenient, but I can pick you up at the airport, and I'll even buy you a snack if you're hungry after your flight. You *will?* Gee, that's great. Okay, you'll know me by—let's see—I'll be wearing my Oyster Stampede T-shirt. It's dark blue with a cartoon of oysters running around on it. My sister gave it to me. And I've got brown hair. Listen, I'll know *you*, don't worry. Okay, I'll see you . . . Thursday? Wonderful. I know we're going to have a good time. I'll see you then."

Was I excited! For days I debated whether I should take the rapid or drive my Plymouth Champ to the airport to pick up Ivana. I decided that since the Champ didn't have air conditioning Ivana might stick to the vinyl seats, so I'd better pick her up on the rapid.

On Thursday I got to the door at the gate so Ivana wouldn't have to look around too much. I mean, she was doing me a favor by coming to Cleveland for a date with a complete stranger, so I wanted to make it as easy as possible for her.

Finally the flight arrived, and the passengers streamed out into the gate area. And there she was with her famous blond hair, carrying a brown leather shoulder bag, wearing a blue sweater and Guess jeans. She looked very attractive. I went up to her and said, "Ivana? I'm Eric.

I appreciate you making the trip, and welcome to Cleveland Hopkins International Airport."

She looked at me critically. "Yes. I see you haf the clems on the shirt like you said."

I said, "Actually, they're oysters, but I hope you like the shirt anyway."

She shrugged. "I haf no opinion of it eider way." I saw I would have to be on my toes with Ivana!

We went down to the rapid, and I paid for Ivana's ride as well as my own. I thought that since we were going to be stopping downtown I would show her a few sights—then we could continue on to Shaker Square on the rapid.

During the ride I pointed out various sights. "Here's the Triskett Road stop," I said. "It's a big, big street here on the West Side." Ivana didn't say anything, but I could tell she was interested. I gave her some Beechies gum, and she chewed it as she gazed out the window.

I decided that since the Champ didn't have air conditioning Ivana might stick to the vinyl seats, so I'd better pick her up on the rapid.

We arrived downtown, and Ivana and I walked around The Avenue. Then I took her to our office in the Arcade, and showed her my desk. I let her sit in my chair, and she ate a leftover banana I'd brought for breakfast the day before. We smiled shyly at each other as she chowed down. I was growing on her, I could tell.

It was a nice day, so I took Ivana down to the Flats, and we walked along the Old River Road. We passed by the bars and nightclubs, and looked at the river. Ivana had no idea the area was such a hotspot. I said, "Well, you know, my theory about that is that people like to be near water. There's something about a river or lake—I don't know, it just attracts people." She looked at me and said, "I tink you may be right about dat." I was really scoring points with her! Maybe I hadn't impressed her with my Oyster Stampede T-shirt, but she had sure liked sitting at my desk and seeing the Flats. I was cooking. Now for the capper. I was going to take her to my apartment and make her dinner.

We rode to the Square on the rapid, and before the driver had a chance to, I called out the stops: "East 79th, 93rd and Woodhill! East 116th!" Ivana was in stitches. "You crazy!" she cried. The driver was getting mad but I didn't care. Ivana and I were having a marvelous time. I was willing to bet she'd never had such fun with Donald.

We got off at the Square and I said to her, "Ivana, this is called Shaker Square. But I call it 'The Hub.' I live right down the street from here, and I can get home from any one of *three* rapid stops in this area. Plus, I can walk from my apartment to the supermarket, the coffee shop, the cleaners—and there's a Revco on the corner for my toiletry needs and you know, odds and ends."

Ivana was wide-eyed. "You can get to all dose places by valking?" I nodded. She shook her head in disbelief. "It *is* a 'hub.'" Zing. Another point on the board.

In the lobby of my building, I pulled out my keys and opened my mailbox. I secretly hoped I would get some impressive mail that she could see, but all I got was the channel guide from Cablevision and a Penney's sale flyer. I tried to joke it off: "Not much today." Ivana was charming in her reply. "I never get nuttin' eider," she said.

In my apartment, I asked Ivana to sit down while I put some music on my CD player. She asked me if I owned a "videocazzit recorder." I had to laugh. I had just bought a new Magnavox, so I unhooked it, carried it over to her, and placed it on her lap. She oohed and ahhed over it. "Looks axpansif," she said. It was more than five hundred dollars, I informed her coolly. With the warranty. Ivana was like me. She liked technology.

I asked Ivana to wait in the living room while I made the sandwiches. I prepared Seaway creamy peanut butter and jelly sandwiches, and since Ivana was a special guest, I cut off the crusts. I garnished the sandwiches with a fistful of Buckeye potato chips and poured us each a glass of milk.

Ivana was surprised by the cuisine, but when she dug in she really enjoyed it. "I don't eat dis much," she said, meaning she didn't eat pb&j's, usually. When we finished, we looked deeply into each other's eyes. I held my breath waiting for her to speak. Finally she looked away and said, "I haf to go. Take me to the airport." I knew she was holding back. But I was, too. We couldn't rush this thing.

I drove her to the airport in the Champ, which she said reminded her of the cars back in Czechoslovakia. I walked her to the gate, and before she boarded the plane she said, "You better call me, you somomagum." Then she gave me a quick kiss, and I saw her eyes begin to brim as she turned to hurry down the corridor toward the plane. She didn't look back. But I knew one thing. This wasn't the final chapter in the story of my relationship with Ivana Trump!

7/12/90

Stop Bothering Me

Our sales manager came back from a party with a bunch of lawyers and told me that the lawyers loved the *Edition* but that one said he didn't want to read about my "navel flint." I laughed scornfully. So now these lawyers say that I'm writing that I have a flint in my navel. So now they claim that I say that I can press the sides of my belly button together and produce flame. What a joke. As if I'd try to pass off such a transparent lie. Lawyers make extravagant, nonsensical statements, so they assume everybody else does too. But I'm telling lawyers: Don't include me in your little world! I've got plenty to deal with in the real one!

Then again, our sales manager might have mispronounced the word "lint" as "flint" while relating this incident to me. The more I consider it the more I think this is the likely explanation, since our sales manager is kind of . . . well, you know . . . a sales guy. "Navel lint" makes much more sense within this context as the lawyer may have been referring to my habit of speaking about personal matters in this column. I would like to state here that I have never once written a column about my navel lint, though I have written about lint screens in dryers, which might easily have confused this lawyer. Yes, I know it seems ridiculous to confuse a dryer with a human navel, but this is a lawyer we're talking about, not a rocket scientist. Try to have a little compassion.

Anyway, what does this pinhead lawyer want me to write about? The environment? Andrew Dice Clay? The school board? The Winbush controversy? Plenty of people will write about that stuff, not to worry. It'll get covered without me putting my two cents in, and believe me, that's all my opinion is worth on these subjects. The essential question is this: If I don't write about myself, who will? Stop and think about that for a moment. If you do, the answer you must necessarily come up with is this: nobody. Not one person. There are no

> **The essential question is this: If I don't write about myself, who will? Stop and think about that for a moment. If you do, the answer you must necessarily come up with is this: nobody.**

major biographies in the works at publishing houses. No movie deals! Nothing! Is it any wonder I do what I do?

Having said that, I realize that perhaps my life story may not be marketable worldwide. Consequently, I've begun to try to think of other money making projects. Why should all those other writers cash in on their stupid stories while I sit here grousing about lawyers? What have they got that I haven't got?

Saleable ideas, that's what. Ideas about atomic terrorists, robot cops, baseball-playing ghosts, Batman, Dick Tracy, hookers, and stockbrokers. The best I've been able to come up with so far is "The story of a young man . . . " That's my big idea. When I'm really cooking, I get as far as "The story of a young man who . . . " and then I'm stumped. What does he do, anyway? Hold Washington D.C. hostage with an A-bomb? Embark on an elaborate scheme to con Qaddafi or Saddam Hussein out of a couple billion petro-dollars? Track down a serial killer who switches his victims' body parts? Be the secret Allied operative who, posing as a Nazi general, convinces Hitler to invade Russia, thus changing the course of World War II?

These may seem like hot ideas to you, but they don't do me any good, because I know I'm not going to write them. I'm more likely to write a story about a young man who steps into his TV, into an episode of *Green Acres*. What he'd do from that point I haven't the slightest idea. Unfortunately, the *Green Acres* idea is more my speed than the lucrative mass murder–Nazi–Middle East–hostage market I wish I could break into. But my brain doesn't work that way. I think more about crackers and cookies.

Really, the ideas I'd feel comfortable working on—ideas that let me write what I know—I just don't see making my fortune. I mean, I just thought of a story of a young man who sprays Formula 409 on a phone and ruins it. How am I going to sell an idea like this? Maybe if I souped up the story, like having the guy spray Formula 409 on Qaddafi. Oh, forget it. You see where my ideas head. Right. On the fast track to nowhere.

I'm going to stop thinking about this. You see what comes of listening to the babble of lawyers and sales managers?

7/19/90

On the Wedding Trip

My twin sister's wedding went off without a hitch up in Michigan, except that the groom—now my brother-in-law—broke out in hives, had a 103 degree fever, wore a collar that didn't cover his tie, and slept in the car during the reception. That's still better than I would have done. I plan to substitute a cardboard cutout of myself at my wedding and hide until it's all over.

My girlfriend Barbara and I drove up to the wedding and stayed at a place called the Archway Motel in Charlevoix. The Archway is clean, inexpensive, and you can sit on the commode in the tiny bathroom and peek out the window at the pool in the back of the motel.

The only thing really wrong with the Archway Motel was the bath mat, a laughable attempt at absorbency.

The only thing really wrong with the Archway was the bath mat, a laughable attempt at absorbency. It was a piece of 8-by-12 paper with a picture of a sailboat on it, and the legend "Your Personal Bath Mat." I felt sorry for it, as well as for the off-brand air-conditioner that you could either have on "Off" or "Cool." No climate control on that baby. No "Lo Cool," "Med Cool," "Hi Cool," or "Fan." Hot or Cold—you take your pick at the Archway. You want subtlety, you have to shell out the cash.

The pool area was no Garden of Allah either, set off in the back in full view of the Union 76 station next door and surrounded by a grim metal fence. It looked like Texas. We did spend a fairly enjoyable hour there one afternoon, playing catch with a little girl who criticized my beachball throwing technique. It was one of those slick balls no one can get a good grip on. I kept throwing it over her head, out of the pool, and she got mad at me. "Stop throwing it so hard!" she cried. I never had the nerve as a child to yell at an adult like that, but she had an Archway scrappiness.

On the day before the wedding, we killed time by going to the beach and playing shuffleboard with my relatives. This was fun, though I did muff several shots. I had the touch at the beginning of the game but soon lost it, sending many disks toppling off the field of play with bogus pushes of my stick. You have to ease those disks down the line. You try to force things in shuffleboard and you're asking for big trouble.

That was it for sports during this wedding foray, except for a round of miniature golf Barbara and I played at Captain's Cove Adventure Golf around the corner from the Archway. We were playing behind a family that let their three-year-old play. He had a little plastic club, and we had to watch him whack at the ball, taking up to 30 shots per hole. They didn't ask us to play through, either, so we were stuck behind the tiny tot, who looked liked he was chopping down a tree rather than taking a skilled approach to holing the ball. We had nowhere we had to be anyway, so there was no problem.

As I said, the wedding went smoothly, except for my sister's new husband's hives, fever, collar, etc., and the reception was nice too. I got to see all my cousins. One, who lives in Grand Rapids, complained that he only worked four hours a week in his government social worker job, and since he had so much leisure time at work he didn't know what to do with his actual leisure time. Four hours! I'd go nuts. I figure I'm kept busy maybe 25–30 hours in my job, which is about right. Anyway, his comment gave me the most food for thought at the reception. I had no big thoughts about the wedding, or that my twin was married, or anything like that. I mean, sooner or later she was bound to get married, and now she is.

That's all I have to say about the wedding. There were a few other interesting things I saw up in Michigan, and both had to do with cows. In Charlevoix I saw a roadside sign that said "All Hail Moo Semen," which really had me confused for a while. Did that mean "All Hail Cow Semen" or was it some wiseass's reference to milk? I couldn't figure it out. Finally I deduced that the spacing between the letters was screwed up, and the sign actually said "All Hail Moosemen," in tribute to a local team.

Also, on the ride home, I saw a bunch of cows hanging around a meadow, while at the exact same time "Oh, What A Beautiful Mornin'" from *Oklahoma!* was on the tape player, with its lines about "cattle standing like statues" and cows in the clover. And there they were. All right, it wasn't the greatest coincidence of all time, but I got a kick out of it. At any rate, a few hours later we were back in Cleveland, the wedding trip over.

8/16/90

Some Birthday

On my birthday last Monday the sales manager hit me in the eye with a rubber band. That was the extent of the fuss made over me in the office on this most special of days. As I rubbed my eye the sales manager exclaimed "Wow! I've never been able to do *that* before!" He was grinning happily. "Next time put a bent paper clip in there," I cried. "You might be able to puncture the eyeball." He still stood there looking like he'd just hit a three-pointer, my sarcasm lost on him.

Not that I expected any special treatment on my birthday. Far from it. In fact, I insisted that nothing be made of it. And believe me, nothing was. I got two "Happy Birthday"s, one solicited. The boss said "Happy Birthday" as if wild horses were pulling it out of him. It was a little strangled thing that barely made it through the air to my ears. "Don't go overboard on this, boss," I thought. "Don't get too sentimental on me." Of course, being gracious, I bowed and murmured, "Thank you," hiding the pain. The only genuine "Happy Birthday" came from the assistant editor, who yelled it at me as soon as she came to work. But did anyone else say a word? Did anyone bring me the smallest of cupcakes, a cookie, a simple card? No.

> **The boss said "Happy Birthday" as if wild horses were pulling it out of him. It was a little strangled thing that barely made it through the air to my ears.**

You see, if I said I didn't expect any special treatment on my birthday, I thought I'd get it. That's how beloved figures are supposed to do things. You're supposed to be modest and disdain attention, but then you're supposed to cash in. You know, like in *It's a Wonderful Life*. People brought Jimmy Stewart money in baskets because he was a nice guy. My delusion was that since I'd been quietly doing for my fellow workers the past several months, on my birthday they'd get together and present me with a microwave or a color TV—and I'd be perilously close to tears, saying, "I don't know how to . . . oh, you all are so . . . oh! oh!" but it didn't go down that way. It went down that I sat at my desk, alone, waiting for the party that never came.

All right. I should admit a few things. I said before that I'd been quietly doing for my fellow workers the past several months, and perhaps that's an exaggeration. But I've certainly been *polite* to them. I've haven't called anyone "Fatty" or "Stupe" or "Dunderhead" or insulted anyone to their faces for some time. I've tried to keep my backbiting to a minimum too, but after all, I'm only human. If people weren't jerks I wouldn't feel the need to rag on them behind their backs or give them the finger over the phone. It's not like they don't ask for it.

I should also note that I don't do much for anyone else's birthday. I mean, let's face it, every day is *somebody's* birthday. It's not exactly a big deal. So I don't feel there's a need for a major festival every time some geek here in the office turns 28 or 31 or some other nothing age. My birthday, on the other hand, was my 35th. A pivotal event, a turning point, a passage, if you will, into the beginning of early middle age. A moment that should be celebrated, reflected upon, and quietly and thoughtfully discussed by all in the office as I open my presents. But it wasn't handled that way here. A rubber band in the eye was the way it was handled.

Before I leave you in your cold rage over this business, I'd like to add one thing as counterpoint. My girlfriend did her best to give me a happy birthday. She presented me with a book, a pair of pants, and a cake, and then took me to dinner at a nice restaurant in horsey Moreland Hills. Unfortunately, we were seated next to a couple of drunk CPAs talking business, which is a sorry spectacle. They talked about team playing and buyouts and salary packages and severance pay, all with the boozy certainty that their Art of the Deal babble contained astounding insight. They'd sit back in their seats and declaim as the rest of the dining room listened. Because they were only slightly louder than the soundtrack of *Days of Thunder*.

But I'll tell you. When those two left . . . and the people in the dining room let out their collective sigh of relief . . . I'll tell you, that was the finest birthday present a fellow ever had.

9/6/90

Fashion: Pants and Stains

You might have noticed that the *Edition* now has a fashion columnist. And you should see the way this guy dresses. I have pants envy of him. One day he came in with pants that ended four inches about his shoe line—and he got away with it. He looked dynamite, like a dancer, like Gene Kelly. If I tried that I'd look like a Beverly Hillbilly, though not quite as good. Some people can do what they like in terms of pants, and fashion. I can't.

Since I don't wear suits to work, I have to make a fashion decision every morning and live with it the rest of the day. The shirt I choose has to go right with my pants or I'll feel like a dork—and there's no turning back. "Boss, can I go home and change? I can't stand this ensemble"—that doesn't fly in the real world. I try to wear what I call "universal" pants: pants of solid colors that go with anything. So I have light and dark pants. These go with my light and dark shirts. But not always.

> "Boss, can I go home and change? I can't stand this ensemble"— that doesn't fly in the real world.

Here's a concrete example. Last week I wore a white polo shirt, but one of those smooth ones, the ones without the breathing holes in them. You know, a cheap one. With it I wore my (once tolerated, now despised) sky-blue Dockers, which are about an inch too short and simultaneously hug my hips and billow out at the sides. Clown pants, of which I own more than anybody I know. Plus I wore blue socks and brown shoes.

All right. My strategy was to present a summery aspect, a light, festive image to cheer the eye. Unfortunately, I had locked-in orange stains on both my pants (in the embarrassing crotch area) and my shirt, stains that I couldn't see in the dull light of my bedroom but that jumped out in the fluorescent lighting here in the office. They looked like Gerber's stains, situated in places where an infant would drool, and the pastel nature of my clothes made me look even more like a large baby. My stomach hangs over my waist a little, too, so all in all I felt like the biggest schmuck in the building. I could hardly wait to go home and peel that crap off.

I've worn a pumpkin-colored polo shirt with purple Dockers, as well, which looks seriously bad, but I only made that mistake once.

Usually my color coordination is mediocre, not humiliating. It's the aforementioned weird stains that derange me. I get key stains: little marks showing through my pockets made from the pointy ends of my keys. I have to keep rubbing my pockets with a gum eraser to get rid of them, which makes me appear to be engaged in disgusting antics from the rear. Of course, this only concerns me with my light pants. My dark pants just have fade marks (from my wallet, in the hip pocket) and a mysterious, overall fading in the zipper area. All my pants somehow make me look like a degenerate. The only good thing about them is the belt, which I've worn every day for 15 years. It's so supple and worn it feels like string licorice when I pull it off.

I'm happy, though, that summer is nearing its end, so I don't have to worry about shorts anymore. My shorts problem makes my pants problem look like a day at the beach. I've got running shorts, but I'm not about to wear them around town like a Californian, carrying my wallet in my hands. I do have a shred of dignity left. But my walking-around shorts, which have plenty of storage space in them, are the wrong length, ending mid-thigh, when I guess they're supposed to end just above the knee. I pull them down so they're lower on my legs, but then they're low-riding my butt, a look I'm not going to adopt. They also climb up the insides of my thighs at a 45 degree angle, the ultimate loser effect. I generally don't wear these shorts unless I don't care if I look stupid, but if someone I knew caught me wearing them I'd still feel the need to explain and apologize. No, they probably don't care one way or the other about how much of a dink I appear in my shorts, but why take a chance? I've got to let them know that I know, that I'm self-aware about this thing. I'd explain about my big feet, too, and everything else, right on up to the top of my head. No one's going to catch me with my pants down!

9/12/90

Attack of the Kitten People

I wouldn't exactly say I'm afraid of the new kitten, but I would say I'm fearful. I hear her running and sneezing behind the sofa as I sit watching TV. When the rustling stops I turn around and peer down at her. Nine times out of ten she's staring up at me, tensed, ready to jump. So I quickly turn again, and she leaps, clawing and chewing the hair on the back of my head. It feels just like someone working one of those small staple removers on your scalp. I pluck her off the back of my head, set her down, and she takes off.

It's hard to eat with someone standing on your shoulders.

The kitten was brought in to replace the cat Tootie, who moved out with my sister. We got her at the Animal Protective League. I think she was taken from her mother too early, as she nurses on her own tail. Am I supposed to stop her from doing this? I don't see the harm, although the tip of her tail is always wet. But that's none of my business.

She doesn't have a real personality yet. She performs all the standard kitten functions. She bats around crumpled pieces of paper and ignores the Hartz toys I buy her. The $30 cat condo we got her is the only furniture in the apartment she doesn't claw and jump on. She's always on the attack and on the run. I'm frightened when she's not in sight, because she'll come flying at me out of nowhere, targeting on my crotch. Mealtime is the worst. I'd have to eat crouched on top of the refrigerator if I wanted to be truly safe from her. I eat off a tray in front of the TV, and she comes up and puts her nose in my food. I push her aside, but she walks back the same way every time, like a film loop repeating or the cat on the commercial doing the "Chow Chow Chow."

Drinking my morning coffee is hard, too, because she's all over me after spending the night alone. I can't blame her for wanting some affection, but one day she's going to nose the coffee cup out of my weak, early-morning grip, and then there's going to be coffee all over my newspaper and pajamas. "Why don't you put her in another room and close the door," you say. Because I feel sorry for her, that's why. She's been locked up all night and wants to play. She's a kitten, for God's sake. What's your next suggestion, send her to a prison for the criminally insane? Go make her be a cat in a crack house? Man, this is a tough town.

So I let her do what she wants, within reason. I mentioned that she pounces at my crotch, and naturally I nip that in the bud. Uh . . . I mean I stop that posthaste. Sometimes, too, she stands on my shoulders while I eat, and I don't like that much. It's hard to eat with someone standing on your shoulders.

That's it for the trouble. She knew how to use the litter box when we got her, which I think is the most convenient thing in the entire domesticated animal world. It's fantabulous that cats can do this. And all we humans have to do is scoop and throw the litter out once a week. It's a beautiful system.

You're probably wondering what the kitten looks like and what her name is. She's a calico, and her name was hard to come up with. We thought of Sneezy, as she does this a lot, but we didn't want to name her after a dwarf. We thought of Fally (she fell off the bookcase once) and Necky (she has a scrawny neck), but let's face it, those are stupid names. Irving, Birdie, Flip, Don, or Raymond aren't much better. I thought of naming her after members of the Cleveland School Board: Gary, Mildred, Ralph, Stanley, etc., but those are too depressing for a frisky young kitten. We thought of local broadcasters: Wilma, Robin, Denise, Don Olson of the Akron Bureau, Leon, Casey, Joe Mosbrook—it was driving us crazy, as you can imagine. So we settled on Daisy, which has been evolving into Dizzy. So it's basically Dizzy, and she seems happy with that.

9/20/90

Impending Domestic Bliss

My girlfriend moved in, and I'm not going to be alone anymore. I like being alone in many ways. I spend a lot of time fooling around in front of the mirror, playing air trumpet along with my new idol, Herb Alpert. I bought his and the Tijuana Brass's Greatest Hits, mainly because I love "Casino Royale." You know, the one that goes "Bup bup ba, bup bup ba/Bup bup bup buppa bup buppa bup bup ba buppa ba bup bup buhhh buhhh . . . " It's an instrumental. I purse my lips together and finger the air, dipping now and again as Herb would do. This is huge fun, but when you're playing an imaginary trumpet to "Tijuana Taxi" or "Spanish Flea" you don't want someone walking in on you. Especially when you're vamping and trying to be a sex idol like Herb Alpert.

When you're living with somebody, you have to watch yourself, at least for a while. You can't be as dog-careless in your personal habits—which I won't spell out here.

When you're living with somebody, you have to watch yourself, at least for a while. You can't be as dog-careless in your personal habits— which I won't spell out here—but you get used to certain things, certain ways you hate to change but you should because they might gross somebody else out. You repress instinctual acts; at least I do, because I'm a tidy person, and I don't want anyone to think I'm so disgusting I couldn't even be shown at a carnival. That's the way I feel now, but I know that in a couple of months I'll be as relaxed as John Goodman on *Roseanne*, burping and being mangy and jerking around. Yes, I'm going to be Mr. Excitement, or at least Mr. Enjoyment. Maybe Mr. Mild Fun, depending on my health.

I can't be alone forever, though I have had many moments of sheer delight alone. I already mentioned the Herb Alpert thing, but on some nights I've sat by myself watching TV or reading and thought "this is great!" and laughed a little. These are the times when the fact that nobody's bothering me gives me sensuous pleasure. I'm almost hugging myself I'm so happy with my company. It's true love. I don't need anybody or anything, not beer, not sex, not nothing, just my own self.

Of course, you have to look down the road. Maybe you're giggling on the sofa today, but what if something happens? What if your appendix bursts while you're watching *Murphy Brown* or *The Flash*? The person who wasn't bothering you before is the same one who won't take you to the emergency room. It's the same person who won't spoon your soup into you after you've had your stroke, or the one who won't tend to your iron lung. You're saying "Take it easy, man. That's not going to happen." I have just one thing to say to that. *Prove it.*

Besides, I don't want to get too set in my ways. Getting too set in your ways is kind of like a small death, isn't it? I don't need to eat at 6 P.M. exactly every night, be done by the sports segment, and start getting ready for my vigorous walk while watching the first cartoon of TNT's *Bugs Bunny and Pals* show at 6:30, do I? I don't need to leave for my walk at precisely 6:45 and get back 58–62 minutes later every single time. So what if it works for me. There's life beyond this routine. And I'm going to find out what it is.

With somebody else around I'll be forced to vary my days. Is there some law that says I have to be in bed by 11:30–11:40 weekdays, midnight on weekends? Maybe I should stay out late once in a while. Maybe I should play poker all night and smoke cigars. I used to go to bars every evening and stay until last call. Maybe I've gone too far the other way. My movements are so predictable these days I'm a candidate for kidnapping. There's no work involved in figuring out where I'll be at any given time.

It will be easier to get out more now, easier to be away from home and thus add a little mystery to my personality. "Hi, we're not home right now (implied: we're out and about, doing fascinating stuff, maybe even in New York City) so please leave a message after the tone." That's the way it should be. I can't do it alone, and I don't want to. If I want to fool around in front of the mirror, I can always close my door.

10/4/90

Yet Another Injury

And now the true story of how I threw my back out this past weekend.

On Saturday I was supposed to go to a wedding in Westlake with my girlfriend Barbara. I complained bitterly about this—after all, I have a reputation to maintain—but I was basically resigned to going. I remember thinking that morning, however, how nice it would be to come down with a sudden illness. Nothing serious. Just something bad enough so that nobody could ask me to go to Westlake or anywhere else.

Saturday morning, then, I was in the kitchen babbling away at Barbara, when I bent over to pick up the plastic margarine tub the cat Daisy uses for her water dish. On the way down I felt something pull in my back, causing me to bellow and then fall to all fours. "My back," I groaned. "My back. Oh, my back." Much like Jack Lemmon in *The Odd Couple.* I managed to crawl onto the carpeted dining room floor, because I didn't want to die on linoleum. There I stayed for several moments on my hands and knees, panting like a dog, and hoping fervently I hadn't slipped a disk or dislocated my spine.

I managed to crawl onto the carpeted dining room floor, because I didn't want to die on linoleum.

I couldn't get up for some time. I looked up at Barbara, attempted to smile, and said, "Well, it looks like I pulled a muscle or strained something here." I didn't want to worry her too much, as it was obvious I was going to survive this thing. Of course, I didn't want her to think I was faking, either. There was no sense going through all this pain and not getting out of the wedding. So I worked at making my smile brave yet sickly, like in a TV hospital drama. I didn't mention the wedding right away, though, as I didn't want to appear too eager to claim that I had sustained a social-obligation-ending injury.

I shouldn't have worried. No way was I going to any wedding, much less one in far-flung Westlake. I wasn't about to be in pain in Westlake, away from everything. I spent the whole day with my back feeling like it had been whacked with a baseball bat. I walked with little, mincing steps, emitting chirps of pain as I went. Not even the mighty ibuprofen helped.

I was in distress. Would I have to spend my life on a board? I'd heard about back problems like this, with people who weren't allowed to bend for months at a time. Where would I be if I couldn't sit? What good's a man without his chair? All these years I had taken sitting down for granted. Now this back injury threatened what had become a major activity of my life.

I didn't want to go anywhere, but I figured I'd better go to Revco and buy a heating pad. I shuffled painfully over to the discount drug store with Barbara, and bought an $11 heating pad. Despite my discomfort, I was pleased at this solid value. Eleven bucks, and I might never have to buy another heating pad again. A heating pad is like an iron, an item you can buy for less than $20 that could conceivably last 20 years. This heating pad could serve me through many back strains in years to come, I thought.

When I got the heating pad home, however, my satisfaction quickly turned to disillusion. There were more warnings on the pad than in a nuclear power facility. "Do not" do this, "Do not" do that. How about this one. "Do not lean on, sit on, or crush pad. Place pad on top of injured area." What a ridiculous notion. Have you ever seen anyone use a heating pad that they weren't leaning on, sitting on, or crushing? Leaning or sitting on a heating pad is the very essence of using a heating pad! I'm supposed to lie on my stomach and put the heating pad on *top* of my back? These heating pad people better get wise to themselves. I'm going to set up my heating pad on the back cushion of my chair and lean against it, the way I learned as a boy. And heating pad manufacturers better learn to like it.

That night, while Barbara was at the wedding—she had somebody else to go with anyway—I sat home and watched videos, *F/X* and the second half of *The Music Man*. During *The Music Man* I got stuck on the floor. I was lying there, watching the spirited musical, and I couldn't get up because of my back. I started to spin around there on the carpet, sort of like Curly of the Three Stooges, but believe me, this was no comedy! This was a Cleveland guy in big trouble. Finally I was able to drag myself up onto the sofa. But it had been a dicey moment.

My back started feeling better the next day, midway through the Cincinnati–L.A. Rams game. I guess it wasn't a serious injury after all. But I sure wasn't about to risk permanent damage to my back by going to a wedding in some faraway place, so I'm glad I decided to stay home and take it easy. You never know about these things.

10/18/90

Before the Trip to New York

I'm going to New York City this afternoon to see my brother and his family. I'm flying in to LaGuardia at 4:15. Then I'm going to take a cab to my brother's apartment off Central Park instead of to his office, to avoid the midtown traffic.

LaGuardia. Midtown. Central Park. I've got the lingo down.

I know all about New York because I've been there before, in 1983, for a publishing convention. I adapted to the pace of the city more easily than I thought I would. People walked fast and looked depressed, which is no stretch for me. I didn't see anybody twirling around like Marlo Thomas, filled with wonder at the city, as she did at the beginning of *That Girl*. If you twirl around today in New York City everyone gives you a wide berth. People who twirl around in New York City today aren't Marlo Thomas. They're martial arts experts who've just flipped out and are chopping at everything in sight. That's the way it is in New York nowadays.

One thing I might do while walking down the streets of New York is mutter to myself and make vague arm movements to ward off potential trouble.

I remember stopping for just a few minutes at Penn Station between trains several years ago as well. The minute I stepped off the train a guy came up to me and asked me my name. Like a rube, I told him. He jumped up and down and cried, "Wow, man! That's my name too!" Then he tried to sell me a record album. He was a hustleh, as they say in New York. Today I guess you can't move five feet without somebody putting a touch on you. "Hey mistuh, got a dollar?" Either I'll give them a dollar or move along. I'm not going to lecture them or tell them to get a job. I mean, I wouldn't hire them, so why would I say such a thing?

I don't expect to be bothered, though. One thing I might do while walking down the streets of New York is mutter to myself and make vague arm movements to ward off potential trouble. Sure, this is in questionable taste, but I've got a wallet to protect. You think I'm going to give up my brand new driver's license and Asset card to some street scum just like that? You think I'm not going to take measures? If this doesn't work, I have my fist with its secret weapon: the ever-dangerous extended foreknuckle. Try to shake me down and *bip!* you won't know what hit you. You'll be eating soft food at Manhattan General if you fool with me. Just a word of warning to anybody in New York who might think a sitting duck is flying into town.

Of course, there's more to going to New York than having street smarts. There's shopping, restaurants, and theaters. I guess if you really like being treated like a dog, go to a camera store in New York. For some reason clerks in camera stores are permanently enraged, and they take it out on customers. I hear they're not too friendly at the danceterias, either—that is, if you care to take the chance that you won't be dancing with some stranger now and getting strangled later. New York's good for ending your evening tied up in some wacko's car trunk, too. So I'm basically going to steer clear of the clubs. I'm a little too wholesome for that kind of stuff.

What I will do, during the day, is sit in Central Park and look at the stockbrokers and the mimes. The mimes run around and teeter on the edge of ponds. Don't ask me why. That's not all the park offers. The joggers will rush past you and holler "Woddya, woddya." Activists for all kinds of causes come up to you, argue, then burst into tears. Messengers on bicycles will zip by you and cry "Woddya, woddya," just like the joggers. There's all kinds of street theater, too. Students from acting schools will stare at you and sway back and forth. Modern dancers will hop and twist around, interpreting the budget crisis for you. I'll probably even see somebody chewing the bark off a tree. There's lots to do in the park.

I'm ready to go. I've got my New York face on.

10/25/90

New York, New York

When I returned from my trip to New York, I had traveler's arrogance. *Hello peasants. You know where I've been?* New York City! *Hahahahaha.* I got over that soon enough. All I had to do was remember the way the city made me feel. I sure wasn't cocky walking down Fifth Avenue!

I was nervous even before I got on the plane to LaGuardia. I'm not an experienced traveler, and my stomach was jumping. As I rode the Red Line to Hopkins Airport I kept repeating my stomach-calming mantra, "Coats, Soothes, Protects," from the Pepto-Bismol box. It really works. Plus I took deep breaths.

> As I rode the Red Line to Hopkins Airport I kept repeating my stomach-calming mantra, "Coats, Soothes, Protects," from the Pepto-Bismol box. It really works.

The plane ride was uneventful. After I arrived at LaGuardia I stood in line for a taxi. My brother had told me what route I should be taking to his co-op on Central Park West, so the cabbie wouldn't rip me off by going by way of New Jersey. I didn't really listen to him, figuring I wouldn't know the difference anyway. So I'm a chump. If the cabbie was going to screw me out of a few bucks, big deal. That's New York.

He didn't, though. He even offered to knock a dollar off my fare since he made a wrong turn! His name was Nbr Nbram. Or maybe it was Nbram Nbr. Nbram was on top, Nbr on the bottom of his posted identification. I wondered what kind of nickname a guy named Nbr Nbram would have. Nibs-Man? Nibby? Whatever. He was a good cabbie and I gave him a big tip.

That night my brother and I walked down to Broadway's Great White Way from his place. I saw the Ed Sullivan Theater, Radio City Music Hall, the Rainbow Room, the Imperial Theater. I saw that *Cats* was still around. I saw worried-looking hookers on Times Square. We were rushing around, so everything went by in a flash. It was better than seeing it on TV, but to be honest, not much. You have to linger there at least a little so it'll sink in.

The next day, when my brother and sister-in-law and niece were at work and school, I was on my own. I crossed Central Park and went to the Metropolitan Museum of Art. This is when I got intimidated by the city. I rushed back to my brother's place and cringed there for a while until I got the courage to go back out. Then I walked around on Columbus Avenue and sat in a few restaurant bars. I had non-alcohol beers, and they calmed me down, or the dark of the bars did.

From that point on, the trip was great. My sister-in-law had her purse—with her keys in it—stolen from her office, so my brother and I spent my last day in the city changing locks on the doors to his apartment. This was no treat for him, but it was fun and novel for me. We went to a locksmith on Broadway to get new cylinders and keys for the locks, and my brother tried to install them himself. Then we had to wait all afternoon for the building's maintenance guy to come undo my brother's handiwork. I totally enjoyed these shenanigans and pretending to help. I mean, what did I care? I was on vacation.

Over the weekend my brother, sister-in-law, niece, and I drove to their place on Shelter Island, New York. It's a two-hour journey they make every weekend to escape tension-rife Manhattan. My brother is a partner in a law firm, and my sister-in-law is an attorney for the city of New York, so they can afford both places. On Saturday we drove to the ritzy Hamptons so I could see the big oceanfront houses and maybe spot a celebrity. I didn't see anybody, and I didn't think it was that much better than Bratenahl. But the sky and the ocean were blue, and I did my obligatory reflective-standing-on-a-beach thing I like to do on trips.

The highlight of the entire trip, however, happened on the way back to LaGuardia from Shelter Island. We stopped at a petting farm in Peconic, New York, called Punkinville, given the cutesy name because it sold all kinds of pumpkins. Punkinville had goats, chickens, pigs, rabbits, deer, and prairie dogs that you could feed and pet, though there were some rams there I didn't want to take a chance on. I did feed a goat, who ate out of my hand. He surprised me by not rubbing his teeth against my palm—I worried about it, thinking he might gouge me—and his tongue was nice and dry. He was dainty and a clean feeder. He didn't leave a particle of spit on me.

You really ought to feed a goat some time. I'd do it again, for sure.

11/1/90

Thoughts on Dizzy

The cat Dizzy continues to fascinate. We got her as an eight-week-old kitten on Labor Day, and she's finally starting to grow into her large ears. Soon she'll be too big to ride on my shoulders like a parrot, which is all right by me, because this gives me a neck ache. The more she grows, the more I have to hunch over to give her a flat plane to stand on. It's not that great a trick anymore anyway if I have to be bent over like this—it smacks of labored antics. You have to know when to retire certain stunts from your cat's repertoire. You're not doing anyone any good by staying at the party too long.

A yell won't do. I have to scream in a strangled, psychotic fashion or it's no good.

Dizzy's activities aren't unique to her. As an adolescent cat, she does normal stuff. You hold up a length of dental floss in front of any cat, and it'll bat at it and try to eat it. Cats don't care if it's used or not. Similarly, Dizzy has tried to eat not only used dental floss but a chewed-up cookie directly out of my mouth, which maybe is unique to her. She tried to lick it right off my molars. I didn't let her, because, as someone at work said when I told her about the incident, "Who knows where that cat has been licking before?" I'm on my toes enough to know where cats lick, and I did stop Dizzy before we swapped any serious spit. I mean, I know not to French with animals, but to tell you the truth, I'd rather French with Dizzy than with many, many people I know. And you can think what you want about that.

(Speaking of teeth, we were surprised to find one of Dizzy's as we were playing with her the other night. It looked like a shark's tooth. I didn't know cats had baby teeth and lost them. At least that's what I hope happened. I'm not too worried. How many rubber-lipped, toothless cats do you see walking around?)

Dizzy's the second cat in a row I've lived with that's liked human food, like beef stew and cake. As I've mentioned before in this space, I eat my dinner in front of the TV, on the sofa, and Dizzy sits on my shoulder and watches intently as I do. This gets on my nerves plenty.

She physically impedes my food getting to my mouth, and since I'll upset my tray if I attempt to throw her off, I have to scare her off by screaming. A yell won't do. I have to scream in a strangled, psychotic fashion or it's no good. Even then she's back within seconds. I'm talking a banshee howl here, from the heart, but Dizzy doesn't care. She wants the beef stew and cake, and I can scream forever.

She likes regular cat food too. Every time I pour her food into her bowl from the Dairy Formula Kitten Chow container—shaped like a milk carton to fool cats into thinking they're getting the real thing—she jumps up and tries to tackle the box as I pull it away. Sometimes I hear her go "woo, woo" as she's eating. Really. I've heard it a couple of times. This can only mean she's in ecstasy. It also means she's probably going to end up like her predecessor, Tootie, the Victor Buono of the cat world.

Right now, though, Dizzy's svelte. She's coltish. She springs and leaps and scrambles around. She plays fetch. It's odd, but she does. You throw a crumpled Salem Lights pack across the room, and she'll run to get it, carry it back, place it at your feet, and wait for your next throw. Another odd thing she does is hang around my bathroom as I perform my morning toilette. She sits on the bath mat as I take my shower and doesn't mind being dripped on when I step out. Usually cats are long gone at any hint of water being dripped on them. She also stands on the rim of the sink, looking into the mirror with me as I shave and brush my teeth. What the hell can she be thinking about?

11/8/90

Chips: The Greatest

Potato Chips: The "Mr. Versatility" of Foods—What other snack can be eaten on its own, as well as in conjunction with other foods, like dogs and burgers and chicken? The answer is, None. Not corn chips, not tortilla chips, certainly not pretzels. Corn and tortilla chips are both derived from the heavy corn plant; both form thick globules of saturated fats in your digestive system. Pretzels, from the baked family, don't do this, but are totally inappropriate for the garnish role. Who eats burgers or dogs with pretzels on the side? You'd have to be nuts. What's that leave? Yes, the light, crispy chip, the food that dissolves off your molars far more quickly than other snacks. And that's the secret of its success. That's why chips really "get around" in the food and eating arena.

> Yes, the light, crispy chip, the food that dissolves off your molars far more quickly than other snacks.

Best Flavors for Chips—You know what flavor I like best in my chips? Potato. "Wait a minute, smartass," you say. "We know chips are made out of potatoes. You made it sound like you were going to tell what kind of chips you like best." I just did! *Potato.* Plain. No sour cream, no onion, no barbecue (though on occasion I can get into Dan Dee Hot, as opposed to regular barbecue, because they really coat the chip with the hot powder, both sides, top to bottom. On the regular barbecue the hot powder coating is spottier. And some of the chips in the regular barbecue bag don't have *any* powder on them. Forget that!). I don't need that junk on my chip. Which leads us to . . .

Dips: Yes or No?—As a rule, I'd say no. If you must dip, stick with the reliable French onion job from your grocer's dairy case. Sure, you're going to enjoy an artichoke or spinach dip at a party once in a while, but you can't run out to a Convenient in a pinch and grab one of those. Don't spoil yourself. Get used to what's readily available, and that's French onion. Better yet, don't get used to anything, like me. Then you'll never find yourself behind the eight ball dip-wise.

Hints for Livelier Chips—Having said all this, I will concede that, on the very rare occasion, chips can use a little goose. Here's the situation I found myself in at lunch just today, for example. I was eating grilled ham and cheese with chips on the side, plus a kosher dill wedge.

I ate about half my chips and thoroughly enjoyed them, but for fun I decided to squeeze my pickle on top of the remaining chips. "Whoa, Nellie!" you might say, but what is a pickle, anyway? cucumber and . . . yes, *vinegar*. So I wasn't doing anything weird at all. I was doing what millions enjoy doing to potatoes, only with a pickle. They were good, too. There's nothing wrong with being creative with your chips.

Chips on Your Plate: Is Less More?—This question has puzzled the great thinkers for centuries: Is it better to have a lot of broken chips on your plate, or a few big ones? I'll tell you what I prefer. I prefer the big ones. I can't stand shoving greasy chip particles in my mouth with my fingers like a chimp. I'm a human being, and I want to snap half of a big old chip with my teeth the way decent people do. Maybe you get more weight by volume with a pile of crumbs on your plate, and maybe you don't. All I know is the peaceful feeling I get when I see large, whole chips sitting next to my sandwich.

Chips on Film—In *The King of Comedy*, Rupert Pupkin (Robert DeNiro) eats from a bag of Wise potato chips. Wise is my favorite brand—is it more than a coincidence that our greatest actor, DeNiro, is seen eating Wise? Also, in *The Sunshine Boys*, an old geezer auditions for a part in a potato chip commercial and then only pretends to eat the chip, making chewing and smacking noises. The exasperated director says, "Could you *eat* the chip?" The geezer shrugs saying, "I can't; I got gallstones." From this I learned I didn't want gallstones if they stop you from eating chips. There are countless other examples of chips on film, but I can't think of any more right now.

When to Serve Chips—Any time is fine to serve chips. That's the way I feel about it.

11/15/90

Dream Boyfriend

The other day I was sitting on our couch quietly weeping. My girl-friend Barbara came up to me and said, "Are you crying, honey?"

"Yes, I am," I replied, "I was crying tears of joy, thinking about how lucky you are to be going out with me."

And I was. I was so happy for her. Imagine, fortune blessing you with a perfect boyfriend like myself, a snappy, peppy bundle of good looks and charm mixed with a childlike sense of wonder. Imagine Lady Luck bestowing on you such a dynamic formula for a boyfriend, made up of equal parts virility (the large, bushy eye-brows), keen, probing intellect (the high fore-head), and imposing physicality (the big breasts and shoulders). Is it any wonder I was moved by this? It's like a little miracle, every day, for Barbara.

> **What about romance? There's certainly a place for that in any relationship.**

Now you fellows out there might be thinking, How do I hitch my wagon to this guy's star? Well, I'll tell you: it's the little things that matter. I know by bitter experience that it's sometimes not enough merely to be wonderful. Sometimes you have to give a little, too. I know it hurts. But I do it. And knowing that I do contributes to the overall warmth and joy I feel when I think about my girlfriend's marvelous gift and blessing: namely, me.

For instance, when Barbara calls me on the phone at work, I say, "Yes, *How* may I help you?" This is: 1) politeness. There's no reason not to be polite just because it's your girlfriend; 2) a genuine and sincere inquiry. The accent on "How" says to Barbara, "Just what is it *exactly* that you want?" She appreciates the desire for specificity; 3) much better than the grunted "Whut?" that you probably give your mate. Now isn't it? Alternatives: "Yes. How delightful to hear from you" (for the lighter moment) or "Yes. What can I do to help you today?" The little things.

At home, I'm just as cordial. When Barbara does something wrong, I don't get angry. I smile and say, "Now that's not the way we do things. That kind of trash doesn't fly here." When she's bothering me, I respond by crying out, then running into my room. But after a few minutes I come out, saying "I have decided to forgive you," waving my hands around magnanimously like the Godfather. This shows true humanity—not to mention true class.

What about romance? What about *toujours, toujours, l'amour?* There's certainly a place for that in any relationship. Just last night, I was in the supermarket with Barbara, and I saw an attractive woman go by me in the aisle. I stood there smirking and nodding in approval, much like the fellow in that auto parts commercial several years back. You know, the guy who sold auto parts to those chicks wearing the Daisy Mae outfits, the checked blouses exposing their stomachs and the hot jean shorts. You remember the ad. Anyway, I did that to show Barbara I was a romantic person with a heart alive to love. And I think she appreciated it.

When Barbara speaks to me romantically, I know how to give it right back. How important is this? Plenty. When somebody tells you they love you, you don't say "That's *your* problem." You act nice. You give a response in kind, as I do. When my girlfriend says, "I love you," I say, "That's very commendable. Thanks so much." Or "Who can blame you?" or its variant, "I don't blame you." The confident "Doubtlessly." The cocky "And why wouldn't you?" The regal "As you will." But my favorite is the tender response—those three little words.

"I do, too."

12/6/90

Baby Shower

We threw a baby shower for my sister a few Sundays ago. It wasn't my idea. This is what people do.

The party consisted of nearly 20 women and me. My girlfriend and I were nervous preparing for it. We cleaned and cleaned. I cleaned my bathroom, which had to serve as the guest bathroom, but I couldn't totally wipe out its socked-in grime. It was hard to believe that this had come to pass: 20 women might have to use my bathroom—my buddy—where I smoked and dripped and where five-year-old dustballs nestled in the corner behind the toilet. I had to be tough about it. I could get out the surface dirt, but there was no way to get rid of the yellow film that accumulated over the years, and it was fruitless to worry about it.

Some of my sister's close friends hung around for a while and started talking about breast pumps. Their gross talk nearly bent me over in disgust.

It turned out only one person used the bathroom anyway. When the guests arrived at 3 o'clock they sat down immediately. We had plenty of food and drinks: sodas, wine, and vegetables and dip, cheese strata and artichoke squares. I wondered why they didn't dive right into the food, and I stood by the tables eating to give them the idea. Soon they wandered in from the living room and chowed down. Then everyone went back into the living room to watch my sister open her presents.

This wasn't too exciting for me. Baby items don't interest me. My sister opened things like bath wraps, which I guess you wrap the baby in after it's been dipped in a bath. It had a hood on it. She got a bottle dryer, a baby swing, and a stroller. She got a receiving blanket to wrap the baby in after birth, which I'd never heard of. Doesn't the hospital have these kinds of supplies on hand? Do you have to bring towels to the hospital, as well, so the doctor can wipe the baby off after it's born? They'll pry money out of you for anything.

Some of the women made more of a fuss over the wrapping paper than they did the presents, "Oh, that's so pretty." Big bamooch. Tear it off, crumple it up, throw it away. You're going to congratulate Hallmark for every little product? They saved the bows and ribbons, too. I suppose it makes sense to recycle these, but to have to think about that is for me a slice of Hell. It certainly wasn't my place to say anything, though.

After the ceremony the people started going home. Some of my sister's close friends hung around for a while and started talking about breast pumps. Their gross talk nearly bent me over in disgust. They talked about stretched nipples. This was another thing I'd never heard of. You put this breast pump on and it sucks the milk out of you. I'm not making this up. I thought if women had trouble nursing they just got the milk at their grocer's dairy case. Or they bought Lactaid and poured that in a bottle. How would I know? (I asked one of the salesmen here what Lactaid was, and he said it "cleaned metal." I'm not the only one who doesn't know what's going on.)

That wasn't the only unpleasant surprise, either. My sister let me feel her stomach, which I've never done before; that is, feel a pregnant woman's belly. The instant I felt it I pulled my hand back in revulsion. My God, it was as hard as a nut! I thought it was supposed to feel soft and floaty—I thought the baby was surrounded by albumen or sputum or something of this nature, and it would be like marshmallow whip. I touched it again so as not to offend, but I couldn't imagine putting my ear to it like they do on TV. The whole thing made me queasy.

After everyone left, we cleaned the place up. As I mentioned before, only one person used the bathroom, and it had been a toddler who'd been brought to the party. Of course I didn't have to worry about her doing a white glove test in there. I found it ironic that the toddler's mom had to go in the bathroom to check that her child didn't do anything weird that she'd have to clean up, when I had been afraid all along that one of the women would find something weird that I had done in the bathroom already. So it was kind of like the old switcheroo.

Anyway, the baby shower was over in time for me to watch *60 Minutes*, and that was good.

2/21/91

Again, Ahead of the Pack

The cover story in last week's *Time* magazine is titled "The Simple Life: Rejecting the Rat Race, Americans Get Back to Basics." Symbolizing this on the cover is a picture of a pair of walking boots and a bicycle, both looking like they cost a fortune, but what of it. It's the thought that counts.

I don't want to crow, but . . . *ain't I been living this way all along?* Where's everybody been? *Time* surveyed 500 adults, and 69% said they want to "slow down and live a more relaxed life." And so, we read about former corporate sharks who are now looking and acting like a bunch of Amish. They're putting on aprons and plaid shirts and their old knockabout pants and running little markets and cider mills. They're eating cheese-covered casseroles. The men are shaving with brushes and soap instead of Foamy or Edge. (For further details, see reruns of *Green Acres* on Nickelodeon every night.) Now I find myself on the cusp of a trend.

> I long ago rejected the fast track, because I feared others on the track would run me down, back up, and run me down again.

For a long time I've been knocked as a piddler and a putterer, a do-nothing. But I knew all along the nation would come to my way of doing things—or not doing them, as the case may be. I long ago rejected the fast track, because I feared others on the track would run me down, back up, and run me down again. I don't have to slow down and smell the coffee, because I already smell lots of stuff, all the time. Suddenly, I'm vindicated. I look smart.

Take cars, for instance. People are getting rid of their expensive, hard-to-maintain foreign jobs in favor of still expensive, but easier-to-maintain foreign jobs. Big sacrifice: they're trading their top-of-the-line German cars for top-of-the-line Japanese.

Now I'll give you *genuine* simple. I had a 1982 Plymouth Champ, a fuel-efficient, peppy little deathtrap I sold to a salesperson here at the office for $200 cash and a couple of dress shirts. What car did you get to replace it, you ask? None. Not one. I'm a non-polluting, mass transit guy. I take the rapid to work every day and ride in my girlfriend's Escort other times, shouting and singing along the way. I let her drive because I'm afraid to—not that I'm not skilled at it, but because I have a low tolerance level and I can see myself ramming into things—other offending vehicles, slow-moving pedestrians—in frustration. Or what if during one of my frequent daydreaming episodes I cross the center line and *whammo!* Or what if my tires go spinning off their axles on I-90? These things happen, believe me. At any rate, I've gone back to basics on this one.

I've dressed simply all these years too. I've never worn a $1,500 suit. I frequently wear polyester blend shirts and have worn shiny, utilitarian polyester pants in my day as well. I don't wear the pants any more, as they began to stiffen up on me and cut into my thighs, but I sure didn't wear them for style's sake or to make a statement. They were *clothes*, designed to keep the cold out and to cover what needed to be covered so people wouldn't go screaming into the streets. I never cared about designer labels, except maybe Big Yank, which is okay for a simple guy like me.

Fifty-six percent in the survey said they wanted to find more time for their hobbies and interests; they're starting to "cocoon." I don't have anything to say about that, except that you might take note of the name of this column—the name I gave it four years ago. *Four years ago.*

America, *Time* magazine, get with it. Cleveland's way ahead of you. As usual.

4/11/91

Bat!

I got the Bat Call last week. My mother phoned me Tuesday night and told me she had a bat in her apartment. Then she said she thought she might have two bats, one swooping one way, one the other, thus supplying an instant answer to the question "What's worse than having a bat in your apartment?"

"Are you sure it's not a bug?" I asked.

"Yes," she said. "It's as big as an eagle."

"I'll be quite frank with you, Ma," I said, "I hope that's not the case."

> **I did feel sort of guilty walking home, leaving Ma alone with the bat.**

Though I was busy (I had been sitting in my shorts, looking at *Time* magazine with the TV going) I went over to her apartment. I had no game plan formulated. My father used to swat bats with a tennis racket or a broom and flush them down the toilet. Here's the fun part of that: lifting the toilet lid to check if the bat flushed or if it is still swimming around in he bowl. I could have a coronary just thinking about it. No, I would try to whoosh it out.

After the bat took a couple of dives at my head in the dark of my mother's front hall, I decided to go home. My mother was safely locked in her bedroom, and she could call the apartment building's maintenance man in the morning. I'm a young boy with a whole lifetime in front of me. I couldn't be having a rat with wings sucking the juice out of my neck. But I did feel sort of guilty walking home, leaving Ma alone with the bat.

When I got home my girlfriend Barbara was there, and she was eager to go after the bat. We went back to my mother's place, this time with a flashlight, baseball glove, and shoebox. I don't know what we expected to do with the shoebox or the glove. We stood in an alcove beyond the dining room, shining the flashlight on the bat, who was struggling to find a way out via the dining room window. We wanted to get a living room window open, because that seemed to be on the bat's flying route. Neither of us had the nerve to open the dining room window with the bat right there, beating its wings and squirming around.

I walked slowly into the living room to get the window open. After I opened it, I headed back to the haven of the dining room. As I walked back, the bat was suddenly on me. I shrieked and ducked. The bat flew by.

I heard my mother's faint voice from behind her bedroom door.

"What did you say?" she asked.

"I was screaming, Ma," I said.

I heard her say "Oh." As long as it's nothing important!

Barbara and I stood watching the bat for a half hour. Every minute or two the bat would fly by, and Barbara would leap back, landing on my feet, and I'd cuss her. How was I expected to back her up with her jumping on me like that?

Soon the bat began creeping around on the floor in the front hall. The poor devil was tired. He was lying on the floor a foot from where I was standing, and I shined the flashlight on him. I felt sorry for him. He wasn't so bad looking. If I'd had a jacket or towel I could have ended the whole thing right then by throwing it over him, scooping him up, and tossing him out the window. All we had at hand was the shoebox, though, and that would have taken precision placement. I'll admit it: I was too scared to try. If that thing had flown up at my face while I tried to place a box on him it could have been the end of me. Oh—no way? People die jogging and shoveling snow and no way would I die from a bat attack? All right. I'll take your word for it.

He rested only for a minute, though. He went back to his swooping. We thought we could draw him out the living room window by standing in the den off the living room shining the flashlight. He flew by a few times but didn't get the idea. Then Barbara backed up and accidentally turned on my mother's Vornado fan with her foot, which made me swear. For some reason the sound of the fan enraged me, and I kept swearing until we managed to turn it off, which took some doing. I was beginning to get very tired of the whole business.

I think my mother was beginning to get tired of it, too, with the noises, the light flashes, and the swearing, so she told us to go home. The custodian would take care of it in the morning. We all hoped— especially my mother—that the bat would be hiding in the drapes in the morning and she could sneak out to work.

The next day my mother did find the bat, hanging in the den window. She carefully slid the den doors shut, closing the bat off from the rest of the apartment. The custodian took it from there.

I think if I were to give myself a grade in this affair, it'd have to be an F, since we failed to get the bat out. I would, however, give myself an E for effort, and, if it improves my main grade any, I did *dream* the bat flew out the window. The whole thing still ended better than my aunt's bat incident. She called an exterminator when she had a bat flying in her house, and when he came down after going up to her attic with a flashlight, he was grinning.

"Wow, lady," he said. "You got *thousands* of them up there."

Thousands.

6/6/91

The I-Team Nightmare

WJW-TV's *Newscenter 8* 6:00 newscast: Nov. 11, 1991, 6:09 P.M.

ANCHORMAN TIM TAYLOR: Recently Carl Monday and the I-Team took their investigative cameras to the offices of the weekly newspaper the *Cleveland Edition* to look into various charges and accusations against entertainment and listings editor Eric Broder. What they found was a shopping list of violations: personal misconduct, questionable work ethics, and general negligence. Here is Carl Monday with the Special I-Team Report: "Disgrace in the Newsroom."

CARL MONDAY: We'd heard things about Eric Broder . . . lots of things, and all the time. Things about his personal and grooming habits . . . his interpersonal relationships in the office . . . and a work ethic that can best be described as doubtful. But were these things true? We decided to find out.

What we did was hide our camera behind the wall next to Broder's desk. The *Edition* is an open office, with no doors to separate employees. Broder's desk is in the corner of the room, where he thinks no one can see what he's up to. But the I-Team saw. (*The video runs as Monday provides commentary.*)

Here's Broder arriving for work in the morning. So far, so good . . . he could be any employee coming in to work. But we didn't have to wait long to see some highly questionable behavior.

Here's Broder brushing his hair at a small mirror on the post behind his desk . . . and what's he doing now? He's looking . . . just *looking* at himself in the reflection. As you can see, his face is only about an inch from the mirror . . . and look what he does now. That's right—he *kissed* the mirror.

But that shouldn't have surprised us. Broder just can't seem to leave himself alone. Here he is tucking in his shirt . . . and *tucking* in his shirt . . . and tucking *in* his shirt. A psychologist might call this obsessive behavior. But not quite as obsessive as Broder giving himself the Special K Pinch. *Various shots of Broder feeling his stomach through his shirt all day long.* Or patting his hair down with his hand repeatedly throughout the day. What the heck: it beats working

Indeed, working doesn't seem to be a part of Broder's job description at all. If it was, he wouldn't be staring into space, doing nothing, as he is here . . . and here . . . and here. But don't get the idea that all Broder does is stare like a zombie. No, we saw him reading a magazine at this desk; or *was* it a magazine? (*Close-up of what Broder is intently examining.*) No, actually it's a catalog from a local lingerie shop. Broder doesn't want his co-workers to know how frisky he is, though; when another *Edition* employee walked by his desk, Broder quickly covered the spicy catalog with some papers.

And don't get the idea Broder is deskbound, either. He's up and at it all day. Up and at what, you ask? Well, apparently not anything to do with the paper. Broder left the office for a half-hour at one point. We thought maybe he was on assignment. And, in a manner of speaking, he was: Assignment Tootsie Roll. Yes, he'd spent that time in a candy store. Here he is, back at his desk, spending another 15 minutes eating the Tootsie Roll. Those noises you hear are Broder snorting as he eats. And God help you if you want to phone Broder while he's eating his candy. (*Shot of Broder, mouth full, yelling "I'm not here!" as he's paged for a phone call.*)

"Here's Broder arriving for work. So far, so good . . . he could be any employee coming in to work. But we didn't have to wait long to see some highly questionable behavior."

If you're wondering how Broder can hold on to his job, you're not alone. We did manage to get a shot of him proofreading articles with his superior; how it works is, his boss reads the articles to Broder, and Broder checks for mistakes in the galleys. What you're seeing is Broder proofreading stories by various *Edition* writers—he doesn't look too happy doing the work. But what's this? Why is Broder suddenly animated, slapping his leg and laughing? You guessed it. The boss is reading Broder's *own* work to him. (*Shot of Broder, absolutely delighted, saying, "That's a good one, huh boss? Is that dynamite or what?"*) But he wasn't happy for long—the next article *wasn't* by him. (*Shot of Broder looking glum again.*)

At the end of the day we confronted Broder. (*Shot of Broder looking quizzically into camera. Monday approaches him, saying "Mr. Broder? Carl Monday with the I-Team. Could I ask you a few questions?" Broder appears confused. Monday says, "How often do you read porno magazines and eat candy when you're supposed to be working?" Shot of Broder grabbing a copy of the magazine* Entertainment Weekly *and attempting to cover his face with it as he runs out of the office. Shot of Broder peeking around the corner into the office to see if the camera is still present. The last shot is of Monday running toward Broder and Broder disappearing from sight.*)

MONDAY (*on the Newscenter 8 set with Taylor*): Obviously Broder didn't want to talk with us. But I think the videotape did the talking for him.

TAYLOR (*shaking his head in disgust*): It sure did. It's a "disgrace," indeed. Thanks, Carl.

11/6/91

Why I Am a Sex Machine

There are many reasons why I am a sex machine. I think the main ones have to do with *appearance* and *attitude*. Let's start with appearance, if that's okay.

Appearance of the sex machine. Clothes make the man, and I'm no exception. All the clothes I wear are made of the sex fabric, cotton. Cotton breathes with the skin, wicking perspiration, and as it and the skin become one you end up with, you know, a sexy look. That's why I'm constantly being undressed by women's eyes as I walk around the office building here, because they want to, you know, see me naked, I'm pretty sure.

My hairline recedes on some days, and on other days comes charging back. You know what it is? That's raging hormones.

My hair is real sexy too. It's brown, the sex color. You know what they say about men with brown hair. The same thing they say about men with receding hairlines. My hairline recedes on some days, and on other days comes charging back. You know what it is? That's raging hormones, and you better believe that's got everything to do with sex, sex, sex.

Framing my sex-filled brown hair are my ears, as you might suspect. They're quite big, and that means something too. They stick out from my head, which is a sure sign of potent . . . ah, you know . . . potent sex. Clark Gable had ears like mine, and they called him the King of Hollywood. He was big box office, but he was big in other fields as well. My ears are just like his, so you can draw your own conclusions, if you want to.

To the direct right and left of each ear are my eyes, which are really quite suggestive. I've hypnotized women with my eyes, because they're very powerful, like Svengali's. They bore right in on you. I'm afraid to look people in the eye because I've got this frightening power, and I could easily misuse it. Don't you think? So when I don't look you in they eye, it's not that I'm squirrelly but that my hypnotic sexual eyes would put you in a trance, and that's not necessary in everyday business. But, as I said, I can and have hypnotized women with them, and, you know, may do so again.

Many a time a woman has said to me, "You have a sensual mouth." I think the strength of my sensual mouth is in my lips, which are crimson slashes that cruelly bisect my face. Actually, they're a little lower than that, but "bisect" is a well-known sexual buzzword. Most of you got that, right? At any rate, the mouth is very sensual, which spells t-r-o-u-b-l-e for the woman I'm kissing, if I can get personal here.

Attitude of the sex machine. On to attitude, which might be even more important than appearance to a sex machine. I have a devil-may-care attitude that really is catnip to most women. Which is to say they find it very appealing, not that women could be influenced like cats are with catnip. But if they could—and mind you, I'm saying *if*—maybe they'd react to my devil-may-care attitude in a way that's similar to cats and catnip—that is, by wriggling around on the floor and having breathing difficulties. But maybe you'd get the same reaction if you tickled them, I don't know for sure.

Anyway, a sex machine has to have an attitude of "I don't care what you think, I'm me, and I like being me!" darn it. Which is what I do. For example, I had a stress zit on my forehead last week, and I covered it with a big Band-Aid. Now most people don't look too good with a Band-Aid plastered across their foreheads. But here I turned disadvantage into advantage. I didn't tell people I had a stress zit on my forehead; I used a special strategy. I walked on the balls of my feet with my arms dangling loosely at my sides—just like a cocky, bantamweight fighter. Women weren't thinking, "Look at that loser covering that zit on his forehead with a Band-Aid." They were thinking, "That monkey's been in a scrap. I'd like to place a cool, moist towel on his injury. I hope he's not hurt in *every* part of his body, that big sex machine."

God, I hope that's what they were thinking. I looked like such a shmuck.

6/27/91

Going to the Grocery Store

In these hot summer months, if you can't get to a cool spot I recommend going to the grocery store and hanging out as I do. It's cold and there's lots to look at.

My girlfriend Barbara and I usually end up at the grocery store around 2:30 on a weekend afternoon. As soon as the crisp, refreshing store air hits me I start snapping my fingers, ready to get at it. Meat! Fruit! Crackers! Dairy! Convenience foods! Get down with your bad selves because here comes Grocery Man to look at you!

We begin at the left of the store as you enter from the parking lot. Then we go up and down the aisles, meats (in the back) to checkout, checkout to meats, until we're done. The first aisle is fruits and vegetables, with plenty of plastic bags on the rolls. Barbara looks at the vegetables and selects items to let rot for five weeks in the Nice 'N' Fresh drawer in our refrigerator. I say to her, "Ain't nobody going to eat that lettuce, babe." (I have kind of a swinging attitude in the grocery store.) Me, I pick four nice pieces of fruit and bag them. Four pieces are a week's worth for me. Apples, plums. Members of the citrus family are too much trouble, with their squirting and their need to be sectioned and peeled. Peaches are hairy, and pears look like somebody threw them on the floor. Nectarines and tangelos? I don't know a thing about them. I leave the berries alone, too.

> **People don't buy saltines because they love the taste of baked flour. They want *salt*. If Premium won't supply their customers salt I guarantee you they'll find a cracker that will.**

I'm happier in the cracker section, anyway, next aisle over. This is where a man can make a real decision. Zesta? Premiums? Ritz? Town House? Triscuit? Club crackers? Those Keebler elves are no slouches. Tiny guys with big baking talent! Premium better get wise quick. People don't buy saltines because they love the taste of baked flour. They want *salt*. If Premium won't supply their customers salt I guarantee you they'll find a cracker that will. I'm not kidding about this.

While we float in and out of the aisles we take occasional detours over to the meat case. I can't help staring at the pig stuff, the knees and knuckles and shoulders. And the whole fish packaged up in plastic and styrofoam. You can't get much deader than that. I'm sure not about to buy anything with the eyes still attached. Sometimes I look at the fish and imagine I see it breathing. I have to walk over to the cold cuts to get my perspective back. I forget my disgust at the pigs and the fish when I see good fresh bologna and olive loaf.

I start to get giddy around the canned goods—the Spaghetti-Os, Beefaroni, Dinty Moore, Manwich, Beans'n Weenies. This is usually when I do my Slo-Mo Man routine, too. When Barbara asks me what I want to get in this section, I say, "I . . . don't . . . know . . . what . . . do . . . you . . . want," like I'm in slow motion. Barbara doesn't like it when I do this, but you can't keep me down when I'm feeling mischievous. The rich bounty of the canned goods section makes me frivolous. A lucky American blowing on the horn of plenty!

When we stroll through the freezer section I calm down because here I have to make tough choices. I don't like frozen dinners, but sometimes that's all I feel like making myself after a hard day's work. Le Menu, Budget Gourmet, Stouffer's Banquet, Swanson—they're all kind of lousy with the stunning exception of Le Menu's Cordon Bleu or the odd chicken pot pie. It's no fun choosing between the lesser of evils. The freezer case dilemma is redeemed shortly afterward, though, because the next aisle over is potato chips, and nobody, but nobody can say choosing between chip styles is anything but a good time. Maybe it's the best time. Those chips sit nice in their bags in the store, don't they? Those first few chips out of the bags are all right, aren't they?

We end our time at the store at the dairy case and fooling around the breads. I say "fooling around" because at this point I've had about enough of the grocery store, and I'm always mad that I can't find my favorite kind of bread, Bavarian Rye. Bavarian Rye is chewy like white bread and has a crust you can tear off and suck on. I can't find it anywhere, though, and I don't like that multigrain oatmeal stuff that seems stale the day you buy it. That is some dry, puritanical bread they're loading the shelves with now.

So that's it, we get all we need, and we head to the checkout line. A few weeks ago on our way to the checkout I looked down the soda pop aisle, and I saw a girl dancing past the Vernor's. Yeah, she knew about the grocery store too!

7/11/91

The Greatest Vacation of All Time

The best part of going to the northern woods of Michigan is swimming in the green lakes up there. I get wet slowly, by wading into the lake waist-deep, then patting water on my shoulders and stomach. I may look like an old guy doing this, but isn't that better than risking shock or perhaps instantaneous death by jumping right in? How macho is it to be lying in some small-town Michigan morgue? Not very, I'd say.

> **My gravestone would read, "He didn't look right, but they made him work anyway, even on vacation."**

Once I'm completely submerged, I like to blow air out of my lungs and sink to the rocky bottom. I pull myself along the rocks, pretending to be a bottom feeder or a parasite. This de-evolution is very relaxing. After coming out of the water I towel off and sit in the shade and read about Nazis. Is that a vacation or what? And the birds would chirp: *Foo foo fweet. Foo foo fweet. Whoop, whoop.*

At night we'd go into town and walk along the pier that goes out into Lake Michigan. Then we'd walk around the harbor in town where all the cabin cruisers are docked. The people sipping cocktails on board the docked cruisers would look at us, and we'd look at them. I didn't envy them, because I like crawling along the bottom of the lake better than sitting on top of it in a boat.

We went on boats anyway. We paid $20 each to go on a cruise on an 85-foot schooner. There was no wind, so we drifted and ate Eagle brand potato chips they sold on board. We also went rowing on a rubber dinghy, with me battling the waves with nothing but brute strength and two aluminum oars. I didn't even get a chance to crack open my Diet Pepsi, I was so busy fighting the current like an Eskimo. Our dream of floating peacefully in the middle of the lake and drinking our pops was crushed by Mother Nature.

But they say man is more brutal than nature, and this was proven by my sister during the trip, when she asked me to move some of the house's deck chairs when I wasn't feeling right. "No!" you say. "Not on your vacation!" Yes. When she started moving the chairs and I just stood there she said coldly, "Will you help?" Despite the way I felt, I did. At my funeral, people would ask my sister if I died from moving things around when I wasn't feeling right, and she'd wave her hand dismissively and say, "Nah, he was just sick." But my gravestone would read, "He didn't look right, but they made him work anyway, even on vacation."

You might think the whole trip was ruined by my sister's inconsideration, but I forgave her and continued to have fun. I'm always on the lookout for animals up in the woods, and we saw a lot of them. We saw a raccoon mother and her kids. Raccoons' main function in life is eating garbage and giving people dirty looks for bothering them. Even the baby raccoons look bitter. Geez, if you don't like it learn a trade, like a beaver or a woodpecker. We also saw a great strapping deer run across the driveway. "Where you going, honey!" I yelled at him. And of course we saw rabbits sitting around.

My favorites, though, were the seagulls, who are just pigeons in sailor suits but look good to me anyway. We fed them bits of ice cream cones in the harborside park in town. Gulls are garbage eaters, too, but don't have the attitude, and when you see one perched on a dock, or better, on a piece of driftwood—boy, that's maritime. That's nautical. And if birds could talk, gulls would never shut up. They're hustlers, like New Yorkers: "Hey, listen, hey listen, whattya gonna do with that sugar cone? Hey listen, hey listen, throw that over here. Say, whattya got there, hey, hey." Gulls are all right.

The entire vacation was all right. Those were just the highlights I was talking about, and you might find different kinds of fun up there in the northern woods, like water-skiing, or camping, or whatever. I personally probably wouldn't care for the activities you choose, but what the hell, I've had my vacation, now you have yours!

8/1/91

You'll Hear from My Psychologist

"The loss of a historic building such as Adelbert Hall can have a devastating impact on the CWRU community. To help people deal with any potential emotional trauma, counseling is being made available"—CWRU's *Campus News*, June 25, 1991: "Counseling Available for CWRU Employees, Others"

I am a former Case Western Reserve University student. When I saw my former administration building, Adelbert Hall, burning on the local news broadcast, I was shattered. While I was nowhere near the fire, I have had many disturbing and traumatic episodes as a result.

> **When I saw the top of the building burning on TV, I was forced to take a drink—and I haven't stopped drinking since.**

As a student at CWRU, I not only passed by Adelbert Hall *nearly every day*, I often went *inside* the building, and it holds many memories for me. I would go to the cashier's window and cash checks there, and as I did I would look around and see the numerous fine features of the building, such as chairs, tables, walls, rugs, etc. These things were a part of my life; they were familiar to me. To know now that many of these items have been smoke damaged in the fire has put me under severe emotional distress. It is as if my memories—and so my life—have been destroyed.

When I saw the top of the building burning on TV, I was forced to take a drink—and I haven't stopped drinking since. Therefore this event has propelled me into the illness of chronic drinking and the attendant byproducts of this disease, such as missed work, blackouts, bar fights, destructive behavior in gift and card shops, and one episode of armed robbery. When I saw the flames coming out of the windows of the building I felt violated, and this feeling caused me to lash out at others whereas before this event happened, I, you know, wouldn't. I have also smoked crack cocaine because of this tragedy, becoming addicted to it, a sickness I attribute directly to the university's negligence in letting this fire happen to me.

I have had even more trauma due to my memories of a seminar I took as a student within the confines of Adelbert Hall. It was a seminar on the work of John Milton, and the class was held in a room on one of the upper floors that was completely destroyed by the fire—a room I had personally sat in only 14 short years ago! While we didn't study Milton's epic poem about God, the Devil, heaven, and hell, *Paradise Lost*, the fire caused me to have nightmares relating to this poem, though I have never exactly read it, per se. There have been moments, too, when I have experienced a vague uneasiness thinking about issues of heaven and hell, and I attribute these emotionally disturbing feelings directly to the fire and its link to *Paradise Lost*.

Too, I have not been able to function at work because of the emotional toll of the knowledge that a building that I had a day-to-day relationship with has been severely damaged. My assigned tasks at my workplace have gone undone thanks not only to my drinking and cocaine use but also to the awful thoughts of the fire damaging not only the chairs and tables of my youth but the file cabinets and other aids to the administration of my education. These thoughts have caused me severe emotional distress, not the least of which is my hurt at my supervisor's reaction to me calling in sick due to the fire. His skepticism and extreme sarcasm in response to my inability to work because of the fire's effects have been very painful to me and have made my recovery from the fire that much more difficult. Therefore my self-esteem has been "really burned" as well, if I may make a small joke.

Finally, and perhaps most hurtful of all, the fire has caused me to pull away from my loved ones and forced me to seek comfort not only in pornographic videos but in the arms of prostitutes, taking a financial as well as an emotional toll. I feel degraded after these episodes and cannot even escape them at home, as I am now on the mailing lists of Leisure Concepts and Caballero Films, who send me catalogs of their Triple-X sizzling-hot adult products that further tempt me and cause me considerable anxiety. I have spent thousands of dollars on these products, money I can ill afford to spend. This has been one of the worst results of the Adelbert fire.

Consequently I am suing the university for 12.5 million dollars in damages.

8/8/91

Ask the Cat Man

I wouldn't give you two cents for no cat. You mess with me and my German shepherd will tear your throat out. A cat don't do nothing but sit around and look at you. What are you always writing about cats for?—Dale, Cleveland

Cats are my pals. You think cats don't do anything but sit around? Listen to this. When I get home from work, I like to lie down on my bed and just unwind. The cat Dizzy won't let me, though, unless she can do it too. If I close my door she meows piteously until I let her in, then she comes rushing in with a yell and jumps on my bed with me. She walks around in circles, then curls up right next to me, whereupon she begins sucking her tail and digging her claws into my side. You know what that is?

That old German shepherd of yours will eat you up if you have a heart attack at home and fall down and don't move for a while. Alive or dead, he doesn't care.

That's l-u-v, baby. That old German shepherd of yours will eat you up if you have a heart attack at home and fall down and don't move for a while. Alive or dead, he doesn't care. He heard the dinner bell the moment you fell down, and there won't be anything left to find of you but a chewed up hip bone. He'll be happy, but where will you be? That's why I like cats.

Sometimes when I go over to my girlfriend's house and fall asleep on her couch the cat jumps onto my stomach from a height, and when I wake up there she is staring at me with her ears back like she's going to attack me, then she jumps off and runs away. Why?—Howard, Cleveland Hts.

Why? She's busting your hump, that's why. That cat knows you don't like her, am I right? Do you ever pet her or talk to her—even a "How you doing?" You ever give her a Pounce treat or some kind of nibble? I thought not. She's just trying to spook you. You show her a little respect and maybe she'll leave you alone. Then again, maybe she won't. She might be nuts, for all I know.

My cat is such a bitch I can't believe it. She's affectionate when she feels like it, but whenever I want to pet her she looks at me like I'm some kind of leper and runs away. When she does that I feel like kicking her arrogant little butt.—Tina, Lakewood

I know how you feel. Our cat acts like Jackie Onassis all the time, too. "I'll be affectionate when it serves me, but don't you touch me, peon." Some cats are like that. Our previous cat, Tootie, was always affectionate and always liked to be stroked. She was a big eater, too. She was a fat animal that enjoyed being manhandled and rubbed. What can I tell you? Different kinds of people, different kinds of cats.

You know, I really think my cat Shasta was an Egyptian queen in a previous life, maybe even Cleopatra. She has a regal bearing and we have psychic communication as well, where she gives me imperial commands and predicts the weather. I also wear a mystical cat amulet around my neck and Shasta sometimes communicates with me through that.—Rena, Lyndhurst

It sounds like your cat ought to be pooping in a rubber litter box and you, too. You're crazy as a bedbug.

What does it mean when my cat hides behind the couch cushions and flattens her ears and crosses her eyes? It's quite alarming.—Steve, Cleveland

You're telling me! Our cat does it too (see picture). All I can think of is that it's a psychotic episode; I'd like to pretty it up for you, but that's what I think. It's almost like a hostage situation when they're like that; you try to talk them out. I wouldn't put my hand anywhere near their heads when they're psycho. Gradually their ears will pop back up and their eyes will straighten out and everything will be back to normal. So to speak.

My cat Trudy sits upright in chairs with her legs spread and her arms hanging over her stomach and it looks really bad and not at all catlike. Is she maybe a slob or a loser or something? – Traci, Lakewood

I wouldn't worry about it; she probably wants to look like you when you're sitting in a chair. It may be her way of saying, "Hey, look at me, I'm just like you, and I should eat that way, too." Don't bring out the Cheerios and the steak quite yet, though. Cats ought to eat cat food, and it may be that your cat is just informal. Nothing wrong with that either.

8/15/91

A Trip to Gander Mountain

Got my Gander Mountain catalog. It wasn't addressed to me, actually. It came to my sister, the cop, who's more of an outdoors person than I am.

Gander Mountain specializes in "sportsman supplies" for hunters: parkas, binoculars, hats, boots and waders, camouflage outfits, tents, sleeping bags, and the like. I'm not interested in any of this stuff, except maybe the Rattlers Snake-proof Cordura Brush Busters, which keeps rattlers from biting your legs and ankles. They have good photos in the catalog of rattlers being foiled by the Brush Busters. They're shown trying to sink their teeth into "1,000-denier Cordura fabric and 2-layer protection below the knees in the prone area." Fat chance, I say. Let's see any snake on earth get even 500-denier! They'll creep away with chipped fangs. I contend your prone area can get by with 200-denier. Any more denier than this, and you're being a major-league wussy. (There's

> Hey, I can find you a dead squirrel easy on Lee or Mayfield Road without spending $5.99 on a Lohman Blow-type Squirrel Call.

also a photo of a snake howling in frustration next to a couple of snake-proof boots: *Aaoooooooh! Aaoooooooh!* These things must really work.)

The catalog is kind of boring until it gets into the hardcore hunting supplies. I'd gone past the Dog Boots (which look like moccasins with two holes in front for the dog's toenails) and the Automatic Kennel Silencers ("for controlling persistent [sic] boredom and night barking") until I finally got to the guns: pistols, shotguns, blackpowder rifles, big old revolvers like they used in the days of *The Rebel* and *Alias Smith and Jones.* And of course, the Turbo Tumblers that separate the media from the cases once the cases have been polished and deburred. I don't know what the hell it means either, but it sure sounds good, even if the Turbo Tumblers do look like West Bend automatic corn poppers.

Come on, I'm thinking, let's get to the game. Lions and tigers and bears! But when I turn the page the first thing I see is the Mr. Squirrel Whistle: 162 pages of catalog and *squirrels* are the prey? This has all been leading up to squirrels? Yes, I see—squirrels and deer and rabbits. Hey, I can find you a dead squirrel easy on Lee or Mayfield Road to use the Mr. Squirrel Skinning Aid on without spending $5.99 on a Lohman Blow-type Squirrel Call that "produces the bark of an excited squirrel and the soft purr of a sunning squirrel." They bark like dogs and purr like cats? I didn't know. They never let you get too close, and now I know why. Too many guys have barked and purred at them, then blasted away. No wonder they zip up trees every time they see you coming.

Same thing with deer. I mean, what chance do deer have when you're using the Quaker Boy Bleat-in-Heat Call, imitating "perfect doe-in-heat bleats and meek fawn distress calls"? Or the Knight and Hale EZ Grunter Plus Doe Bleat that's a bisexual call: you can be an "aggressive rutting buck" or a "hot doe in estrus" with this device. And people worry about Pee Wee Herman! These guys imitate the mews of fawns to attract does, and they grunt to enrage territorial bucks. What a life. And if you're a Canada goose you'd better watch out. This catalog has more calls designed to shoot your butt out of the sky than any other bird. The Big River 200 Long Honker Goose Call imitates the Canada goose perfectly—"and you don't even have to 'hut' to make this call break to the high note." Again, I don't know what this means, but it sounds like man has outwitted goose once again.

Once you've bumped off your quarry, you can put it into your Deluxe Reusable Big Game Bag (keep that baby in the *garage*) or if it's a deer, onto the Warren and Sweat "Mule" Big Game Carrier. You have to get the "magnum size" for large deer, bear, sheep, or elk. Sheep? Maybe that's for shepherds in case one of their flock dies of natural causes, because I didn't know you could hunt sheep. I'd just get a magnum anyway, so there will be extra room for my squirrels.

Gander Mountain. This is a man's man's world.

8/22/91

How to Sit with Babies

Babies hate my guts. That's what I was thinking as my girlfriend (er . . . fiancée) Barbara and I watched my seven-month-old niece Jane E. Frazier during the Bears–Bills game two Sundays ago. My sister had gone out for a few hours, leaving the infant in our care. For a while, Jane E. Frazier, honked off that her mom had left, cried and looked at me like everything was my fault.

I don't know nothing about baby-sitting babies. It's a good thing Barbara was around, because that baby would still be crying if I'd been there by myself. She'd be crying through adolescence and into college. I never would have thought of turning down the sound on the football game and putting on soothing music, as Barbara did. I would have continued to sit on the sofa, waving my arms around and going "woo woo" to calm her down. What a waste of time. The baby had no interest in my tepid riffs. What's seeing some guy bounce around on a couch making stupid noises, compared to nursing on a mother's soft breast? If I was a baby, I'd think, "There's no comparison." I'm just glad Barbara came up with the music idea.

Jane Frazier cheered up considerably after this move and began to take an interest in her surroundings. We put her toys around her. She chewed on her yellow worm, which wore a cap and glasses and held a book. She had a plastic phone, a toy accordion, a key chain with big keys, and stacking cups. I think she felt good when we got down on the floor with her, as she then felt she was dealing with equals, though of course we knew better. We knew she'd still be on the floor for the next several months while we'd be back on our feet soon, walking around. We're bipeds all the way.

After awhile, the baby began rocking back and forth on all fours to the music, saying "Guy guy guy dai dai dai guy guy guy." This was all right. There was nothing to this. Put on some tunes and you'll have no problem with babies. But then we discovered the baby had gone to the lavatory in her diaper. Barbara cleaned her up and changed her, while I held her feet up and almost gagged. Earlier, I had in actuality gagged after touching the baby's gummed and wet Stella Doro cookie fragments. The baby was going "Huh huh huh hee hee hee hah hah hah." Then, when we threw the used diaper aside, the cat Dizzy sniffed it and looked up at us with her eyes crossed and her mouth ajar. I had to shake my head at the entire business.

During the last hour of our baby-sitting experience, nothing much happened. We put some old Ethel Merman music on the boombox, and Jane Frazier went "Aaahhhhh aahh huh huh *hunh*." I was going to rub the baby with my Pollenex electric massager, but Barbara didn't think it was a good idea. I did touch her leg with the Pollenex on "low," and she did look surprised, but hardly electrocuted as Barbara had feared. I wasn't totally comfortable with using the device on the baby anyway. None of the pictures on the Pollenex box showed babies being massaged; just guys with mustaches with cricks in their necks or old folks with arthritis. However, there were no specific warnings: *Not to be rubbed on babies' arms or legs.*

I also idly wondered in the waning baby-sitting moments if I should draw a couple of crossed daggers and snakes and the legend "Born to Raise Hell" on Jane Frazier's arm with a felt tip pen, then tell my sister we took the baby out to be tattooed. I don't know if new mothers go for that kind of gag, even though my sister, a Cleveland cop, probably has lots of friends on the force with tattoos. Maybe she would have thought it was a great idea—who knows? But I would imagine most moms would like to be present when their babies get tattooed.

When my sister returned, Jane Frazier was going "Bah bah bah bah bah," and another football game (49ers–Raiders) was on. My sister scooped up Jane Frazier, thanked us, and left. Barbara and I congratulated ourselves on a job well done, and I myself slept like a baby that night.

10/10/91

Pretzels: The Inside Story

Pretzels: "Death, Get Outta Here"—Pretzels are among the most healthful of snacks, rich in life-giving nutrients. When you eat pretzels, you're in effect saying to Death, "You get on outta here. I'm not eating corn chips or pork rinds or other fried foods, I'm eating pretzels, ground from nutritious wheat and then baked like bread, with no fats or oils used in processing to give me a heart attack or stroke, so get the hell out, I'm eating pretzels now." And Death will take off, because it knows not to mess with anybody smart enough to eat pretzels all the time.

> Unfortunately, Mr. Salty, the pretzel/sailor who was once the universal symbol of crunchiness and saltiness, has fallen on hard times.

A Pretzel Memory from the Troubled '60s—I used to watch TV shows like *The Mod Squad* and *The Monroes*, lying on the floor on my back with my head propped on a pillow, eating beer pretzels, the nubs at the bottom first, sucking on them like sourballs. I'd stare at then-young actresses Peggy Lipton and Barbara Hershey with longing, and dread the next day of junior high. But I'd savor the beer pretzel, because I knew the supply was finite. Now, as an adult, I can get all the pretzels I want, there's no more school, and I don't need to worry about Peggy Lipton and Barbara Hershey anymore.

Pretzels in and out of Context—Naturally, most people eat pretzels in the comfort of their homes. But pretzels are especially good when you shouldn't be eating them. Off-brand pretzels, like Lance, taste fairly good at your desk at work (*out of context*); however, you wouldn't give Lance pretzels the time of day *in context*, or at home. Conversely, out of context, the best pretzels become soaringly delicious. Example: when I was visiting my brother in New York, he had a supply of Bachman Pretzel Stix, which come boxed in individual snack packs. These sticks, baked to the perfect brownness, are unapologetically covered with salt and as crisp as an autumn night. They're hard to find in Cleveland, so out of town they tasted as good as roast beef. Another roast beef–quality pretzel is Harry's Sourdough, which, eaten at your desk, is the ultimate out-of-context treat.

El Pretzel Memory Español—My junior high school Spanish teacher, Miss Tucci, was understanding when I had just gotten braces and rubber bands on my teeth and could not respond in class when she called on me. *"Es difficil para usted,"* she said sympathetically. But when she caught me eating pretzel sticks in her class—my cheek misshapen with the edges of the sticks—it was a different story. *"Ernesto!"*—this was the closest equivalent of "Eric" in Spanish she could come up with—"Take those out of your mouth!" And that was the end of *los pretzels* in Spanish class.

A Tale of Two Pretzel Brands—Recently in a *Detroit News* survey, Rold Gold was voted the best pretzel brand. I have no problem with this. For years Rold Gold was great—particularly the rods—but then went straight to hell. What happened? No one knows. But in the past few years, at the end of the Go-Go '80s, Rold Gold made a remarkable comeback, particularly in the salt department; by which I mean they got rid of whatever Rold Gold employee it was who made their salt decisions. Whoever it was, he or she was one stingy booger. Now the salt's back on, and Rold Gold's back on, too—back on top.

Unfortunately, Mr. Salty, the pretzel/sailor who was once the universal symbol of crunchiness and saltiness, has fallen on hard times. The pretzels in the Mr. Salty boxes are now wan, mushy, and only fitfully dotted with salt—shadows of their former selves. And talk about your contents settling during shipping! Those boys lie dead in the box. It's sad to see a once-proud pretzel reduced to this.

Various Recommendations and Conclusion—Personally, I'm in a sticks-and-rods period; I'm generally leaving the twists alone. For sticks and rods, I'd say go with the already mentioned Rold Gold and Bachman; Reisman puts out awesome rods, too. For Bavarian-style (fat) pretzels, go with Snyder's of Berlin. Not Snyder's of Hanover! Of Berlin! *Edition* sales executive Matt Bruns likes Snyder's of Berlin, too. He says, "They're good." That's all you need to know.

In summation, I would recommend looking for dark pretzels that sport a dangerous-looking amount of salt. You can always brush off extra salt, but you can't put it on. Don't let anyone tell you you can just shake some on; that's not the way the world works. Also, look for broken pretzels in the bag and check their interiors—you'll want a brown, toasty appearance. You see that, you've found a winning bag.

10/24/91

My Hot Date with Katarina Witt!

Katarina, I thought, Katarina. I had seen the famous figure skater Katarina Witt in the new ads for Diet Coke on TV and in magazines, and I knew that somehow we had to "happen" together. She was so attractive, gliding around the ice in her little outfit, then stopping to sip her Diet Coke. I decided to call and give it a shot.

"Diet Coke, Home of Refreshment!" sang the voice on the other end of the line.

"Hello," I said, "May I speak to Katarina Witt?" "Just a minute, please," said the operator. I heard a faint "Katarina Witt, line one" go over their office loudspeaker. I waited a few moments.

"Ja?" Her voice was like rose petals falling—spinning—onto lilypads.

"Katarina?" I was nervous but I forged ahead. "My name is Eric, and I'm calling from Cleveland. I was wondering if perhaps you'd like to come to the North Coast and maybe go out to dinner with me. I can show you my desk and even Tower City if you'd like."

> "The Honor Snack system, Katarina," I said, "is a method whereby my co-workers and I can purchase assorted snack foods through the honor system."

At first Katarina was doubtful, but when I told her I was the Indoors columnist for a weekly newspaper she quickly agreed to come. I hated to resort to this kind of power play, but what the hey, it got her on the plane.

I told her where our office was, and she said she'd arrive the next day around 3:30 in the afternoon. I was very excited and thought about what clothes to wear.

The next day at work went slowly as I anxiously awaited Katarina's arrival. I was wearing my alluring brown pants made of all-natural fibers and my one white shirt without the greenish pit stains. I had my blue tie rakishly loosened, as well, for the Barney Miller look.

I was sitting at my desk when she walked in. She was stunning. I leapt up to greet her and introduce myself.

"Hello, Katarina, I'm Eric, and you might say this is 'Indoors Central,'" I joked, referring to my desk.

"That's my boss over there"—I pointed at him and he waved—"and those are my co-workers." I gestured vaguely at the various people in the room. "And that over there is our Honor Snack supply."

"Vas ist los, 'Honor Snek'?" asked Katarina. She had walked right into my tender trap!

"The Honor Snack system, Katarina," I said, "is a method whereby my co-workers and I can purchase assorted snack foods through the honor system." I led her over to the Honor Snack box. "See this slit? You put money in there, and then you can take your choice of whatever snack you like." I casually flipped a quarter into the air and caught it. "Two of these will get you a candy bar, or gum, or chips, or beef stick, or what have you. So what'll it be, Katarina?"

She looked over the selection for quite a long time. As she did, I drank in her beauty. What a lucky guy I was, to have a famous skater in my office, choosing snacks!

"I vant der peanuts, ja? Undt maybe chips for later."

"Done." I got out my wallet and very smoothly began fingering the bills inside. "I think this should take care of it." I slowly pulled out a crisp new dollar, folded it carefully, and stuffed it into the Honor Snack box while grinning suavely at Katarina.

"You just help yourself, Katarina," I said huskily. "The financial situation is all set." I was turning her on mercilessly! As she munched on her peanuts she gave me the hairy eyeball.

"Der ain't no one like you back in Deutschland," she said. I winked at her. We were connecting like crazy.

After her treat we walked over to Tower City and got on the Van Aken rapid. I took her to Thornton Park ice rink. I rented a pair of skates; Katarina had her own, of course. I hadn't told Katarina the last time I skated was about 25 years ago, but I wanted her to feel comfortable here in Cleveland, and I figured an ice rink would fill the bill.

Katarina laced on her skates and began zipping around. I hobbled out onto the ice, and tried to stay balanced on the blades. I got about eight feet before I toppled over onto the surface.

Katarina skated up to where I was lying and knelt by me.

"Did you fell down, liebchen?" she asked sympathetically.

"I've fallen and I can't get up, as they say on TV," I said, giving Katarina my most winning smile. She hauled me up and I sneaked a little peck on her ear. "You naughty!" she said, pushing me back down. So she wanted to play. I tore off my skates and chased her around the ice, sliding in my socks. I finally caught her—which was exactly what she wanted. I held on to her hand and she began towing me in my socks all around the rink. We glided and dipped together as the other skaters applauded. Unfortunately, when Katarina accidentally let go of my hand as she began a pirouette I went sliding off and smashed into the Plexiglas wall. She gasped and skated up again to my inert form. I had my eyes tightly shut. I was playing possum.

She nudged me with her foot. I grabbed her leg and pulled her laughing down on top of me. She called me a "schweinhundt" but covered me with relieved kisses.

Soon we were back on the rapid, on the way to the airport. Katarina had come to Cleveland perhaps hoping to advance her career through me and my power as a columnist, but instead she'd encountered an understanding American who'd given her free food and skated with her. She'd come expecting little, but left with it all.

At the airport, we smooched at the gate until her flight boarded. I watched her plane take off, Katarina kissing at me through her window. I was moved beyond measure, so much so that the next day at work I dug out the dollar I had stuck in the Honor Snack box to keep as a souvenir of Katarina's visit.

Auf wiedersehn, my darling! Ach du lieber, did we have a great time or what!

1/16/92

Mr. Hospitality

In this press release from the National Tour Association there's an item: *Search Begins for Cleveland's Most Hospitable Person.* "Show off your North Coast hospitality, and you could win big! Many Cleveland attractions have donated prizes to be given to the most courteous hospitality person in the city. Prizes include a gift certificate to the Galleria, tickets to the Ringling Brothers Circus, etc., etc."

I feel I should win the award for Cleveland's Most Hospitable Person. Though I don't want people in my home during the week, many's the time I've had guests over to watch Sunday football games on my TV. If you ask these people who come over—particularly my friends Joe ("I heal sick minds") the psychologist, Howard, and *Edition* sales executive Matt Bruns—how they feel about my hospitality, they'll tell you no one is nicer to them or gives them more fun beyond the confines of the televised games.

To illustrate: Several weeks ago Joe and Howard came over to watch the Browns' final game of the season, against the Steelers. Now in dealing with guests my primary aim is to *provide enjoyment.* You don't just sit your guest down in a chair and give him a glass of water to suck on and not talk. You give them kosher dogs at halftime, as I did, and keep the conversation moving along.

Here's a game I thought up to make football more interesting. You use the players' names to comment on the action as it happens and as it involves that particular player. For instance, when tight end Ozzie Newsome was playing, he'd make a great catch, and I'd say, "Ozzie's making a *Newsome* of himself again." What laughs that got, even after the 75th or 80th time I'd say it. And now that safety Vince Newsome is with the team, you can still use it. A few more: "Leroy's *Hoarding* the ball again." "Eric sure *Turnered* him around." "Lee's *Rouson* the ball well today." "Webster *Slaughtered* him on that play." You can see how much fun it is. And as the host, I'm the Grandmaster of this very enjoyable activity, and my guests look to me for leadership in this department.

I also make sure everybody's comfortable in my home, asking if they're too hot or too cold, and then making the appropriate adjustments. If it's too hot, I blow the fan on them, and if it's too cold, I close the window. I asked Howard and Joe, "Is anybody cold?" and Howard, thinking I was speaking in the general sense, replied "I'm sure they are!" but after this misunderstanding was cleared up I discovered that they—Howard and Joe—were just right, not too cold, and not too hot, either. So I didn't do anything. If it ain't broke, don't fix it. Leaving things alone when they're fine is an important aspect of hospitality.

As Cleveland's Most Hospitable Person, I also take time to listen to my guests, their hopes and fears, their cares and anguish. As I was loading dishes into the dishwasher, for example, Howard commented, "You know how to load a dishwasher." And I do, too: back to front, glasses on the upper rack, plates on the lower, silverware sorted by type. Howard told me that his wife loads their dishwasher wrong. "She puts a bowl and a spoon into an empty dishwasher, and it's full." Howard felt he could confide in me because I present a sympathetic face as host. I could have said, "Who gives a s---?" but didn't. I nodded and said, "That's no good." Being understanding of your guest's anxieties is a crucial part of hospitality too.

Leaving things alone when they're fine is an important aspect of hospitality.

When *Edition* sales executive Matt Bruns came over to watch the Denver–Buffalo AFC Championship game a few weeks back, we did far more than merely sit in front of the TV. We tossed around a deflated football. We volleyed a foam ball with plastic rackets. We threw darts for points, my darts representing Buffalo, Matt's Denver. Matt watched as I drove the cat's ball toys into the sofa using a seven iron. Matt will tell you he got more exercise watching TV with me as host than by going to any health club. And you can't beat exercise.

In summation, I'd like to say I supply far more than a TV while entertaining. I give my guests food, fun, and enjoyable conversation as host. I should be named Cleveland's Most Hospitable Person and be given those tickets to the circus.

1/23/92

Mutual Interaction with the Animal World

We've just returned from a trip to our place in the woods of Northern Michigan, land of crystal clear lakes, blue skies, and towering cedar and fir. We had a great time there, smack in the middle of nature. We'd stand among the trees and breathe in. Oxygen! I'd beat my chest while inhaling that sweet air, like Eddie Albert at the beginning of *Green Acres*. Breathing in and going to restaurants, those are my two favorite things.

But that's not what I'd like to talk about here. I'd like to discuss our *interaction and mutual cooperation with the animal world*.

When you're in the middle of the woods, it's good to share your unwanted food with the timid woodland creatures who live around you: deer, raccoons, rabbits, birds, ducks, chipmunks, and the like. These animals, always environmentally appropriate, serve as living garbage disposals for your waste. By giving them your various leftovers, you're sustaining the earth cycle, which is, you know, fairly important.

But it's also smart to be on good terms with these animals. If they remember you as a person who gave them a snack or two, and not as some bonehead potting away at them with a shotgun, they may very well give you extra consideration should you find yourself lying wounded and helpless in their woodland home. The timid creatures that once scurried away at your approach can easily become savage predators against you if they smell weakness. You've seen the films on the Discovery Channel and PBS. Those boogers will strip your body clean in 20 minutes and I don't mean your wallet and jewelry. Do I have to spell it out for you? You better interact with them first or they'll interact with you, and on *their terms*.

At any rate, to guard against this possibility, we gave these animals fried chicken, potato chips, baloney, eggs, and cookies. I'd like to deal with the methodology and strategy of dispersing these foods on an individual basis, if I may.

Now throwing fried chicken into the woods is easy—a straightforward chuck—but baloney slices are a different story. In an early attempt, I had thrown a baloney slice with bites (mine) taken out of it. Not good, it went only a few feet, a wounded duck. But as for the rest of the slices, I went for a frisbee effect, and this succeeded spectacularly. The baloney whipped through the air several yards, deep into the woods, where the not-very-particular raccoons could have a feast.

We felt the cookies were deer food. They were moist oatmeal affairs, and we put bits of them where we hoped the deer would see them. (We figured the raccoons would be happy with the chicken and baloney and leave the cookies alone, although this may have been naïve. But you think of raccoons as hearty, meat-eating types, less interested in delicacies than the gentle deer. I mean, who can visualize Bambi tearing into a steak? It's ridiculous.)

For rabbits and miscellaneous animals, I ran through the woods holding a Jay's potato chip bag upside down, trailing chips in a line going nearly 20 feet. This way, you have one set of animals enjoying chips at one spot, and another set enjoying them down the line. Then everybody's happy, and no fighting.

Now, throwing fried chicken into the woods is easy—a straight-forward chuck—but baloney slices are a different story.

As for the eggs. We thought it best not to leave any lying around, as this might lead to confusion among the birds. So we heaved them too into the woods, where they busted and dribbled down the sides of the trees, convenient for licking purposes.

After distributing the food, we could then leave our place in the woods and return home to Cleveland with peace of mind. When you cooperate and interact with nature, you empower yourself within that world. And then, hey, you're in good shape, am I right?

9/30/92

Hardened Earwax: The Inside Story

You've probably been wondering, "Has this guy had any problems with his ears lately?" Funny you should bring it up. I recently had an ear incident that may be of interest to you, the reader.

Here is how the situation "went down." I had just returned home from my vigorous evening walk when the phone rang, and I ran to get it. My Walkman earphones were dangling around my neck, and somehow, during the course of my phone conversation, the earphone and telephone cords got tangled up. Trying to disengage the cords, I became increasingly frustrated. My neck and head began to get hot, and I was sweating profusely.

> "There's a big chunk," said the technician, referring, of course, to the rogue wax that was now rocketing out of my ears.

I finally got the cords free, but I was still keyed up when I got into the shower. So there I was, stressed out, wet, soaping my ear holes but not rinsing them properly. I can sense all of you out there nodding your heads and saying, *"There's a combination that'll harden your earwax."*

Right on. That's exactly what happened. But I didn't know it at the time. When I stepped out of the shower my ears felt clogged, and shaking my head sideways didn't help. I thought to myself, "this feels like swimmer's ear. I'd better go to Revco and get some drops." But all the drops did was make a thundering noise in my ears when I put them in. This was the point where I began thinking of hardened earwax.

I've never had hardened earwax before. I always thought it a joke ailment, like bunions, athlete's foot, or hangnails. But this was no joke. I couldn't hear! The only thing clearly audible to me was a constant noise like a crashing surf. And when people spoke to me they sounded like Munchkins talking from behind their bushes. For the life of me I couldn't clear my canals.

"Did you try popping your ear hole with your index finger?" you ask. Yes, but that gave me only momentary relief. And that night, as I sat through dinner at a restaurant with my fiancée Barbara and our friends Pete and Julie, the crashing surf in my ears and the inaudible mutterings of my friends and loved ones began to drive me crazy. Though Pete and Julie were coming to our home to visit, I determined at that time I had to give myself a home flush immediately! Company or no company! So after dinner we all went together to a drugstore and bought earwax softener drops and an ear bulb for this purpose.

It didn't work. I didn't know what I was doing. I squeezed water into my ear, but it just crashed against my ear hole wall and dribbled out. Pete had success doing this one time to his own ears, but I didn't feel it was appropriate to ask him to do it for me. He was drinking beer in the living room with Julie and Barbara, and though I had put earwax softener in my ears in front of everyone, I thought flushing might be a more private matter. Besides, who was I to ask guests to flush out my ears? That's no way to entertain.

It was heartbreaking. Everybody was having fun in the living room, and there I was in the bathroom, squirting water in my ears, water that just fell right out into the sink. What a loser, doing a home flush that didn't even work while everyone else partied. Finally I just gave up. I decided that if I had to take my ears to professionals, I would.

And I did. I went to an urgent care center the next day, and they did the job. It was exciting. A technician shot water into my ears as I held a cup up to them to catch the fall-off. Now this was a flush. It felt like cascading rapids in my head or Niagara Falls. What refreshment! "There's a big chunk," said the technician, referring, of course, to the rogue wax that was now rocketing out of my ears. When the technician was done, I grinned and my eyebrows shot up like a person experiencing fast relief on a TV commercial. I could hear again.

The one thing I regret is that I was too bashful to ask to see my earwax after it had been ejected. I could have run a photo of it for you. Now it's too late. Health care facilities only hold on to your earwax for a couple of weeks, right?

10/7/92

My Congressional Campaign Speech

I know it's a little late, but I've decided to run for the congressional seat in my district. I don't know which district it is exactly, but one of my first acts as your congressman will be to find out. And I won't rest until I do—you can depend on that.

The reason I've decided to run is many-faceted. The first facet is that I *care about people.* As a congressman I will stand up for my constituents. No corporate or special interests will dictate to me how I'll vote on the issues. Gifts? Perks? Junkets? Special privileges? Sure, I'll take them. But when it gets down and dirty on that congressional floor, I'll do the right thing for the people I represent. That's a promise—from me . . . to you. (Here I'll point at audience, my other hand placed on my thrust-out hip my campaign trademark.)

> I'm going to perk up my ears, put them to the rail, and wait for that train that's the voice of the people to come rolling into the station.

The second facet is that *I want to help people I care about.* What good is caring if you don't help those whom you care about? I'm going to help my constituents; just see if I don't. If I don't, you'll know the reason why! I won't hide under my desk or behind the sofa or take a quick trip to another state. I'll be there if you want to complain, or whine, or give me a hard time. I'll be there for you. If the line's busy, just keep trying. If I'm not there, I'll be there later. Just leave a message. I'll get back to you. Count on it. (Pointing again.)

Thirdly, and perhaps most importantly, I want to be an *instrument for change.* Change is a hard thing. It involves risk. It involves daring. It involves turning old notions on their heads and trying new ideas.

That won't be necessary with me. I can implement change without all that risk stuff. How? With *people.* That's right. With you! With my constituents. You've had enough of us in the Congress telling you what's what, and what's best for you. What we need are congresspersons who listen to their constituents; I mean really *listen.* This is what I plan to do. I'm going to perk up my ears, put them to the rail, and wait for that train that's the voice of the people to come rolling into the station. When it pulls in, my head will be on that rail, listening. So . . . *all aboard* . . . for improved service in your congressional district! All aboard for change! Woo, woo! (Here pantomiming pulling a train whistle.)

But what are my programs? What are my plans to improve health care, produce jobs in the private and public sector, stimulate growth, and relieve the gridlock in Washington that prevents so many fine plans from being implemented?

I have a Four-Point Plan—a Five-Point Plan, if you count private and public sector job production as two separate things, because there are two different sectors, but originally I thought of it as one big thing: job production. But they wouldn't give them different names if they weren't different things, correct? The way I see it is, public sector jobs are like jobs in government agencies, and private sector jobs are say, jobs in art galleries. You can rest assured one of my priorities as your congressman will be to find out the difference between the two, and let you know as soon as I do. *Promise.* (Point, hip thrust.)

At any rate, Four-Point or Five-Point, take your pick. I don't have time to get into specifics, but let me just say that each point—whether it be the First or Second or Third or Fourth (or Fifth, depending on which program you prefer)—will be given equal attention by me and my staff. We're not going to spend months on the First point and then, because we run out of time, not get to the Second or Third. That's not the way I'm going to do things. Why? Because that's not the way *you* do things. You don't run your household that way. If you did, you'd be out of a job. The least your congressman can do is budget his time and delegate his responsibilities so his points can be implemented, the way you do at your home and business. Who says we congresspersons can't learn anything from our constituents? (Laughing warmly here.)

Please consider voting for me on November 3. Because, really, a vote for me is a vote for *yourself.* And I think yourself is a *pretty good* person to run this district. (Nodding sagely as I walk off stage to thunderous applause.)

10/28/92

Why I Am Anal Retentive

 I don't see what's wrong with being anal retentive. I really don't. I've been "accused" of being anal retentive many times by my co-workers, but these people don't realize that they're not insulting me. They're *trying* to insult me, granted, but when they say, "You're anal retentive," what I hear is, "You're a tidy fellow who gets the job done ahead of time and is considerate of others." So my reply to them is always, "Thank you."

Naturally, like everyone else, I'd love to sit around and drink coffee and chat with others deep into the afternoon, putting off all the tasks that need to be done. That's "fun," that's "enjoyable." Yet what happens when we procrastinate until the 11th hour? *Panic* when the clock strikes 12. Frenzied activity to finish the job. Frayed tempers and raw nerves. Long-simmering resentments bubbling to the surface. That's not so "fun" and "enjoyable," is it?

I personally get my assignments done three to six days ahead of time. Contrary to what you may think (and to common sense), this doesn't win me any popularity contests in the office. Because my articles are finished, in the system, and ready to go long before my co-workers', I am able to sit back and relax on deadline days while they work feverishly to get their work done. I smile and make jokes while they slave over their word processors, their little minds in high gear, trying to compose their articles for this paper. "I finished mine last Friday," I remind them. "I'm done. Get it? D-o-n-e. Done." Sometimes I write "I'm done" on a sheet of paper and put it in front of them. And then I see their necks and ears get red.

When I try to be helpful and say, "Now isn't that something you could have written last week?" they just look at me, their eyes brimming with hate, and make bitter remarks about the relative tautness of one of my nether regions. One co-worker, Jeff Hagan, makes frequent comments of this nature to me, as well as making kissing noises with his lips in office meetings when I am praised for always hitting my deadlines. Smacking lips, I assume, means I'm a "brown-noser" and "teacher's pet." As if I would be offended by these designations!

When I'm ridiculed by my colleagues—when their negativity flows over me—I maintain serenity. They tell me that their articles require legwork, phone calls, and research, followed by extensive thought; and that this column demands no more than a few hours' work a week, with its source material readily accessible to the writer. "You don't have to *do* anything," they say. "You just write about your own boring life."

That's right. But I write about my boring life *three to six days ahead of time*. That way, if it's too boring, I can always soup it up for you, the reader. It's simply a matter of planning ahead. This is what I tell my colleagues. I tell them if they start earlier, their articles will be better, because then they can improve on their work before the deadline.

And I tell them that, *especially* in their cases, extra time for thought isn't going to help. That extra time won't be filled with thought, anyway. It will be filled with *anxiety* about the job hanging over their heads. Even if that time *was* filled with thought, I say to them, let's be frank, you're not going to be any smarter a couple of days from now. You're drawing from a limited well of intelligence to begin with. So you might as well get it over with.

> **When they say, "You're anal retentive," what I hear is, "You're a tidy fellow who gets the job done ahead of time and is considerate of others."**

But do they appreciate my advice? Do they take it to heart? No. They respond with taunts and name calling, obscene gestures and disgusting personal remarks. And as a person who has only love to give, my only response to them is to sing softly, "All we anal retentives are saying . . . is give our kind of behavior a chance." Then I add, "By the way, I'm done."

11/18/92

A Thanksgiving Menu Plan

The editors of this publication have asked me to present a Thanksgiving menu plan to you, the general readership, as a service to benefit you this holiday season, so you can study it and serve your family a sumptuous feast as I have mine the past several Thanksgivings. Good luck and *bon appétit*! (*Important:* Do not follow directions in menu plan.)

What you will need:

Gas or electric range

1 turkey of desired poundage with pop-up thermometer and gizzard bag

1 package frozen peas

1 1-pound bag cranberries

1 loaf of generic white bread, preferably with clown on package

1 1-pound bag potato chips

1 pretty small bag shelled walnuts

Plenty of margarine

Assorted spices (any that are there)

Portable radio or audio cassette player

Water (available from tap)

Cooking time: 1–8 hours

Serves 2–11 persons

Set aside peas and cranberries. Open turkey and pull out gizzard bag. Take gizzard bag outdoors and discard. Carefully read directions on turkey and then set on top of range. Turn on radio to preferred station or select cassette tape from music collection and play. Turn volume up or down, depending on preference.

Examine package of peas and put in freezer for later use. Draw water from tap, testing temperature with finger. Keep in 12-ounce tumbler by side of sink. Drink when thirsty.

Take large-ish pot from cupboard. Remove cranberries from bag and place in pot, covering them with lukewarm water. Soak for six hours. Sprinkle in assorted spices for flavor. Drain water from cranberries after six hours, but dinner may be over. If this is the case, set aside for later use.

Place two slices of clown bread in toaster and toast until golden brown. Spread margarine over slices when done and eat. Have a nice soda if available from icebox, or perhaps a small glass of fruit juice.

Look at turkey on top of range. Plan on pre-heating oven. Rub turkey for good luck. If legs of turkey are untied, re-tie them. Look inside turkey and make sure all gizzards are out. Go outside to check that gizzard bag was indeed discarded. Return indoors.

Take package of frozen peas from freezer and set on counter. Crush with kitchen mallet. Empty crushed peas into small metal bowl and cover with lukewarm water. Drain water after several minutes and put peas in pan. Cook on lowest setting for one hour. Discard.

Place turkey on center rack of oven. Set oven temperature to 275 degrees, remove turkey, and wait for oven to pre-heat. Look at turkey and untie legs again. Check for gizzards one last time, then replace turkey on center rack of oven. Close oven door and wonder if you should have put the turkey in hours ago. If so, increase the oven temperature to 300 degrees and dig around pop-up thermometer with fingernail to give it a little boost.

. . . The turkey should be far from done, but this can be remedied by continuing to push up on pop-up thermometer with finger.

Empty bag of walnuts onto counter and crush with kitchen mallet. Brush crushed walnuts off counter into open palm. Walk around kitchen with crushed walnuts in palm until container is found. Empty walnuts into container, cover, and refrigerate.

Look in oven to check status of pop-up thermometer on turkey, again nudging thermometer with fingernail. *Do not touch heating elements in oven at this time!* Now press thickest part of turkey with thumb. If skin bounces back, turkey is cooking. If thumb goes all the way through turkey to gizzard cavity, turkey is papier-mâché and should be removed from oven immediately.

Go outside and remove gizzard bag from trash. Empty gizzards into pan, cover with water, and put on to boil. Turn off radio or tape player if annoying. Stare at pan of gizzards cooking for a half hour, then cut heat to lowest setting. Remove pan to another burner and set heat on first burner to "off."

Open oven door. The turkey should be far from done, but this can be remedied by continuing to push up on pop-up thermometer with finger. When the entire thermometer is exposed, turkey is supposedly done. If this is not the case, set aside and have someone who knows what they're doing cook it later.

Open bag of potato chips and snack. Discard gizzards.

11/25/92

Raymond Burr in a Lump

I have many methods of dealing with insomnia, none of which work. I'm going through a sleepless period now, and I've found I just have to tough it out.

A big problem is my pillow. It's dying. Where it used to be spirited and fluffy, it's now hard and unforgiving. The impression my head makes on my pillow is the cavity I have to live with the rest of the night. There are no second chances with my pillow. I try to puff it up, but the hole my head makes at the onset of bedtime is socked in for good, and the bottom of the head hole is flat and hard. Some nights the pillow makes a brief comeback, displaying its old pep, but those nights are few and far between.

> **A big problem is my pillow. It's dying. Where it used to be spirited and fluffy, it's now hard and unforgiving.**

Most nights, though, the main problem is I'm just not tired enough, but I go to bed anyway because I've had enough of being awake. Sometimes I go to bed hungry, too, which is a big mistake. Then I have to get up an hour or so later and eat 25 or 30 saltines and 5 or 10 cookies. You say, "Why don't you go to bed later and eat something immediately beforehand?" My response to that is, I just don't know.

When I'm flipping and flopping in bed, I don't worry about my life. Most of my insomnia time is spent with assorted junk running through my head, mostly '60s TV themes and commercials. The theme from *Mannix* goes through my head, as does the one from *Room 222*, and the semi-circular theme from *Dennis the Menace*. Just last night the opening siren-filled theme from *Ironside* kept running through my head, along with the image of Raymond Burr lying in a large lump after being shot and before being confined to a wheelchair. Do you know what it's like to not be able to sleep and have Raymond Burr in a lump dominating your thoughts at the same time? It sucks.

Some of the commercials that plague me are '60s Ford jingles, like "Ford/It's the going thing/It's what's happening" and "Only Mustang makes it happen/Only Mustang makes life great/Only Mustang/Only Mustang/Mustang, Mustang, '68." Also, "Smile a little/Frown a little/Give a little grin/Every time you use your face/Dry skin lines set in/You need new Deep Magic Dry Skin Conditioner." Another one I can't shake is the old commercial for Score, the hair cream. "Baugh baugh bup bup baugh bup baugh baugh/Baugh baugh bup bup baugh bup baugh baugh/Baugh baugh that's the Score/That's the Score/That's the Score."

Many '60s songs bother me, too, while I try to sleep, like the Rolling Stones' "She's a Rainbow." I've spent many hours lying in bed, thinking "Have you seen her dressed in blue/Have you seen her dressed in *gold* . . . She comes in colors *everywhere*/She combs her *hair*/She's like a ra-a-ainbow." Ever since the Syndicate of Sound's "Hey Little Girl" came out 25 years ago it's been running through my head. "Hey little girl I don't want you around no more/If you come round knocking you won't get past my door. *Hah!*" It's hopeless when that one starts up.

If I am able by some miracle to get this crap out of my mind, I then attempt to hypnotize myself to fall asleep, which fails miserably. I try to visualize a timepiece swaying in front of my eyes, but I can't get it placed correctly in my mind's line of vision. It's always off to the left somewhere. I tell myself, "You can't keep your eyes open. Your legs are getting heavy. You're getting sle-e-e-epy." But I'm not.

I also try the counting-backwards-from-100 technique, in the hope that I'll fool myself into thinking I've been given anesthesia like before an operation and I'll knock myself out, but my body's not that stupid and stays awake. I've even tried counting sheep, which was totally laughable. They're supposed to be jumping over a fence, right? That's how counting sheep is done in cartoons, but maybe the original idea was a head-count of sheep in a field. At any rate, it doesn't work worth diddly. Nothing does.

12/16/92

Big Plans for '93

In 1993 I resolve to:

Eat executive-type cereals. The cereals I currently consume—Alpha Bits, Cocoa Pebbles, Frosted Flakes, Froot Loops, and the like—are strictly for punks. A fellow pushing 40 shouldn't be eating food endorsed by Fred Flintstone, no matter how good it tastes. It just isn't right for an adult to have a cupboard full of cereal boxes with cartoon animals on them. A high-powered executive type like me should be eating Total and Mueslix and Grape-Nuts, cereals with fiber and grain and nuts and fruit. That'll give me the right start to the day. I'm also going to cut down on the fudge and weenies. That's not executive fare either.

> What executive sings to his cat and then sings her imagined response? Not one.

Keep my mouth shut at work. I'm fed up with the complaining, backbiting, whining, kibitzing, second-guessing, and peeing-and-moaning in our office. In '93 I'm going to put an end to it. This could render me totally silent, but so be it. I'm going to zip it up and keep my comments to myself. Even when everything around here goes to hell without my advice and helpful suggestions, I'm not going to say a word. I've pledged before that I would assume the attitude of the wise old owl who sees all and says nothing, and this year I'm going to do it, even if these people don't have the slightest idea of what they're doing.

Cancel my Time-Life Your Hit Parade disc series. A few years ago I ordered a series of compact discs, Your Hit Parade, featuring all the top hits of the years 1939–1960, 25 songs per disc. They've come fast and furious, filled with songs by Kitty Kallen, Mitch Miller, Perry Como, Teresa Brewer, Andy Williams, Louis Prima, Percy Faith, Mantovani, Xavier Cugat, etc. I have more than 20 discs, and now they're beginning to send leftovers, throwing together songs that didn't make it onto the other discs. There's only about a 30 percent good song rate on these discs, which is very poor considering the investment. I was hoping to round out my knowledge of pop music with these discs, but all I've learned is that I'm going to have to sell them, and that rock and roll didn't come a moment too soon.

Stop acting like such a dork in my home. I've always been active in my home, singing, shouting, dancing, working on my impressions (of Ed Sullivan, Ted Baxter, Jack Lemmon in *The Odd Couple*, etc.), doing voices, talking and warbling to the cat Dizzy. You know: like a dork. I often do this when I'm home by myself, and the next door neighbors can hear me, and this isn't the executive-type image I want to convey. What executive sings to his cat and then sings her imagined response? Not one. They must think they've got Pee Wee Herman living next door. Not only that, I talk normally to these neighbors when I run into them in the building, so they also must think I've got multiple personalities. At best they consider me mildly psychotic the way I carry on with my cat.

Get over my thing with cars. Owning and driving cars has always been a problem for me, and this year and I'm going to at least co-own a decent car and also become a stud driver. I've never liked to drive, even though I've always had good hand-eye coordination and been skilled behind the wheel. But I go months at a time without driving, thus reinforcing my phobia about it. Owning a car is actually scarier to me than driving one, as I've owned two—a Catalina and a Champ— and both have ended up crumbling away in my care. I sold the Champ because the lower section of the driver door that pushed in the button that turned the interior light on and off rusted away, and the interior light stayed on after I closed the door and the battery ran down. Don't you hate that? And the Catalina, a '68, had long-dead bees lodged between the dash and the front window; not to mention I couldn't see out the greasy back window and had to keep a padlock on the hood to keep miscreants from stealing the battery. Every time I turned around the tires were flat. And as I watched the guy hook it up to the junkyard's tow truck I said, "Good-bye and good riddance, you dog." In '93: a quality late-model automobile with your man behind the wheel.

1/6/93

Eating Healthy Organic Food

When you work with other people you're bound to have disagreements. In this office we have many conflicts but resolve them peaceably, except for that one day when the staff writer, Hagan, whipped at me with his belt. Old Mr. Commie Vegetarian Liberal Peacenik couldn't control his temper that time!

Anyway, quite a few of our disagreements are in the area of food. People around here eat weird things during the day. Our office is near a food co-op, with its odd selections. It's filled with "organic" products, the kind of stuff squirrels like to hold in their paws and break open with their front teeth.

> **And how would you like to eat a beautiful piece of prime rib without salt? You might as well buy salt-free pretzels. And some people *do*, for God's sake.**

I know organic is good for you, but I personally can't live on nuts and seeds and little half-apples. My co-workers bring in tubs of this crap, and I peer at it while they eat. They put pale strips and lumps of gray material into their mouths. *That's* from the earth? What *is* that? Those are the kind of thoughts I have while I watch them eat. But because I have respect and love in my heart, I don't make remarks—unlike them, who feel a need to comment every time I bring in a breakfast egg sandwich from McDonald's or a pack of Zingers or Ho Ho's from the vending machines downstairs. Yes, they certainly make free with their opinions on meat, cheese, sugar, fat, and cholesterol whenever your man is chowing down.

Let me just say something about meat, cheese, sugar, fat, and cholesterol. *There's nothing wrong with them.* Of course you shouldn't overdo it, but a little meat, cheese, sugar, fat, and cholesterol never did anyone any harm. I'm not saying you shouldn't eat greens and fruit. You should. But a Ho Ho here and there isn't going to kill you.

Neither will salt, while I'm at it. Once I bought a salt-free slab of Swiss cheese by mistake. After I tasted it you know what I felt like doing? I felt like squishing it against the bathroom tiles. Because that's caulk, not cheese.

And how would you like to eat a beautiful piece of prime rib without salt? You might as well put a pile of sugar-free cough drops on your plate and eat those for all the pleasure you'll get. You might as well buy salt-free pretzels. And some people *do*, for God's sake. Voluntarily! If your doctor says you should, that's one thing, but to do it just so you can "cut down"? Wake up, I'm warning you. No one's waiting for you at the gates of heaven keeping track of whether you buy salt-free pretzels or not. I say, Get pretzels with salt. You only go around once. Don't defeat the point of pretzels by trying to make some kind of impression.

"What about chili?" you ask. "Have you ever had bulgur wheat chili?" Yes I have. My mother served it unbeknownst to me while my aunt and uncle—who are on some kind of a health kick—were in town. I started eating it and thought, What the hell *is* this? It tasted like wet cardboard. Then my mother told me what it was. I sat at the table and looked at this bulgur wheat chili, which was piled on a baked potato. This is health food, I thought. This is what my co-workers think I should eat. Never mind that I'll starve to death since I can't choke it down. That's not important. The pathologist will be thrilled that my organs are in such good shape because I ate healthy. "Here's a man who ate plenty of bulgur wheat and other organic foods."

This is the final word on nutrition to my wisenheimer co-workers. If you're in good health you can eat just about anything as long as you throw in a banana here and a carrot stick there. Exercise vigorously at least four times a week. Don't go out and get hammered every night or smoke 60 Chesterfields a day. Most importantly, *stop bothering me* and let me eat my Egg Macs and cream-filled treats in peace.

1/27/93

The Joy of Mel

What's better than getting mail? Nothing, in my opinion. Sex or travel, maybe, but mail delivery is *every day* (except Sunday and holidays). Every day there's a chance of getting something interesting in the mail. Every day there's a chance you'll get a letter from someone telling you they're hot for you. Every day there's potential for getting a package. What the hell's better than getting a package? Maybe inside the package there are dozens of compact discs featuring your favorite artists and a letter from someone attractive saying you've got a great body and they're in love with you. Huh? Doesn't that sound good? Well, that's mail.

I personalize mail by calling it "Mel." People think I'm an idiot, but I don't care. I love getting mail so much that when I see a pile of mail on my desk or in my box I say, "All right, Mel!" I call the mail delivery person Mel, too. Like, "Mel's gonna bring something good today." To me the word, Mel, connotes "the delivery of good times, sex, and money."

You say, "All this Mel stuff is fine, except that usually Mel only brings bills or *Ohio Motorist*. You have to be some kind of a dork to think something spectacular is going to happen through Mel."

What I'm talking about is the *possibilities* of Mel. For example, I got a letter recently from Paul C. Forstrom, in which he said, "I am sending you this letter with my business card to introduce myself to you as Paul C. Forstrom, Vice President-Special Accounts of Citizens State Bank, Clara City, Minnesota." Paul C. Forstrom is with the Reader's Digest Sweepstakes, and he's the guy who's going to give me the check if I'm the winner. At a special luncheon. A check made payable to "M-R-. E-R-I-C- B-R-O-D-E-R." The somomabeetch even spelled my name out for me!

You say, "Paul C. Forstrom isn't going to give you a check." I know that. And I don't care if he's a real person or not, either. The point is that—through Mel—I can fantasize about receiving a $167,000 check from Paul C. Forstrom, who I see as being a chubby guy in a suit, in his late forties, with gray hair, mustache, and glasses. He'll give me

$167,000 a year for 20 years, and if he dies along the way, Paul C. Forstrom Jr. can take over. You can't beat that. Mel just generates good vibes.

Sure, in reality Mel is mostly bills and catalogs, but what's wrong with that? You've got to pay your bills, don't you? You may blow a lot of money and be getting billed until the end of time, but that's hardly Mel's fault. Look at it this way. The more you buy, the more offers you get through Mel. Then you take the offers—like ordering a book on back pain or a subscription to *Playboy* so you can get *Playboy's Foxiest Ladies* thrown in for free—and mark the "Bill Me Later" box. That's your choice. Mel's not marking that box. So anything you get is what you asked for. And that's what keeps this economy rolling. That's a big positive, too.

Here would be a perfect Mel day for me. I'd get three packages. Each one would be filled with brand-spanking-new books, videos, and CDs. Balance due: 0.00. Then a letter: *You're so hot. I fainted thinking about your body today. You're a sex machine, and all my girlfriends agree.* Then my income tax refund check. Finally, a letter from Paul C. Forstrom: "I am indeed real, and it is my pleasure to inform you that you have won the *Reader's Digest* $5 Million Sweepstakes. This is no joke. *Reader's Digest* will send a private jet to pick you up and take you to Clara City, Minnesota, where I'll hold your elbow and present you with your first check for $167,000. You're the main man and I'll see you later."

There can hardly now be any doubt in your mind that Mel is one dynamite government service.

2/3/93

Indoor Tips for Gents

I was wondering how you keep up with paying your bills and keeping them organized so they don't get out of hand. Your credit history is perfect, and I wish I was like that—Deric Roder, Lakewood

What I do, Deric, is tuck my bills into my checkbook as I receive them, putting them in the chronological order in which they're due; in other words, putting the ones that are soonest due on top. By keeping my bills with my checkbook, I thus associate the two: to wit, the statements are forever linked to the means of paying them, so I harbor no illusions concerning what needs to be done. I look upon my checkbook; the bills are within; the only way to remove the bills is to pay them. I don't run away from the problem by stuffing my bills where I can't see them. Because when you hide from your bills, Deric, you're hiding from *yourself.* Do you understand what I'm telling you, Deric?

As for the "Lather, Rinse, Repeat" controversy: Simply ask yourself who wins when you use twice as much shampoo as you need and therefore have to buy it twice as often. Is it you?

What do you do to handle unsolicited sales phone calls from credit card companies and the like that always seem to come at the worst times? I bet you handle them good, you dog, you.—Rick Boder, Lyndhurst

Well, Rick, it's amusing you should mention that. I have happened upon a technique for dealing with unwanted phone solicitation, and it's really so simple I'm surprised I hadn't thought of it before. I would take those calls—usually right in the middle of dinner—when the person would mispronounce my name and then make a pitiful attempt at small talk like, "How's it going there in Cleveland tonight? . . . Good, good. Now, Mr. Broader, this is a courtesy call from . . . " and I'd listen for a few moments and then say "I'll pass," because I don't wish to be rude. I mean, these poor devils have to make a living, and they don't want to call me any more than I want to hear from them. So here's my solution. I simply say "He's not home right now, may I take a message?" Their inevitable reply is "No, we'll call back at a more convenient time," and the matter is completed. So I am a bit of a "dog," aren't I, Rick!

*You're always so impeccably groomed. Do you have any shaving and sham-
poo tips you can pass along?—Eric Floder, Willowick*

Eric—and that's a marvelous name; did you know "Eric" means
"king" in Danish?—I'd be happy to. Re shaving: I always splash the
hottest water I can stand on the regions I'm going to shave, then apply
a *quality* cream. Bargain shaving cream is no bargain, my friend, if it
doesn't supply a clean, close, comfortable shave. I leave the cream on
for a full minute to soften my beard. *Muy importante*, this leaving-it-
on-a-minute strategy. Then stroke down gently and evenly with the
blade. Never up, as the cretins on the TV shaving commercials do.

Shampoo? Eric, I can't choose your shampoo for you. This is something a man must do for himself. I would advise buying a quality shampoo, one that supplies body and manageability and won't leave you
looking like a lunatic. I leave the shampoo on for a full minute for conditioning purposes. Skip the conditioning step at your own peril. As for
the "Lather, Rinse, Repeat" controversy that has been raging for years:
Simply ask yourself who wins when you use twice as much shampoo as
you need and therefore have to buy it twice as often. Is it you? Are you
the one who wins, Eric?

*I hear you cut your own hair on occasion, and I have to say it looks sensa-
tional. Are there any rules of thumb for home hair trimming you'd care to
share with us, the readers?—Dirk Droder, Berea*

I must admit, Dirk, that I shouldn't cut my own hair, for as I've
always maintained, "A man who cuts his own hair has a fool for a barber." But what can I do? I happen to have a skill in this area. Ever since
I got a free Trim-Comb with a tube of Prell Concentrate back in the
mid-'70s—a Trim-Comb I still have, Dirk—I've been chopping away
at my own hair, tearing and pulling it out, and sometimes, frankly, leaving large bald spots on my head. However, I can tell you that if you
take great care while trimming your hair, you can effectively rid yourself of those fly-away chunks of hair that stick out from your head and
that make you look like one of those shirtless unfortunates who always
seem to be getting shoved into the back seats of police cars on the TV
news. And yet the selfsame look may result from careless trimming!
Let me switch gears a bit, Dirk, and advise you to take your hair to a
trained professional, and leave the home hair-cutting to persons such
as myself. Your attempt could easily end in tragedy.

2/10/93

Why I Am a Finn

After watching the recent *60 Minutes* report on Finland and its inhabitants, I thought, "These are my people."

The Finns' dominant national characteristic is melancholia. The *60 Minutes* camera swept over dozens of Finnish faces, each one glummer and more downcast than the last. When the Finns spotted the camera, they quickly and guiltily looked away. On a Finnish bus, the riders looked as if they were being driven en masse to a community proctology exam. Finns apparently are terrified to have strangers talk to them, and God help you if you should try to hug one.

One way the Finns cut loose is by getting together and tangoing. The dancers looked as I did when I went to dancing school: like they'd just received death sentences.

I have no problem with this. What some might consider pathological unfriendliness or squirrelly behavior I consider good manners and letting others have their personal space. I often don't look people in the eye, because I've always thought it bold and forward. If someone stares at me as they speak, after a while I think, "Get the hell out of here." It unnerves me. I don't need to be gaped at. Neither do Finns. I like that in a people.

I don't see what's wrong with being perpetually downcast, either. It doesn't indicate anything except that you're not a grinning nitwit. I've had people tell me to cheer up when I've been in my best moods. So it doesn't translate to my face. Big deal. Who knows what Finns are thinking? They could be coming up with great stuff as they sit there brooding. The world could use a lot more brooders and a lot fewer dinks going around shooting off their big mouths! Sorry if I got out of hand there.

Neither do I like having strangers attempting to start conversations with me. What earthly benefits could talking to me possibly have for a stranger? One minute they're telling you they like your jacket, the next they're asking what kind of bank accounts you have and how do you withdraw your funds. The old withdrawal scam! That's what talking to strangers gets you. And I've had smelly guys sit next to me on the rapid and say, "Hey, how you doin', *ha ha ha ha*," or point at my book and say, "Is that a good book? *Ha ha ha ha.*" You think keeping that kind of conversation going is in your best interest? These are the little chats that begin on the rapid and end with you buried in a landfill. So I keep up my forbidding, Finnish demeanor and I don't get bothered.

Here at the office, Miriam, one of our sales executives, always gives the staff writer Hagan hugs and neck massages. As a Finn, I don't go for this. I'm not physically demonstrative and don't think people ought to be hugging and massaging each other in the workplace. When these two start doing this I groan and scowl at them, causing them in turn to make yet more personal remarks about the tautness of my nether regions. But I say, Move to California, where they squeeze each other in schools, offices, restaurants—wherever—if you want to do that. You're in Cleveland now, a Finnish-type city if there ever was one.

Even our cat Dizzy is a Finn. Dizzy's an isolated character who's often tense and nervous and runs away if you try to hug her. She sits on the sofa at times looking utterly dejected, or like a sullen teen who's just been caught smoking dope. And she'll bite you if you offend her, which could be at any time, for any reason. But she's often very affectionate—*at the proper moments*. It doesn't come cheaply. What's the worth of love and affection if that's *all* you give? You've got to mix the sugar and spice. Dizzy, along with Finns, understands this.

60 Minutes showed that one way the Finns cut loose is by getting together and tangoing. The dancers looked as I did when I went to dancing school: like they'd just received death sentences. Maybe dancing gloomily isn't the best way to dance, but that's how I dance, so I doubly enjoyed watching the Finns go at it. My heart filled with identification.

I couldn't believe it—a whole country filled with people like me! The notion elated me so that at one point during the broadcast I got up to my feet. Briefly.

2/17/93

I Am an Auto Consultant

Worked on the car this past weekend. A little auto maintenance, you understand.

It's my fiancée Barbara's car, actually. Since she drives me around, I feel I should take part of the responsibility for the car, a 1986 Ford Escort. I function as a sort of consultant. When the car breaks down—usually in South Euclid or Mayfield Heights, for some reason—I'm there. I have no choice. I'm in the car. And as a consultant, I point out to Barbara the probable source of the breakdown: *a lack of preventive maintenance on her part*. Not only do I not get paid for this kind of consulting work, it seems to make Barbara angrier as the car glides to its dead stop.

What a hollow charade. Now I was pretending to be a guy who knew so much about cars he could screw wheel nuts on backward and not give it a second thought.

(As I get older I realize more and more that helpful remarks are not only not appreciated, they often honk people off. What can you do? I won't be silenced, however. I'll continue to speak the truth in my role as a consultant.)

Anyway, this past Friday morning we went down to the apartment building's garage and saw that the car had a flat front tire. Barbara was mad, but I kept my cool. We opened the hatchback and searched for the jack, and I pointed out that if there was less trash piled back there, the tools we needed would be easier to find. More truth, more ingratitude as a result. We finally found the jack, but it looked incomplete to me. It was a little thing with a wire sticking out of it. I held it in my hands, turning it over and pulling at it, but I couldn't figure it out.

I called the garage guy over, who stuck the device under the car and began twirling the wire. The jack immediately lifted the car. The garage guy then took the lug wrench—which I was carefully examining—out of my hands, stuck it on each wheel nut, and loosened the nuts by kicking down on the wrench with his foot. That's the way to loosen those boogers, I thought. I took over and got that baby off.

After running around doing his job, the garage guy came back and mounted the spare. But I'm the one who put on and tightened the nuts. *Okay, job's done, the spare's on, let's hit it. We'll finish this business over the weekend.* That was the attitude I had. We gave the garage guy 10 bucks and we left.

The next day we went to a gas/service station on Lee Road and had a kid test the flat and replace it, as it was beyond help. Now whenever I go with Barbara to service stations for car repair purposes I go into my full auto consulting mode. Since I'm nearly 5'10" and have a full beard, I can make a feasible appearance of a guy who knows something about cars. So I stood by, silent, unsmiling, my arms folded, maintaining a stolid expression that said, Hey, I've been under the hood, my man, I *will know* if you try to rip us off.

I was gazing ruggedly out over Lee Road when I saw the kid beckon to me with his finger. He pointed at the spare and said, "You screwed the nuts on backward." I tried to save face by grunting "Yeah, I knew that." What a hollow charade. Now I was pretending to be a guy who knew so much about cars he could screw wheel nuts on backward and not give it a second thought. It wasn't fooling anyone anyway because the kid proceeded to give me a brief lecture on changing tires. After he did the job we tipped him a couple of bucks and left.

I felt good about the whole episode despite the backward wheel nuts fiasco, and when we then went to Beachwood Place I walked through the mall saying loudly, "Yeah, we worked on the car. Did a little *tire work.*" My hands were still greasy—I had helped Barbara roll the tire over to the work bay at the service station—and I was filled with scorn for the elite Beachwoodites surrounding me. I was willing to bet those Beachwood guys in their puffy sweaters didn't have grubby hands from tire work like me. And the ritzy Beachwood women were probably looking at me admiringly and thinking, Now there's a man who's equally comfortable in both the world of high-tone shopping *and* auto consulting work.

And I am, too.

3/3/93

No Cocktail Tacos at This Wedding

My fiancée and I are planning our wedding and reception again. We were forced to postpone the original date last September, so now it's going to be in May. May! When I called my out-of-town brothers and sisters and told them the new date, to a person they said, "You're really going to do it this time, right?"

Big surprise, and typical of the disrespect I get. I longed to say, "*Maybe*. You're just going to have to fly out here and take your chances." These people must think we postpone weddings for laughs. "Hey, I'm bored, let's postpone the wedding again." Or, "Let's do a last-minute postponement while everyone's in town." Or, "This time let's postpone it and not tell anyone." But I simply replied, "Yes we are, and thank you for your concern." Answer people with dignity—that's your best shot at making them feel small.

> If only I could still find frozen cocktail tacos in my grocer's freezer case. These little fellows had a dusty, Texas taste to the tortilla and contained a small dollop of mudlike meat.

Now, however, we have to do the nuts-and-bolts planning for this thing. There's no sense getting torqued out of shape about it. *It's only a party. It's only a party. It's only a party.* That's what I keep telling myself.

The most important thing to figure out is what food and beverages to serve. I don't mind helping decide this. We have a caterer's list that I've been studying. Since this isn't going to be a sit-down affair, we're serving hors d'oeuvres. Marinated artichoke and mushroom caps . . . country liver pate . . . carmeled brie with grape clusters . . . ham roulades . . . melon and Prosciutto . . . petit puff pastry . . . none of this stuff gives me a thrill. None of it's substantial. It's the kind of food that just slides down, and then out.

My dream has always been to serve pigs-in-a-blanket—which I always thought were cocktail weenies wrapped in dough—and have a big bowl of ketchup people could dip in. But I guess they're not cocktail weenies. People in the office tell me they're sausages wrapped in pancakes. Forget that. Another dream flushed down the toilet.

I don't suppose I could get cocktail weenies wrapped in bacon, either. Liver or water chestnuts, that's the choice. On the list it says

"Water Chestnuts with Crisp Bacon." Won't crisp bacon break if you try to bend it around a water chestnut? I'm not even a caterer and I know better than to do that. If this item is just a long strip of bacon with a water chestnut pinned to it—well, then, I don't know what to say.

If only I could still find frozen cocktail tacos in my grocer's freezer case. When I was a young boy this was my favorite dish. These little fellows had a dusty, Texas taste to the tortilla and contained a small dollop of mudlike meat. I never knew what was in that meat, but I didn't care. Sometimes I'd undercook my cocktail tacos and leave a bit of frozen meat filling in the tortilla. Mmm. Nothing has replaced cocktail tacos in my heart. They disappeared from the market years ago. Maybe it's just as well, because they'd be such a hit they'd distract from the event itself. It'd be a cocktail taco function instead of a wedding reception, and you can't have that.

Same with my idea for a Wise potato chip display. I was thinking of getting a huge Wise potato chip owl figure and beneath it present an unlimited supply of Wise potato chips, my favorite. (The owl would symbolize our commitment to quality chips.) Or maybe get a real owl from the Natural History Museum and have it sit near the potato chips. But this is another case of the snack overpowering the event. What if instead of sitting quietly by the chips the owl begins to hop around and leave droppings and chase guests? You have to consider these possibilities when you're planning a wedding.

Beverages shouldn't be hard to figure. Beer, wine, pop. We can't be pouring gin and Four Roses on a Saturday afternoon. This isn't the '50s, and it's not Mardi Gras week, either. We have to have a little decorum. Frankly, if there's vodka there I might drink it, and me drunk is a pitiful spectacle. I sag to the right with my eyes half-closed and my mouth ajar. I realize that's how many grooms look, but I want to appear to be at least 45 percent alive that day. A tall order, but I think I can do it.

Of course, you realize all this wedding and reception talk is academic if the Cavs have a playoff game that day.

3/10/93

Behavior In and Around Bathrooms

I went to a party recently at a house in which the bathroom was situated smack in the middle of all the activity. It was between the kitchen and the dining room, people were congregated around it, and if you needed to use it you had to shoulder your way through guests and tell them to move so you could shut the door. Because I drank so much beer I had to use the bathroom several times, and each time I considered giving the other guests the customary "don't listen" command. But if you tell people not to listen, then they'll listen for sure.

Call me "square" or "out of it," but I don't feel I was put on this earth to embarrass others as they go to the bathroom.

Let me clarify that. *Some* people would listen. Personally, I wouldn't. Call me "square" or "out of it," but I don't feel I was put on this earth to embarrass others as they go to the bathroom. If someone told me "don't listen" I would consciously go to another part of the house, so I wouldn't even be tempted. That's how strongly I feel about it. I can sense your mounting applause and murmurs of approval, but this is nothing more than simple common decency.

I try to comport myself with dignity on a daily basis around bathrooms. Here at the office, for example, when I walk into the men's room and see a fellow employee working on himself in front of the mirror, I don't say "It's no use" or "Why bother, loser?" or "There's nothing you can do about that hair" or other remarks of this nature. I give him a thumbs up and a "Lookin' good!" no matter what I personally believe is the genuine worth of his efforts. "Isn't that lying?" you ask. Yes, but of the white variety. If others—even mistakenly—think that they're "lookin' good," it's good for everybody. Offices operate far more efficiently when people believe they are "lookin' good."

Conversely, when a fellow employee bursts into the bathroom when I'm fooling around at the mirror—say, slapping myself on the cheeks to get the blood flowing, washing my nose, or singing—I continue the activity no matter what. This is to convey the idea, *You've caught me doing something stupid but I'm not ashamed. I'm 100 percent all-man.* It's the very essence of machismo. *I will do what I will do. Should it not be so?* You need to develop this tough attitude as there are always going to be people sneaking around in their soft shoes outside of bathrooms and then popping in.

At this office, however, I have another problem: what to say to women employees I encounter on our respective ways to the bathroom, because the men's and ladies' rooms are next to each other. Now, I know these women are going to the bathroom. There can be no denying it. Up until recently, my reaction when I would have an unexpected encounter with a woman on the way to the bathroom was to grunt "*hunh*" and cast my eyes downward. This was to indicate that I was sorry I caught her doing something of a personal nature, that this wasn't my choice—it was pure chance, and it wouldn't happen again. But that's not reality. It *will* happen again. For the rest of my life I'm going to run into women heading for the bathroom. This is the world we live in.

So my solution is to acknowledge our common humanity. Instead of grunting and looking down, I now say, "You going to the bathroom? Me, too." And then add a suave chuckle to show that this is, indeed, a lighter moment. Like "Lookin' good!," "You going to the bathroom?" is an expression that speaks volumes more than the words themselves. The subtext is sophisticated, knowing, and so very adult—with a hint of *joie de vivre*. It shows I know my way around bathrooms and suggests I know how to behave when I get inside them, too. That's good.

3/17/93

The Truth About Cussin' Jobs

Reading David McCullough's biography, *Truman*, I ran across the phrase "cussin' job." For the young farmboy Harry Truman, raking hay was a "cussin' job." So was milking cows, as they "flipped their manure-soaked tails in his face."

This was an eye-opener to me. Being hit in the face with a manure-soaked tail has just replaced pulling on a fat disgusting udder as my top reason for why I don't milk cows. Probably the main fear we all have when it comes to milking cows is getting kicked off the stool by an enraged cow whose udders you are ineptly trying to manipulate. But to now know that even if you *don't* get kicked off your stool, the very least that can happen is that you'll get slapped in the face with a manure-soaked tail . . . well, I'll just continue to pick up my milk at the store. Plus I had no idea cows' tails were soaked with manure; although, if you think about it, why wouldn't they be? I must have been living in a fool's paradise thinking cows moved their tails out of the way when they went to the lavatory.

> **Being hit in the face with a manure-soaked tail has just replaced pulling on a fat disgusting udder as my top reason for why I don't milk cows.**

Anyway, this cow thing made me think about cussin' jobs, jobs that make you say swear words beyond their normal, enjoyable, everyday usage. I've been lucky that I haven't had too many of these.

I've had several manual labor jobs that I liked, particularly one when I was part of a maintenance crew in the Cleveland Metroparks system. We'd empty barrels at the picnic areas and pick up roadside trash with sticks with sharpened nails driven into them. This job gave me the opportunity to see animals like raccoons and rabbits, plus hopefully catch a glimpse of full beer cans or discarded pornography. For even more fun we would fling our sticks at the picnic tables; if your stick stuck straight up on the table you . . . uh . . . won.

Where the cussin' came in was when we had to fill roadway chuck-holes with hot tar. We fought over who got the job of raking the tar, and who got the (cussin') job of shoveling it out of the truck bed. With my thin arms I didn't have much control over the shovel, so the hot tar would plop all over me as I dumped it on the ground. And I'd say "f---"

and "s‑‑‑." But at least with filling chuckholes you knew within a few days you'd go back to pleasant garbage duty with its potential for raccoons and pornography.

Not so with my landscaping job, where the thing I was lousiest at—mowing lawns—was the main task. The boss always got mad at me because I couldn't mow in a straight line. I'd go straight for a while, but then my mind wandered and I'd veer off. And when I got to the end of the yard I'd look back at my mow line and say "f‑‑‑!" My mow lines looked like tossed ribbons on the floor on Christmas morning. I never improved, and when I went to the boss and quit, he said, "I'm glad you're quitting, because I was going to fire you anyway."

Another thing that made me cuss was when I was an usher at a movie theater and had to clean up vomit. I only had to do it once, but that was enough. Fortunately the theater was supplied with Vo-Ban, a powder you pour over vomit that dries it up, making it easy to sweep into your usher's helper dustpan. But of course you do have to ultimately confront the vomit, so you cuss while gagging. I'd say "f‑‑‑! (gulp)."

My philosophy is, if your job is more than a certain percentage a cussin' job, you should think about getting out, if it's financially possible. I once quit a house painting job after only two days. I was doing overhead scraping on a carport overhang in unbelievably humid weather, with the paint chips falling on my face, sticking to my sweaty nose, cheeks, and forehead; so I decided to take an early retirement.

Later, when I ran into one of the other painters in a bar, he said the guys wanted to give me the "Most Dedicated" award. Hey, I thought, let them have their fun. I'm not about to spend my life in a cussin' job.

3/24/93

An Excellent Leasing Adventure

When my wife Barbara and I leased a new car this past weekend, I had the opportunity to fully perform in my role as an auto consultant, in which I stand stolidly by as car dealings are transacted and intermittently interject tough questions. I ask the questions I think Mike Wallace or Ed Bradley would ask. Only Mike Wallace or Ed Bradley wouldn't say "Oh, okay" to every response like I do, because I never know what the car guy is talking about.

He winked at us. The message was, *Folks, we're getting away with murder here. Take this deal and ru-u-un.*

Still, we got a good monthly lease price on an econobox. We dealt with a classic car salesman, who looked like an adult Spanky in a checked sport coat. He was a jolly sort who told us that this deal wasn't so good for the car company, but it moved cars. He winked at us. The message was, *Folks, we're getting away with murder here. Take this deal and ru-u-un.*

There were some options on the car we didn't need and told him so, but he said, "They're residuals. Hah? Know what I mean? You gotta take 'em." He began laughing conspiratorially and looking at me, so I felt obliged to laugh too. As I laughed I thought, What the hell are residuals? I didn't ask out loud because having them seemed to work in our favor as we got cruise control and a sunroof, not that we had any interest in a sunroof. I always thought a sunroof was just a hole that water would come in through. This was borne out when the car was delivered, with our salesman demonstrating how to open the sunroof and getting drenched by a stream of water pouring down on his lap. I made a mental note: Keep sunroof closed.

When it came time to pick up the new car, we were excited. This was the first new car deal I'd ever been involved in, where I had actually signed my name to something and been financially responsible. I'd been frankly avoiding it for years. So this was kind of thrilling. Barbara drove the new car out of the lot and I followed in the old Escort.

I was happy and humming until about a hundred yards from the dealer, where the Escort just frigging died on me. I thought I ran out of gas, as I had noticed it was an eighth of an inch below E on the way to the dealer and had chided Barbara about it. It was one of those things you don't believe are happening, so you psychotically announce it to yourself several times. Thus I was saying: "I ran out of gas! I ran out of gas! I ran out of gas!"

I was angry at Barbara and kept saying "I ran out of gas!" to her too when she pulled up. She ventured that the Escort was jealous that we got a new car and was being a bitch. We were right near a gas station, and I told the guy there what happened, and he said "Well, your old car didn't want you to buy a new one." The jealousy theory again! What do I know! I guess it couldn't be anything like there being no gas in the car! But when we put in a gallon and it still wouldn't start, we knew it wasn't the gas.

As we waited for the tow truck, the gas station guy was thinking the problem might be the ignition module. "You know how you tell it's the module, you just pull the wire from your distributor, and if it doesn't spark you know it's out." He was grinning knowingly at me. I grinned back, nodding, thinking *I haven't a clue as to what you're talking about.* What, did he expect me to go out there and pull a wire from the distributor? So I just said, "Yeah!" and by the way he then looked at me I could tell my auto consulting charade was again blown. I felt badly that I had disappointed him, but I wasn't about to go out there and electrocute myself on a seven-year-old Escort.

Finally we got out of there and drove home in the new car. We're happy with it. The monthly payments are low, and the car's loaded with options—the most important being air conditioning (the staff of life). And when we sell the Escort, we can tell potential buyers we put in a brand new ignition module for them. It's a residual. Hah? Know what I mean?

3/31/93

My Nice Time with Madonna!

On the recent Robin Leach TV special, "Madonna Exposed," Robin Leach said Madonna didn't currently have a boyfriend. I figured this might be a good time to invite her to Cleveland to go dancing with me.

I called New York City information and said "Manhattan; for Madonna Ciccone." The operator said "Just a minute." Then I heard the recording: "The number is . . ." and I jotted it down. I dialed the number and a woman answered the phone.

"Is Madonna home?" I said.

There was a pause. Then the woman said, "Ye-s-s-s-s?"

Holy cats, it was the Material Girl herself! I figured some slave or functionary would answer the phone for her, but there she was, waiting to hear what it was I wanted.

> I think she got a little bored when I played my videotape of the 1990 Browns–Bills playoff game, but got her second wind when I brought out the cribbage board.

I introduced myself and said, "Madonna, I'm no 'sexpert,' but I believe you have a crying neediness for attention." I was repeating exactly what Robin Leach said on the special. "I also hear you don't have a boyfriend and are feeling vulnerable right now."

"Maybe I am, and maybe I'm not," replied Madonna. I hadn't asked her out dancing yet and already she was waltzing me around. I decided to be bold and speak a language she'd understand.

"Listen, I'd like you to come to Cleveland and trip the light fantastic with me," I said confidently. "We can go to the Holiday Inn where I happen to know a d.j. who spins today's sounds, and we can just get out on that floor and dance up a storm. How does that grab you?" I paused, then injected the clincher. "*Baby.*"

After a long moment Madonna said, "You know, you got b---s. I like that. I'll come to your Holiday Inn. But you better be ready."

"I'll be ready," I said cockily.

Madonna showed up at the Holiday Inn lounge around 10 that Saturday night with a couple of huge bodyguards. There were only about 15 people in the lounge. They were all somewhat older and didn't pay any attention to her. She was wearing a low-cut black outfit with slacks and stiletto heels.

I approached her, held out my hand, and said, "Welcome to Cleveland, Madonna. May I get you a highball? I'm sorry I don't have any cocaine or poppers," I added, attempting to make a little joke.

Madonna looked around in distaste and said, "Let's just get busy."

As I escorted Madonna out to the small dance floor I said, "I've taken the liberty of giving the disc jockey a playlist of some of my favorite songs. Now, I should tell you I haven't really been dancing since 1984, so it might take me a little while to get warmed up. But then again . . ." I gave a high sign to the disc jockey. "*Maybe not!*"

Suddenly the sounds of Pat Benatar and her "Hit Me with Your Best Shot" filled the room, and instantly my feet were shuffling and my fists were pumping. Every time Benatar belted the words "hit me," I pretended to punch myself in the face. I knew I had to get off to a fast start with Madonna. She looked at me in astonishment. She'd never seen this kind of dancing in her fancy Manhattan discotheques!

When America's "A Horse with No Name" came on I began pantomiming riding a horse, a "horse with no name," which I symbolized by shrugging exaggeratedly at certain moments, as if to say, "Who is this horse?" Madonna was dancing too, but still staring at me. Then the Bee Gees' "Tragedy" played, and I squeaked "Tragedy!" along with the Bee Gees at the refrain. I sang along with the Eagles' "Hotel California," putting special emphasis on the words "they gathered for the feast," and Madonna raised her eyebrows at the heavy lyrics.

As I danced to the Doobie Brothers' "Taking It to the Streets," I said breathlessly to her, "You know, the last time I went dancing in '84 I looked down at my feet and they were really moving fast. They seemed to have a life of their own." I stopped dancing for a moment, pulled her to me, and said confidentially, "I really think some women were looking at me." Smiling suavely, I stepped back and resumed dancing, clapping my hands and kicking my feet out to the beat. Madonna was squinting at me. *Point, game, and match.*

We danced for hours, to songs like Abba's "Dancing Queen," Kenny Rogers' "Lady," and "The Theme to *The Dukes of Hazzard*." We slow-danced to the Commodores' "Three Times a Lady." As we danced to the latter, and after I whispered the lyrics "She's once/twice/three times a lady" in her ear, she said, "Let's beat it out of here." I said, "I understand." But did I?

I invited Madonna to my apartment, adding, "Leave the gorillas behind." I thought we would have a nice chat about Michigan, a state she hails from and with which I'm somewhat familiar. However, after she came up, she quickly disappeared into the bathroom. When she came out, she was wearing her famous leather S&M outfit and carrying a whip.

"Great Scott!" I said.

I backed away from her. She approached slowly, raising her whip. I ran past her into the living room, and she commenced to chase me around the apartment, flicking the whip at me. When it hit me I stopped in my tracks and cried, "Ow! That hurt!"

"On your knees, dog," she commanded.

This was clearly a power move. I wasn't about to let it intimidate me.

"I don't think so, Madonna," I said firmly. "*I don't think so.*"

She dropped the whip. "Okay," she said. I knew it! Madonna wasn't really interested in this kind of thing. It was just a passing fancy.

She changed back into her Holiday Inn outfit, and we sat on the sofa and began talking about the various spots in Michigan we enjoyed. We played cards, too, and watched some taped Bugs Bunny cartoons. I think she got a little bored when I played my videotape of the 1990 Browns–Bills playoff game, but got her second wind when I brought out the cribbage board.

Finally we said good night—early in the morning. I walked Madonna outside, where her bodyguards were sleeping in their airport rental car in front of the building. Madonna banged on the hood and they awoke with a start. Then she turned and looked at me.

"I'm not going to kiss you good night. I know you don't go for that and I respect it. But if we have a second date . . . "—Madonna winked—" . . . you better have those lips of yours in full pucker mode."

"I will," I replied, and gave her the thumbs up as I watched her drive off.

Full pucker mode! What a character!

4/7/93

Assorted Honeymoon Worries

I'm told that on your wedding night you shouldn't just go home. Two people have told me this. Gina, the production manager at our office, says, "I can't think of anything more depressing." And my mother simply says, "Don't go home."

It's not that we were going to go home after the wedding and then act like nothing happened. At the very least we would have cheese and crackers and maybe crack open some frosty, premium bottled beer. We probably wouldn't watch TV, unless it was an emergency, like a Cavs playoff game. We'd have a quiet evening of eating and watching TV (if that emergency arose), then get in the car the next morning and drive up to the northern woods of Michigan. You call that depressing? It sounds like an enchanted evening to me, but what do I know.

> **I'm not about to wrestle with a cat in a Toledo hotel lobby on what should be the most memorable day of my life.**

So we're thinking of going to a hotel, and then continuing on up to the northern woods from there. The critical question is then raised: What about the cat Dizzy? We're planning on taking Dizzy to the woods with us. The problem is, if we head to the woods directly after the wedding and stay in a hotel in say, Toledo, will we be able to sneak Dizzy up to the room?

A cat carrier will definitely tip the hotel clerk off. So will a squirming lump in our baggage if we were to stuff Dizzy into one of our nylon suitcases. I'm not going to put her under my jacket either, as she'll bite and claw me as I walk through the lobby, robbing me of whatever small amount of dignity I have. I'm not about to wrestle with a cat in a Toledo hotel lobby on what should be the most memorable day of my life.

You're saying, "Don't take the cat on your honeymoon." Oh, sure. Leave Dizzy alone in the apartment for a week? She'll be so honked off she'll tear the place up. If I leave her with my mother she'll shred my mother's furniture, which I can assure you won't please Mom in the least. She (Dizzy, that is) is like a razor with ears. Also, if we leave her, who will give her her morning rubdown? I can't ask my mother to give our cat a towel rubdown every morning as we do. She'd say, "No."

I suppose we could go to a local hotel, and then pick Dizzy up the next day and head on north. I've never stayed at the Ritz, or Stouffer's, for that matter. But do you know something? I can't foresee us doing anything at a hotel but watching TV and snacking on complimentary honey-roasted peanuts, or going to the hotel bar and vaguely drinking to kill time.

I take that back. We could swim. But what if we're still buzzed from the wedding reception? I can't swim drunk. The only time I did I was paddling around underwater, and when I attempted to surface I couldn't find the top of the water. Then I thrashed around, going sideways and down instead of up. You think I want to croak in a hotel swimming pool on my wedding day? Thanks, just the same.

And if there's no pool anyway then we're right back where we started from, in the room with the nuts and the TV remote. And paying through the snout for the privilege.

I know what you're thinking. That I'm a dolt. That we should have planned on going to Mikonos or Puerta Vallarta or some other exotic locale. Hawaii! France! Rio!

I've got two words for you concerning these spots: tourist traps. We're Great Lakes types. There's plenty to see around here. Fine sights are just hours away by car. All we have to do is monkey around with this Dizzy problem a little, and we'll be fine.

4/28/93

Tense Shopping Situations

What's harder, buying wedding rings or an air conditioner? I hope to answer that question in this column.

As my fiancée and I are getting married in extremely short order, this necessitates the purchase of wedding rings. We wanted simple bands of gold. We went to Best Products on Northfield Road to get them.

I always imagined a Tiffany's/Fifth Avenue kind of scene when I bought a wedding ring, but at Best we were surrounded by remodeling construction, patio furniture, and microwave ovens. I suppose we could have gone to a jeweler with an oak display case, plush carpeting, and a John Gielgud type waiting on us, but why bother, when Northfield Road is a hop, skip, and a jump away? Why pay for ambiance? These are nice rings. It's not like we got them at the supermarket. These aren't Grocer's Pride or Seaway brand wedding rings. We didn't get them from a bin with a sign that said LOOK!! WEDDING RINGS !!! with two dots drawn in the "O"s to signify eyes. This was no May Madness Wedding Band Blowout. These are genuine rings.

> **My old air conditioner had started sounding its death rattles last summer. It screeched, clattered, and at the end it was moaning and sending out little puffs of warm air.**

(I'm practicing being defensive about these rings because somebody may ask where we got them and how much we paid. I'm not saying they will, but they might. And I want to have my answer ready, even though this is nobody else's business. But wedding time is defensive time. Even though nobody has yet given us a lick of trouble about how we're handling things, I have to be ready, just in case.)

Anyway, getting the rings was quicker and easier than I expected. You always figure you have an off-sized finger or they won't have your size in stock. Or they only carry the style you want at another store. Or the salesperson will be a total dunce. None of these problems occurred, and I was frankly shocked. Particularly because we started the day by crunching the side of our new car on a post in the parking garage. I really thought we were doomed.

Plus I had to make yet another important purchase: an air conditioner. My old air conditioner had started sounding its death rattles last summer. It screeched, clattered, and at the end it was moaning and intermittently sending out little puffs of warm air.

We went to Fretter Appliance, but they didn't have their Carry Cool air conditioners—my first choice, although the last Carry Cool I had fell out my window, which was hardly its fault—in stock yet. They had one on display and I looked longingly at it. Carry Cool! Lightweight supplier of summertime comfort! I pushed at it to get a sense of its weight and heft. I could carry that thing around like a valise. Only 4000 BTUs, but that was enough. I was heartbroken it wasn't in stock.

So we then checked out one of the big department stores at Randall Park Mall. They had an extensive selection of air conditioners. Nearly all were big mamas, but there were a few 5000-BTU midgets that I could afford.

I was about to decide to buy one when I read the caution tag: Do not use with extension cord. *Do not use with extension cord!* You may as well tell me not to plug it in! What am I supposed to do, move my window? I asked the salesman about it and he said, "That's what it says. I can't tell you different. If you want to use an extension cord that's your responsibility." I asked him if I could use an extension cord if it was heavy duty. I certainly wasn't talking about a skinny cord from Revco you'd plug in a table lamp with. He shrugged and said, "I can't tell you to go ahead and do that."

Now the fear had been planted in me that if I use an extension cord with my air conditioner—something I had been doing for years—I would be doing something electrically unsound. I might short the whole apartment building, start a fire, or blow up my room. Now that joker was in the deck. And then the salesman started pitching a service agreement in which a maintenance man would come to my home once a year and check my freon. This was too much for me, and I said, "I-I have to make a *decision* here." I was so nervous I sounded like Nixon. And when the salesman turned away, I ran out of the store.

So, in answer to your question, it's harder to buy an air conditioner than wedding rings. Yes, it surprises me, too.

5/12/93

The Married Sex Machine

"What's it like being a married sex machine," you ask. Well, it's very interesting. Now that women know I'm married, the old idea of forbidden fruit comes into play. They see the simple band of gold on my finger and think, "That sex machine is all married up, and now I want him even more. This desire could send me to women's prison, but I can't fight the feeling. It's like seeing a luscious bon-bon or a jar of the finest caviar up on the shelf just out of reach."

My wedding ring has a message for these women. The message is, "Too bad for you. You didn't win the sweepstakes, this one here [my wife] did, and now you have to suffer." It says, "You can look but don't touch" and "Private property—no trespassing." It's like I've put up an electrified fence around myself. Though these women can no longer run up to me and knock me down, I still feel their vibes. So I have to put out my own vibes: *Don't get too close to the flame. You'll just get burned. And for what?* It's a dream that for them can never come true. I pity them, yet I envy them their fantasy.

> My wedding ring has a message for these women. The message is, "Too bad for you. You didn't win the sweepstakes."

I see these women on the street and in the mall, but what can I do? I feel them giving me the hairy eyeball as they pass by, looking boldly at me and at the crease in my pants. I can't stop every woman and tell her that these are wrinkle-free pants with perma-creases built in, that when I iron slacks myself the creases veer off to the right or the left, and sometimes I double-crease and then there are two lines running down the front of my pants leg so I look like I'm walking in two directions at once. How can I tell these women what they consider fashion mastery in reality stems from a practical decision in the marketplace? Am I to shatter their every illusion?

It's the same with the wallet marks in my back pocket. "Look at the sex machine, he's got a wallet. I wish I could be around when he takes it out of his pocket. Ooh, aah." Do you think I enjoy this? I can't even buy a pack of sheet protectors or Double-A batteries at Rite-Aid without feeling women's eyes on my wallet marks. They're thinking, "He's buying sheet protectors and batteries now—tomorrow it may be shampoo or floss or other personal items. Ooh." Why can't they leave me alone? Am I just a piece of fine, aged Angus beef? I might as well walk around with "Certified Grade A" stamped on my forehead. Would that make everyone happy?

It's oppressive to be a sex machine. To have your hair stared at, and your fingers. Your feet. When I'm with my wife in the mall, all may appear normal to the casual observer, but the sexual tension in the air is nearly overwhelming. What may seem to you to be an inconsequential glance from a woman speaks volumes to me, because I am a man who knows who I am. I've been cursed with this thing.

I constantly have to be on guard, because I never know when I'm going to awaken the savage in someone. It's constant stress. I have to stay on the balls of my feet in the mall, keeping my arms dangling loosely at my side. My wife doesn't know that I'm ready in case women jump out at me from stores. She just continues on. But the women know, saying to themselves, "The sex machine is ready. I'd better cool my jets." Consequently I've never been attacked, thank God.

I know this may be insensitive to the women out there, but in conclusion I would like to present a brief snapshot of my life at home, because I think it will be of interest to the general reader. The other day my wife accidentally trod on my bare little toe, and I screamed and fell over onto my bed and whimpered for several minutes. My wife thought I was a big baby, but when I later shone the flashlight on my mortified toe for her—highlighting a swollen, sharply ridged corn on the bottom of it—she then had a great deal of sympathy and understood why it was I shrieked like I did.

It was a moment of tenderness and understanding for myself and my wife, and while I do realize this is cruel to other women to flaunt our relationship in this manner I thought it might be helpful to you married fellows out there to know that you can shine a flashlight on your toes and your wife will then feel sorry for you. A hint from the sex machine.

6/9/93

The Submariner

Last weekend my wife Barbara and I toured the *U.S.S. Cod* (down on North Marginal next to Burke Airport), the only World War II submarine that remains unaltered from its wartime appearance. It was an impulse tour, and Barbara had to pay for it as I only had a buck in my wallet. Having only a buck in my wallet makes me nervous. It seemed unlikely there'd be a bank machine on board a 1945-vintage submarine. Even if there were ATMs around then, a submarine would hardly be the first place a bank would think of putting one. Who needs to make deposits or withdrawals or balance inquiries underwater? You should do your banking on the *surface* of the earth. That's my opinion.

> **I can take a shower on a World War II submarine or at the Ritz-Carlton. It makes no difference to me.**

In any event, you have to be nimble to get inside the *Cod*. You crawl in a hole and go down a vertical ladder to get into the forward torpedo room. Crewmen slept in bunks above the torpedoes. There was a toilet in there, too, with seven-step instructions on how to flush. You had to "secure sea and stop valves" and "open flapper valve" and a lot of other things until, finally, you had to "open the quick-opening valve, blow head, close quick-opening valve" and then "close the discharge valve and secure air." I was thinking, "That's more trouble than it's worth. I'd just hold it." Of course, on a several-week-long tour of duty this could be a problem. You can't go weeks on a submarine without going to the bathroom. You'd *have* to learn how to open flapper valves and blow head and secure air. You can't ask the captain to surface every time you want to go to the bathroom. He'd say, "Aargh, why don't you use the head, matey." If you then replied, "I don't know how it works," he'd make sport of you. But that's the military.

We then examined the officers' quarters in the forward battery—tiny, close rooms with thin-mattressed bunks piled on top of each other. The bunks appeared spartan but comfortable, like futons. Submarine guys had no secrets from each other in these rooms. You'd hear every snort, every groan. Nocturnal events.

Next door was the captain's quarters, which was more like it, privacy-wise, as far as I was concerned. This is the type of room in which Cary Grant wrote in his log in such films as *Destination Tokyo* and *Operation Petticoat*. And here was another example of a good way to alienate yourself from the captain, by asking if you could have his room with its nice single bunk and writing desk. Yeah, ask him if he'd mind sleeping in your bed above the torpedoes while you take his room! See how far you'd get! I amused myself with this thought as we toured the forward battery.

You're probably wondering, weren't these little rooms hot? Well, they had cool air blowing into them, at least when I was there. Still, they were awfully close. That's what you signed up for if you volunteered for submarine duty. *Clo-o-o-se* quarters. The showers seemed all right. My personal experience with showers and baths is that I can get used to any kind, as I'm so blind without my glasses or lenses on I can't see where I am anyway. I can take a shower on a World War II submarine or at the Ritz-Carlton. It makes no difference to me.

We went into the engine room, which in the movies would house Jack Warden and Arthur O'Connell and others of that ilk. There was plenty of big machinery, diesels, pipes, pumps, knobs, gauges, etc. You think there's an Up-Down lever and that's it? You're living in a dream world. Submarines are a lot more complicated than that. You don't twist and then release a rubber band at their hind ends to make them go, believe me. Maybe one day I'll explain to you exactly how they move.

To cap off our visit we looked through a periscope that was situated on shore, taken off a '50s-vintage sub. As Barbara looked through it I surreptitiously turned a knob on the front of the periscope, and she said, "The image keeps going in and out." When I revealed it was my shenanigans that caused this phenomenon she was honked off, but this was the only tense moment on our otherwise excellent submarine tour.

7/7/93

Life and Death Questions

What if I keep putting off having children until I'm in my 50s or 60s and the kids are so embarrassed at my advanced age they tell their little friends I'm their grandpa? Am I supposed to go along with this charade, or should I croak, "I'm their dad, dammit!" and then hobble off angrily like Walter Brennan?

What if I don't have enough money in my old age to be able to afford a decent nursing home? What if I'm forced to attend nursing home birthday parties where they put a hat on me and I have to watch a magician? What if they make me sing? And if they make us old folks in nursing homes sing, will we have to sing soft rock favorites like "Tie a Yellow Ribbon 'Round the Old Oak Tree"? I can't sing stuff like that. If I just ask them to give me a deck of cards and then leave me alone will they respect my wishes?

If there is TV in heaven, will it show only my favorite programs? If TV broadcasts everyone's favorites, won't the programming be the same in heaven as it is on earth?

What if humankind completely destroys the ozone layer and there is a universal ban on air conditioning? Will they ban it even in restaurants? What if I promise to keep my air conditioner on "LO" and to turn the thermostat to no higher than 5? How would anyone know if I secretly crank it to 8 or 9? Will I be so jaded and cynical by then that my conscience won't bother me about this? Should I hope this happens so far in the future that I'll be an old guy with poor circulation and so naturally be cold and have to wear a sweater anyway, even in an ozone-depleted world?

What if my bad posture turns into curvature of the spine, and I end up a hunchback? What if I wear bright blue polyester shirts and brown polyester pants and hang out at low-rent malls where teens point and laugh at me? And from my hunched over position I just wave irritably at them and say, "Aah, giddadahere!" and they laugh even more? And then I keel over?

What if I die suddenly and investigators find my Leisure Time Products and Adam and Eve catalogs? Will they just assume I order items from these adult specialty houses? Because I don't. I'm just a student of the culture. I don't go for whacked-out love creams or weird battery-operated devices that could blow up on you. I don't even know how these people got my name. Am I the only one who has a hard time throwing out adult material?

If there's everlasting life after death, what are you supposed to do with yourself all day?

Will there be books and TV? How about food? Laundry facilities?

If there is TV in heaven, will it show only my favorite programs? If TV broadcasts everyone's favorites, won't the programming be the same in heaven as it is on earth? Then what's the point? Is it foolish to worry about TV in heaven?

If you don't have your body in heaven—just your soul—how will you find your friends? If everyone's at peace with themselves and thoroughly happy, what will there be to complain about? Won't that limit the conversation?

What if I go to heaven and see Hitler sitting up there in a lawn chair? What if everyone, no matter what they did on earth, gets shoveled off to heaven? How are celebrities treated up there? Will people like Frank Sinatra still be big shots? If you tell the people in charge up there that your favorite earthly food was, say, tacos, would you be committed to eating tacos exclusively? What about going to the bathroom? There definitely won't be any need for cash, right?

8/11/93

A Philosophy on Aging

As I was getting my hair cut recently I looked down at the tufts of silver hair on the barber's bib and thought in disgust, "They could have shaken that old man's hair off before they put this thing on me."

Then I saw the hair falling from my own head matching the scorned tufts. So this was it. The beginning of the end.

I thought about having to get brown hair coloring, like the guy on the Grecian Formula commercial, who after dying his hair kept an unsmiling picture of himself with gray hair on the mantle for comparison purposes. Where was I going to get a picture like that? Did I have to get a mantle, too, or was it all right to put the picture on an end table? And how gradual was the hair re-browning process? Would my entire head turn an unnatural, Ronald Reagan copper-brown, and look like I was wearing some dimestore wig?

> What a terrible thing, to be living in a smelly shelter in your last years and know that you're there just because you went out to lunch too much in the '90s.

This past Friday I turned 38, and this and other concerns about aging have been bothering me. I've been having various troubles. I lost my right contact lens—the superpowered one—in Lake Michigan during my vacation. Driving home from the lake, my wife Barbara, as a vision test, asked me how many people were crossing in the sidewalk 10 feet in front of our car. I said two, which was right, but I had no idea what sex they were. This with partial correction! If I hadn't had the one contact lens in I certainly wouldn't have known the number, and only guessed they were humans through their general shapes and that they were moving under their own power.

Even with both my lenses in I've mistaken tree stumps and rocks for dogs and squirrels. I've said, "Hi, boy" to tree stumps with corrected vision. You think this is going to improve as I get older? I don't. I'm going to be walking into parked cars and wet cement and falling down hills.

I've got a tattered colon, too. I have to take four pills a day for it. It's not like I can skip a few, because then I can feel the colon acting up. I hear it groan. Do you think that's pleasant? It's not pleasant to go to a party either, and have a doctor you know tell you you should just have the colon taken out right away, because sooner or later you'll have to anyway. That was by far my worst party, when a doctor told me to have my colon removed. Later I went to my own doctor and told him what the other guy said, and he winced and said, "Not necessarily." And then he asked, "He told you that at a party?" But that's the kind of stuff that happens when you age, I guess.

You say, "Well, even with your gray hair and lousy colon and terrible eyesight you have an I.R.A. to fall back on when you get old." Wrong. That's another concern I've got. I have no money for my retirement, or anything else for that matter. I've been using my money to live on, not socking it away. Are little things like buying books and CDs and not packing my lunch going to cost me in the end? What a terrible thing, to be living in a smelly shelter in your last years and know that you're there just because you went out to lunch too much in the '90s. They say Social Security is running out of dough, too. That's nice. I'll be living in a single room with a cot and a hot plate and a can of My-Tee-Fine baked beans for company. I'll be lurching around drunk and hollering somewhere with my pants falling down.

The way I figure it, if I take this somewhat negative view of the future now, it will make aging easier on me. I'll be so used to the idea of having no money or colon and being blind as a bat it won't seem so bad when it comes to pass. And if I end up with a little money and my colon and eyesight intact, imagine how relieved I'll be. You just have to know how to think about things.

9/1/93

The Chairman Will Rule

My days of being pushed around at the thermostat are over.

Gina and Anita, the two women who work in production here at the office, are sisters, and both get "cold" if the temperature is under 95 degrees. Consequently, they're always running downstairs to adjust the thermostat to their preferred Flames of Hell setting. Never mind that at 68 degrees everyone else is cool and comfortable and working productively. This is of little interest to these women. On occasion they will brazenly attempt to adjust the temperature in my presence, and I have to jump into a karate stance in front of the thermostat to protect my co-workers from these women's tender mercies.

How'd you like to be driving in a car and see some home fitness system come flying in at you? We'd be looking at one sweet lawsuit, boy.

You say, "Why don't you get a weightlifting machine so you can flex your muscles in front of these women and you won't have to hop around in some phony martial arts deal nobody falls for anyway, and your implied strength will nip their temperature-raising inclinations right in the bud?"

My sentiments exactly. That's why we went to Sears last Saturday to price home weightlifting systems, and how we ended up driving home The Chairman, an incline home fitness system with high-grade virgin natural rubber resistance bands of 5, 10, 15, 25, and 50 increments. I wouldn't have considered buying it except it was 50 bucks. *Fifty bucks.* Even if one of the virgin rubber resistance bands snaps during a workout and smacks me in the head and kills me, so what? It was only *50 bucks.*

The guy at Sears fit the huge, 6-foot-tall box containing the unassembled Chairman in our compact car's trunk, tying it down with string. I hate having big long heavy objects sticking out of the car I'm riding in. What if The Chairman fell out of the car onto the road and crushed a small animal, or shot through the windshield of the car behind us? How'd you like to be driving in a car and see some home fitness system come flying in at you? We'd be looking at one sweet lawsuit, boy. Thank God my wife drives us everywhere. If there did happen to be an incident with The Chairman, I'd let the police begin the discussion with her instead of me. Then after a while I'd gallantly jump in, letting them know buying The Chairman was my idea. I'd try to take responsibility, but they'd probably still think it was her fault. I can't control that.

We lugged The Chairman upstairs, and I tore the box open to look at the assembly directions. You've probably read plenty of humor pieces about writer-types ineptly trying to assemble complicated items, but I will tell you frankly Henry Ford and Thomas A. Edison would have a tough time with this baby. The drawings in the instruction book are like diagrams of the electrical system for the World Trade Center. There are two large plastic bags filled with enough nuts and bolts and grips and springs to assemble a couple of motorcycles.

But I will put it together. I'm going to give my rowing machine to my twin sister the cop, because every time I rowed I'd come off the machine hunched like a gnome and coughing. I'd shake, too, and be unable to grip my soap in the shower with my palsied hand. You call that fitness? And I'm tired of frenziedly pumping my 6-lb. dumbbells—the kind of exercises people like Zsa Zsa Gabor would do. There's no reason I shouldn't be stronger than her.

I'll sit on The Chairman for muscular conditioning, toning, and body building, like it says on the box. Afterward I'll stand in front of the mirror and hum softly to myself and flex my biceps and stand on one leg and look to the left, then the right. I'll work on my pecs, too, so my chest will stop going down. I'll make my stomach look like a professional volleyball player's. I'll turn around, and sneer backwards at the mirror. *It will serve you well to not monkey with me. Don't touch that thermostat.*

10/6/93

Fabio and Me on Love

As I listened to my new CD, *Fabio After Dark*, a collection of brief discourses on romance by the long-haired Italian supermodel (alternating with songs by established artists), I felt his views on love deserve amplification and commentary. I will present his remarks followed by my own, which should essentially cover the subject for you.

Buon giorno. I'm Fabio. An' I'm vary interested in what makes romance work. I want to share wif you my recipe for a perfect evening . . . Wan I plan a date, I want to make sure dat everything is perfect for us. Music is de mos' important thing to set the mood for the night . . . A song can speak for me wan I cannot put my feelings into words. I listen to a solo and I think of a duet. Wan it's dark, I turn on the music, I light the candles. Thar is no timetable for us for a fantasy that we will make come true.—From "Fabio: About Romance"

If Fabio wants to whisper at his date he should rent a video from Blockbuster and do it at home, for God's sake.

What Fabio is saying here is that he sets things up before a date by lighting a few candles and putting a special song on the hi-fi. And the song isn't something uptempo like "The Yellow Rose of Texas" or "Smells Like Teen Spirit," it's slow and romantic—like "Wind Beneath My Wings." When Fabio says, "I listen to a solo and I think of a duet," he's not being literal, he just means when the music's going he's thinking about sex. Then he removes his shirt and it's off to the races.

I would add that you also might want to serve tortilla chips and dip.

[Breathlessly] I can be vary shy when I first meet a woman. But I'll always dream of learning her secrets. First I look into her eyes . . . Thar is a quality in a woman's eyes that show more than her physical being. It reveal her tanderness, and passion. Her inner beauty. I loff to take her anyplace I can devote all my attention to her. It can be a corner of our li'l ressrunt, it can be in front of my fireplace, [whispering] curled up, together. —"Fabio: On Inner Beauty"

Fabio can tell a lot about a woman by her eyes, which he shyly looks into before going to a restaurant. I don't quite understand why he goes on about her eyes revealing her tenderness and passion, then immediately jumps into talking about going to a restaurant. I guess he takes the woman to the restaurant, looks into her eyes, and sees if it's all right to ask her to go to his fireplace, where they can then curl up.

I like to take a special lady to a ceenema, whar we can hold hands in de dark and wheesper vary quietly about what we see. I wonder: Will she kees me . . . like dat? Will I always be de hero of her life? I wish there were more romantic feelms, because romantic feelms can lead to beautiful adventures after we leave de theater. —*"Fabio: On Films"*

Here's where Fabio and I seriously disagree. I don't believe you should talk at the movies, even "very quietly," because that drives me nuts. I go to very few movies, because inconsiderate people like Fabio are whispering at their dates. While he's worrying about being a hero and if he's going to get kissed, I'm trying to enjoy the movie—and I can't, because he's babbling. If Fabio wants to whisper at his date he should rent a video from Blockbuster and do it at home, for God's sake.

There is no place I'd rather be than on a tro-o-pical island. We seem to have it all to ourselves . . . just me an' my special lady. There are no . . . phones . . . to intrude on us. Feesh from de water . . . froots on de trees . . . an' wahnderful silence. The only sounds we hear are de sound of nature . . . and of our hearts . . . beating as one.—*"Fabio: On Tropical Islands"*

Fabio would like to spend time with his date on an island, where no one's calling him on the phone trying to get him to subscribe to magazines or take out insurance on his credit card. Amen to that. I'm not too crazy about his fish idea, as I assume he'd eat the fish, which is no treat, believe me. What's he going to do, wade out in the ocean and catch fish with his hands? Please. I'm concerned about the fruits on the trees, because I don't think islands have normal-type fruits like apples or peaches. I'd rather bring food. Some deviled ham, maybe. I also think wonderful silence would pall after a while, so I'd bring a short-wave radio so I could listen to a little sports talk. But that's me.

11/3/93

A Very Clinton Holiday

This Thanksgiving I got up at five in the morning to put the turkey in the oven. I rubbed the outside of the bird with Sue-Bee honey so it would be honey-roasted, and stuffed the cavity with tiny grilled Velveeta sandwiches on cocktail rye as a surprise for my little nieces and nephew. I also had graham crackers and Hershey bars on hand so the small fry could enjoy turkey s'mores after dinner.

My brother, who covers the White House for the *L.A. Times,* was coming into town and had said he was bringing a "special guest." I worked in a frenzy of preparation for his arrival. My sister the Cleveland cop was coming too, and of course my mother would be there. This was the first time I had hosted Thanksgiving dinner, and in nervousness I kept checking the turkey and slicing at it with a sharp knife so the honey would soak in. My wife stood by and watched disapprovingly.

My slo-roasting idea had turned out to be little better than a joke. I had no food for the president except for undersized grilled cheese sandwiches!

"That's not going to work," she said. "You keep slicing it like that and all the juices are going to escape."

"What do you know about it?" I said, my voice cracking. "What do you know about food? You're the one who thought we should put stuffing in the turkey's hole. Only *my* creativity saved us from that tired cliché. And I'm the one who thought of serving malt liquor exclusively with dinner, too. I'm trying to do something different from the typical petit bourgeois Thanksgiving. But as usual the different are hounded and condemned. It's no more or less than I expect, thank you very much."

I flounced off, my wife devastated by my words. She had tried to interject some of her petit bourgeois morality into my cooking style, but like a wild horse that can't be broken, a stallion that can't be tamed, I bucked and fought and didn't allow her to saddle me and ride me to the constricting territory of the ordinary. That's simply the way I am, no apologies tendered.

My brother arrived at our apartment around noon. Out of our sixth-floor window, I saw him and his wife get out of the car from the front seat. Out of the back seat, I saw my niece and nephew get out, followed by a bulky, silver-haired man in a blue suit.

I buzzed up my brother and standing at our front door, next to my brother and his family, was our "special guest." Yes, it was President Bill Clinton.

He took my hand. "I am *very* glad to meet you, Eric," he said warmly. "I have heard *many* wonderful things about you from your brother."

"You can cut the campaigning," I said. "You already won." Bill pointed at me and chuckled appreciatively.

"You dog, you," he said. "I heard about you."

My sister the cop pulled out her service revolver and started waving it around. "How's that Brady Bill of yours doing?" she asked. I think she had had a little too much malt liquor already.

"Very well, thank you," said Bill politely.

"I guess if you wanted to stop me for waving this mother around you'd have to wait five days 'afore you took me down, rube," my sister said.

"I'm sure you're very responsible with your firearm," Bill said, but I could tell he was getting a little irritated.

"I'm just horsing around," said my sister, and fell back onto the sofa.

"*Please,*" my brother said. This wasn't going at all as he had expected.

We sat down to dinner and I brought out the turkey. It didn't look right. As I started to carve, I noticed it wasn't cooked.

"I told you to turn on the oven higher than 150," sniggered my wife. This was all a big laugh to her, this scene of my ultimate humiliation. My slo-roasting idea had turned out to be little better than a joke. I had no food for the president except for undersized grilled cheese sandwiches! As he munched the sandwiches I saw Bill was growing progressively more uncomfortable. After he had three of the sandwiches, he said plaintively, "I'm still *hongry.*"

At that I burst into tears. "I did my best," I cried. "I had no one helping me." My wife said, "I tried to help you, but you wouldn't listen because you're an idiot."

I pulled her close and said, "Next time I *will* listen." Bill beamed at our affectionate display and started clapping. "That's really beautiful," he said. "This is a heartwarming moment."

The tension had been broken. We drank malt liquor and got to know each other, and what had begun as a disastrous Thanksgiving turned out to be heartwarming, as Bill said, just like *The Waltons.*

12/1/93

Cry of the Timberwolf

In winter I'm generally as tough and adaptable as a Minnesota Timberwolf, but this year a combination of factors has made it difficult for me. And though like the Timberwolf I usually suffer in silence, as a member of the media I feel it's my duty and obligation to reveal how sick I feel, so that maybe my experiences can help others.

Like everyone, I currently have a head cold. However, mine traveled *up* from my chest to my sinuses. As any doctor will tell you, colds normally travel *down*, dripping from your sinus passages into your lungs. This dripping forms a puddle in your lungs, causing what we close to the medical profession call *congestion*.

The congestion in your lungs makes you feel like coughing, but often your coughing just causes the puddle to splash around in there. It's non-productive coughing. That's why you need an *expectorant* (from the root word "expectorate," or "to spit it all up"). You want to spit the puddle up and out, whereupon you can then go on about your business.

You ask, how does an expectorant work? Well, it's a little like the scrubbing bubbles in basin, tub, and tile cleaner. The cough syrup somehow knows to slide down into your lungs instead of into your stomach, where it then breaks up the congestion into tiny particles of what we call *sputum*. It's got foaming action. And, if it's worth a damn, it will make you drowsy.

> Cough syrup somehow knows to slide down into your lungs instead of into your stomach, where it breaks up congestion into tiny particles of what we call *sputum*. It's got foaming action. And, if it's worth a damn, it will make you drowsy.

Unhappily, recent advances in the expectorant field have made it possible to take cough syrup *without* feeling drowsy. I always make it a point to buy expectorant carrying the drowsiness warning on the box, because if you're home, and it's nighttime, drowsy's good.

However, the stuff I just bought didn't have the drowsiness warning—*and yet it didn't carry a "non-drowsy formula" banner on the box*. I assume cough syrup will make you drowsy unless explicitly told otherwise. I felt that perhaps the drowsiness warning was left off in an oversight—or maybe not an oversight. Maybe it was the old bait and switch: to get you to buy their cough syrup they don't tell you it will make you drowsy, and you take it at the beginning of the day. Then you find yourself at work, expectorating and nodding out.

But what these cough syrup people didn't understand was, I was willing to play along. You don't have to tell me it will make me drowsy . . . *just as long as it does*. Do you understand what I'm telling you? I out-witted *myself* in this matter. I overthought the whole thing. My congestion was broken up, but I wasn't properly narcotized.

You say, "You really had a bad experience with that cough syrup." Yes, but you don't know the half of it. After I took the cough syrup my cold traveled to my sinuses, the expectorant doing its work too well, with the sputum traveling up into my sinuses. The laws of gravity had once again let me down, unless I had unwittingly been on an incline during this period. But who gives much thought to the positioning of their heads and feet during the day? We're all far too busy for that—especially me, with my executive-type management duties.

To battle this I took allergy pills. I bought a brand new bottle of pills to replace the (open) bottle of pills I had accidentally knocked into the toilet. (The pills had then met an even worse fate in that particular facility due to my not paying attention to the havoc I was wreaking upon them with my actions until it was too late. Without going into specifics I will candidly say these pills were ruined on every conceivable level.)

But it didn't matter, because these pills didn't have sufficient nasal-passage-shrinking power anyway. I was mouthbreathing in bed, the dry heat parching my throat, so I got up and squirted nasal spray in my nose. This prescription nasal spray had expired in March of 1993, but what could I do? The stuff barely had the pep to make it out of the dispenser, but it still had enough scrubbing action to clear one nostril.

Now I'm going back to the drug store to buy fresh nasal spray and something that will knock me out. I'm going for one that says on the box "May cause marked drowsiness." *Marked*, there's your key word.

1/26/94

A Valentine from the Sex Machine

I may not even get my wife Barbara a card for Valentine's Day, because every day is Valentine's Day for anyone who's married to me. I don't mean to be immodest, but the sex machine is pretty much what the doctor ordered for a woman. I'm the Megavitamin of Love, supplying a far greater percentage than the average man of the Minimum Daily Requirement of what a woman wants and needs. I'm a *time-release* sex machine, too. In other words, there's no end to it. I even work in my sleep.

You say, "But how can a person such as yourself, with frankly global appeal, handle being married?" Well, I think the answer lies in one word: *maturity*. Yes, I could flit around the flowers like a hummingbird, drawing nectar from each, but as a mature person that doesn't interest me anymore. What I am interested in is building a life. Barbara and I have a real relationship. That's what it's all about, love-wise.

Her wanting to kill me is nothing more than passing fancy. Because Barbara knows which side of her bread it's buttered on, and that's me. I'm the buttered side.

The simple things, the joyous things. On the weekends, Barbara and I drive around in our car. Because I nurture the child in my heart, I sing songs or ask Barbara questions about the cat Dizzy. Such as, "Dizzy's nice, huh?" Some people like to keep the conversation going even if there's nothing to say, but fortunately I can always talk about the cat. And Barbara always responds, though not necessarily verbally or physically. I can see her narrow her eyes as I prattle on. Sometimes she'll say, "You're driving me crazy." And I'll laugh, and reply, "No, I'm not." It's beautiful.

When you live with someone you see the power of repetition, too. Because I have only so many jokes and *shticks* in my repertoire, I bless Barbara with repeat performances. If a joke's good once, it must be good five times! Or ten! Or a hundred! Consequently, whenever she asks me a question about my job or family I make my famous reply, "Me no know. Me no care. Me no wear no underwear." Barbara pretends to be angry when I do this—even on occasion pulling the car over and ordering me out—but I happen to know the repeated regularity of "Me no know" comforts her. Anybody can answer a question, but the sex machine answers it with creativity and the principle of entertainment.

When I sing my songs—nurturing that inner child again—I poke Barbara in the ribs and say, "Now you sing." My songs are simple and lovely, oft-times involving no more than the repeated chorus "Dizzy's not here, Dizzy's not here." Doggerel about the cat! No Cole Porter, I grant you, But almost French in its artlessness. And I know Barbara loves my singing, although, again, she pretends she doesn't by saying such things as "You're trying to kill me" and pulling the car over. You say, "How can she even think about tossing the sex machine out of the car?" But really it's just the dance of love. I sing and poke you in the ribs; you stop the car and order me out. That's what marriage is all about.

At home, while Barbara is in the kitchen and chopping vegetables, I love to surprise her by sneaking up on her and yelling in her ear "HOW YOU DOIN' HONEY!" She'll whirl around, knife in hand, and hiss, *"What did I tell you about my ears."* What an actress! She looks like she could easily sink that knife into my gullet and rip it out, but I know better. Her wanting to kill me is nothing more than passing fancy. Because Barbara knows which side of her bread it's buttered on, and that's me. I'm the buttered side. And that's the pure, unadulterated joy of life with the sex machine. You're always treading that thin line between love and hate, which makes life exciting. It's always exciting for Barbara.

Here's a clue to how she really feels about the whole thing. Sometimes, after we go through our little dance, as a way to thank providence for her good fortune, she cries, "Why me, God?" I think that sums it up quite nicely.

2/9/94

Designing Your Indoors

We all know that in designing a room, form should follow function. I can best illustrate this established (yet maddeningly elusive) approach to interior design by describing our own living space.

We moved into our apartment more than six years ago. What we wanted to institute first and foremost was what I call The Viewing Area—that is, a comfortable, utilitarian area where I could watch my favorite TV shows. The primary prerequisite of this area is unobstructed sight-lines, wherein a person's eyeballs are on a straight course to the television screen. Scientific studies have shown that in your own home you have to look directly at the screen, and that angled views are acceptable only for guests, who, after all, will be gone soon; and it is your irritation at said guests or even loved ones taking your seat that leads to untenable stress levels.

If the walls are painted cream white, should you have a cream white sofa? Yes—particularly if that's the sofa your sister gives you.

Therefore, the main sofa—which you can get from your sister, as I did—should be placed no more than eight feet across the room from the television. The middle cushion should be designated as my (or your) cushion for viewing purposes. The left cushion (as you enter the room) should be designated as the eating cushion, as it will be situated next to the incidental table upon which you place the beverage accompanying the meal balanced on your lap on its red plastic tray as you watch TV at dinnertime. Naturally you'll have variations on this arrangement in your own home, but the basic premise ought to remain the same: different cushions for different functions.

We've spoken of function. What about form? If the walls are painted cream white, should you have a cream white sofa? Yes—particularly if that's the sofa your sister gives you. As the sofa was an elderly cast-off, we found that after a few years of our own hard wear its stuffing (also cream white) started coming out of holes in the upholstery. We solved this nicely by covering the sofa with a yellow blanket, tucking it in at the pressure points. Thus our main seating area has sort of an egg effect, yolk on white—but rectangular, of course, for our sitting convenience.

So we've established the color scheme for our living space. But any room sans accent is necessarily dreary, so we enliven the walls of the living and dining areas and small connecting foyer with challenging works of art. In our dining room we've placed a large cardboard map of the world (another item my sister left), and next to that a soft-tip dart board. The map is fading and bending out from the wall, but it gives an international flair to the room. On the opposite wall is a Matisse reproduction of fruit, I think it is. It's definitely a food motif appropriate to the area. I believe, too, there's still that miniature totem pole, appropriated by some member of my family from the Cub Scouts in the late '50s, hanging by the window.

In our living room the enlivening accents include a framed picture of George and Ira Gershwin, a Saul Steinberg poster, an old advertising poster of two boys hunting in the snow, a brown clock, and the *piece de resistance*, a large painting of stampeding horses—you can practically hear the snorts and thundering hooves. Small decorative touches also include a metallic reproduction of an old Chessie System ad depicting a cat covered with a blanket trying to sleep with a model railroad running around it, and a framed piece of sheet music from the show *The Most Happy Fella*. Sometimes, in our lighter moods, we bring out the cardboard baby I received from a friend in California and set that up as well.

Topping off the entire ensemble, so to speak, is our oft-ignored friend, the floor. Our living area has wall-to-wall gray carpeting, which is spotted with its own decorative accents provided by the cat in the form of little urine stains. These urine accents are remarkably consistent throughout the living and dining areas in terms of size and shape and are thus relatively inoffensive. They, too, embody the controlling theme of our home, of form following function.

2/16/94

The Indoor Performance Art Festival

The first annual Indoor Performance Art Festival begins this week and runs through March 16. The audience is encouraged to verbally choose the locations of the performances, where they will then become site-specific. (Dates and times are fluid.)

Feb. 24, 8 P.M.—*Cleaning.* The opening ceremony of the Festival features Deric Roder, a conceptual artist from San Mateo, engaging in a shower performance, asking the audience to stay outside the bathroom so they won't see him naked. After clothing himself, Roder performs a handwashing ritual, soaping his hands while shouting out the names of countries and peoples that "Uncle Sam" (Roder) has abandoned or exploited, thus washing his hands of these countries and peoples. Deforestation of the Amazonian rainforest will be ritualized in a shaving ceremony accompanied by humming and singing, after which the audience will be asked to clean up the bathroom in a participatory performance.

March 2 at 8 P.M.— "Wellness." Chicago's Erik Doder in a performance entitled "I Tell You I Don't Feel Good."

Feb. 25, noon—*Indoor Sculpture.* An indoor installation, filled with site-specificity. Toledo's Derek Floder installs himself on the couch and doesn't move for the duration of *Andy Griffith*, *The Beverly Hillbillies*, and *Gomer Pyle, U.S.M.C.* in a postwar protest against the American involvement in Vietnam during the '60s, accompanied by Floder's wry description of his unsuccessful attempt to donate himself as a living sculpture to the United Nations Building in New York City. Floder mimes talking into the telephone as a commentary on mass communications and concludes by asking the audience to carry him out to his car so he can then drive back to Toledo in a satire of various vehicular modes.

Feb. 27, 8:30 A.M.—*Animal and Human Consumption.* Cleveland's Eric Broder eats a bowl of Alpha-Bits with the cat Dizzy squirming in front of him on his *Plain Dealer Sunday Magazine* in a performance involving a table-and-chair installation and the questions: What do we eat? What role does media play in relation to human and animal consumption? Do we learn what to eat through the coupons in the Sunday newspaper supplement? Broder attempts to answer these through the ritualistic eating of edible items that the audience is asked to bring, along with the items' corresponding coupons. (The coupons will then be affixed to the refrigerator in a magnetized performance.)

Throughout the Festival—*Sleeping*. The cat Dizzy in an ongoing event, a sleeping ceremony followed by a leaving ceremony when the audience arrives. A contextual performance demonstrating our relationship with animals in an indoor environment.

March 2, 3 at 8 P.M.—*Wellness*. Chicago's Erik Doder in a performance entitled "*I Tell You I Don't Feel Good.*" In a particularly apropos performance considering today's controversy over health care issues, Doder describes his ailments while hurling little snips of paper into the audience in a Dadaist pageant of cast-off confetti symbolizing the good health that leaves our bodies as we age. The audience is invited to view Doder as he then takes ibuprofen (buffered aspirin) at the March 3 performance.

March 5, 7 P.M.—*Video Event: Mr. Hobbs Takes a Vacation*. Boston video artist Darique Droder performs the 1962 Jimmy Stewart comedy *Mr. Hobbs Takes a Vacation* by exhibiting the film on her video-cassette recorder, then asking the audience to leave when the film is over.

March 10, 9 P.M.—*Fascism. Fashion*. The direct connection between fascism and fashion is performed by New York's conceptual pagan light artist Erica, accentuating the energy flux of the body and its dressing as she assigns audience members to shine a flashlight on her as she plucks at her garments and yelps in pain. Then Erica will collect and deconstruct the flashlights, tossing the batteries to audience members, who will then be required to give the batteries back.

March 12, 7 P.M.—*Phone Anarchy: "Take-Out Order, Please."* Minneapolis phone anarchist Rick Roader in a Futurist performance in which he calls local restaurants on the phone and orders take-out for the year 2011. Roader examines with the audience the restaurant personnel's reaction to his calls and contextualizes it to 1994 take-out orders.

March 16, 7 P.M.—*Closing Ceremonies*. Cleveland's Eric Broder leads the audience on an anti-capitalist journey by demanding cash—then paradoxically keeps the money in a surreal exploration of art and funding. In an interactive ceremony celebrating closure and circularity, the audience will help Broder tidy up the installation, then be escorted from the Festival by actual police officers as Broder relaxes on-site.

How to Eat to Not Be Dead

As my doctor tells me my cholesterol is starting to nose into the red zone, I've got to think about keeping it down. Unless, of course, I don't mind having a massive stroke, which wouldn't make much difference for me at home but would certainly make performing some of my tasks here at work more difficult. I suppose someone could put a chimpanzee's cap on my head, hang a drool cup around my neck, and I would get by, but at a notch below my usual level of performance. So I better at least look at this sheet of guidelines my doctor gave me.

One side of the sheet has Foods to Use; the other Foods to Avoid. Being a normal person, I hate almost every item on the Foods to Use side. Here is a brief summary of the foods that are good for you: *fish, and 1/2 cup of dried peas or beans.* How's that sound? And don't think that if you eat this you're allowed to toss back a tankard of Nestle's Quik along with it. You can have water, herbal tea, clear broth, or salt-free club soda. Nothing like emasculated club soda! You might as well suck air! A nowhere drink like club soda has to be cleaned up, but you're permitted two servings of alcohol a day. You have to take the salt out of the club soda, but you can have two shots of Tequila or two glasses of Ripple or Mickey's Malt Liquor.

You get to accompany your fish and beans with a slice of whole-grain bread or three soda crackers. *Three* soda crackers. This is bad news for those of us who measure soda crackers by the stack rather than by the individual unit.

Oh, I almost forgot. You get to accompany your fish and beans with a slice of whole-grain bread or three soda crackers. *Three* soda crackers. This is bad news for those of us who measure soda crackers by the stack rather than by the individual unit. You can also have a tablespoonful of peanuts. That's two unshelled peanuts lying in the spoon, or maybe six shelled. What kind of person eats two or six peanuts? Don't even put peanuts on the list if you're going to measure them by a spoon. Don't waste our time!

Now that dinner's ruined, let's think about the next day's breakfast. "Use 1/2 cup of hot cereal or 3/4 cup of cold cereal per day. Add a sugar substitute if desired, with 99% fat-free or skim milk." Three-quarters of a cup of cereal barely reaches the middle of the bowl. Then you're allowed to moisten it with that milk-water and sprinkle sweetening chemicals on it. You're telling me that's healthier than Shredded Wheat with 2% milk and a few modest teaspoons of wholesome cane sugar on top? That's what I eat, and I feel like a million. Occasionally I eat an egg, bacon, and cheese sandwich and a Danish for breakfast, and I bounce around the office like a pup afterwards. But what do I know, I'm not a doctor.

On the Foods to Avoid side, I don't mind avoiding organ meats (kidneys, liver) or avocados. The one fruit to avoid is the coconut, which I don't exactly take home and crack open every night anyway. So a meal of liver and coconut is forbidden—I can deal with that. But also on the Avoid list is cheese, potatoes (except as a bread or cereal substitute), commercial baked beans, potato chips, jams, jellies, syrups, baked goods with shortening and/or sugar, processed meats, luncheon meats, hamburgers, frankfurters, hydrogenated peanut butter.

Yes, I know, everything good in the world is on this list. I don't know what hydrogenated peanut butter is, but I suspect the excellent Jif and Peter Pan fall into this category. I don't have any illusions that my pepperoni-and-cheese Pizza Rolls aren't on this list either, or some of the finer salt-studded pretzels I enjoy. Because here is how life works. Delicious products are made. Then microbe-hunters put a smear of these products on clear slides, peer into their microscopes, and see the cellular make-ups of your Beanie Weenie or your *Hot!!* Bar-B-Q Potato Chips or your Little Debbies. And because the cells of these products have a little pep to them, a little lustiness, where they might incidentally consume one of your healthy cells, these microbe-hunters think they're bad for you.

But I'd rather have zesty Bar-B-Q cells than tofu or humus cells. Or unflavored gelatin or nonfat bouillon cells! I'll die with my boots on, thanks.

3/12/94

The Bitter Truth About Tots

For some time now I have observed the behavior of various tots, including my own nieces and nephews, children of friends, and the young persons in the day care center downstairs from our office. After prolonged observation I'm afraid I can only come up with five words to sum up their behavior: It's totally out of hand.

You say, "What do you expect, they're children, they've got high spirits." Ah. But how do you explain this? The other evening I was at my sister's house, and my niece, the tot Jane E. Frazier, was fiddling with a plate of sliced Honeybaked ham that was sitting on the table and that we were planning to eat for dinner. I stood guarding the ham because Jane E. Frazier has a history of squishing her fingers into food. Food I'm going to eat! I don't want her—or anybody's—grubby little mitts in my food. Is that so unreasonable? Is that a crime?

They're shrieking and squealing and clumsily throwing balls at each other. Guess whose shins these balls invariably bounce off of?

In any event, I turned for a moment, and she grabbed the top of the ham, which was covered, fortunately, by aluminum foil, and started squishing it and squeezing it. I cried "Get out of there!" and picked her up to take her away, but Jane E. Frazier clung tenaciously to the ham, lifting it along with her. The ham was off the ground and being severely manhandled. That's right. My dinner. I can't eat mangled ham that's been carried around and has little handprints on it—though ultimately I did, of course, because I was so hungry. But I'm a sensitive type, and these things bother me. You say, "sure, that'd bother anybody." It's a disgraceful episode, no two ways about it.

But no different from what I see every day. The day care center downstairs is filled with this kind of thing. I have to wade my way through an ocean of tots every day as I enter and exit the building. And they're not sitting quietly on a blanket as I did when I was that age. They're shrieking and squealing and clumsily throwing balls at each other. Guess whose shins these balls invariably bounce off of? That's right. Mine. Because I'm filled with love I pick the ball up and gently hand it back to the offending tot instead of drop-kicking it right out of the building as I should. "Well, you're nicer than most," you say.

Don't I know it. I'm taken advantage of because of it. These people never get out of the way when I'm trying to go about my business. They stand in the doorway of the hall that directly accesses our office. You have to loudly say "Excuse me" and then they'll just look up at you blankly. Hello down there! You're impeding traffic! Let's get off the schneid here if you don't mind terribly! I can't count the number of times I've had to nudge a toddler out of that doorway. This is time-consuming work and I don't get paid for it. But I don't complain.

All I know is, when I was three or four years old I wasn't running around screaming and blocking doorways and bothering decent people. You could place me on any flat surface, hand me a good book, and I'd occupy myself for hours and then quietly go off to bed. I wasn't whining and demanding toys and crying I want this and I want that. No, usually the only words out of my mouth were "May I help you?" I combed my own hair, too. I did everything to make my life easier for my parents.

However, here at the day care center, parents can barely get their tots out of their cars to go into the facility. Once they do, these children poke and shuffle along outside the building while their parents patiently hold the door for them. You know these parents are thinking, Let's make it *today*. My parents never had that trouble with me. I'd jump smartly out of the car, run ahead and hold doors open for them, and then ask, "May I read now?"

In my day, if you behaved like the various tots and toddlers I see hanging around here you'd end up in reform school and then the penitentiary.

4/13/94

Glad You Asked!

How long should you keep food in the refrigerator or cupboard after its expiration date?—Audrey S., Willoughby

There are many schools of thought on how long food can be kept and safely consumed after the "Best if used by ____" date notation on the container. In many cases it's obvious when a food has died and gone to hell, but there are others that aren't quite so clear-cut.

An example of the former is an incident I recently experienced, involving a bottle of ketchup at a local eatery. A co-worker, wishing to use the ketchup, attempted to open the bottle. There occurred a loud hissing sound and, as soon as the cap was off, a small explosion, followed by a reddish gas filling the air. I grabbed the bottle, crisply told my co-worker "This ketchup has turned," then handed it to the proper authorities.

If potato chips wore suits, Ruffles and Lay's would be wearing conservative cuts with tasseled shoes.

An example of a not-so-clear-cut case was the bottle of Sammy's Mean Mustard—a celebrity mustard endorsed by Sammy Davis Jr.—I found recently in the refrigerator. I couldn't tell by the smell if it was bad, but then I remembered something: when I bought the mustard, I recall thinking that Sammy was doing okay if he had his own mustard. In other words, when I bought the mustard, *Sammy Davis Jr. was still alive.* A quick check of my almanac told me that Sammy Davis Jr. had died in 1990, and I had my answer. The mustard was at least four years old, and I based my decision on the general principle that if food is at least four years old, it probably should be discarded.

What are some of the many uses of duct tape? I'm considering buying a roll.—Jim, Cleveland

Ah, one of my favorite subjects! We all know that duct tape is good for taping ducts, but I've been using for it years to keep my air conditioner affixed to my bedroom window. It may be that a heavily taped window isn't the height of contemporary interior decorating fashion, but that AC unit isn't going *anywhere* with your man duct tape holding it in. And you're dealing with a person here who once had an air conditioner fall out of his window and crash onto the street below, so I'm extra appreciative of steady, faithful-as-a-sheepdog duct tape.

Here's yet another use: I recently found to my dismay a hole in my pants pocket, with the result that coins and keys kept falling down my leg and bouncing off my shoes. Did I get out a sewing kit—which I don't have anyway—and try to sew it up? Nope, I taped up the hole with duct tape, and it's adhered beautifully through several washings, to the point where my pants have been fooled into thinking it's part of the original pocket. That's duct tape.

Can whales just open their mouths and fish swim in and that's how they feed themselves? If not, how do they do it?—Bridget, Shaker Hts.

You know, Bridget, I'm just not sure. Certainly a whale could open its mouth and any luckless fish that happened to be in that part of the water would then find itself in the whale's mouth. It would seem that the fish would then drift back into the whale's throat and down its gullet, with no chewing involved. That's nourishment, of course, but where's the taste? Where's the enjoyment? Sometimes, I suppose, whales eat sharks and sea lions and what-have-you, but what do they do—sneak up on them? I would think your animal instinct would tell you a whale was headed for you and in plenty of time. They're not exactly petite, you know. Maybe I'll look this up and tell you later.

What is your opinion of the current crop of potato chips now available on the market?—Buzz, Lakewood

Let's get off on the good foot with my favorites, Mikesell's and Wise. These two chips are the epitome of crunchiness, coupled with pleasing thickness and texture. What you want is a sort of grainy feel to your chip; this means the potato hasn't been emasculated—stripped of its essence, if you will—in the chipmaking process. These two brands *keep the potato alive.* You want the potato to live.

As for Ruffles and Ruffles' parent, Lay's: I wouldn't go too far out of my way for these soulless chips. They're okay, sure. Perfectly acceptable as a side to your tuna sandwich or grilled cheese. But they're corporate. If potato chips wore suits, Ruffles and Lay's would be wearing conservative cuts with tasseled shoes.

The Eagle Brand potato chips are another corporate chip, launched by the mega-conglomerate Anheuser-Busch. Eagles aren't chips for their own sake, but a companion to the company's beers. I consider this a slap in the face to me as a chip eater, as well as to the Potato Chip Institute. I'd bring the Anheuser-Busch people before an Institute tribunal, hold up one of their skinny little potato chips, and tell them, and the world, "This isn't a chip. It's a P.R. stunt." [Since the time this column was first published in 1994, the Eagle Brand chip has been discontinued. More than a coincidence?— E.B., 1999]

New Levels of Being Boring

They say you become more boring as you get older. They're right.

This has been brought out in my own life, with my behavior around the house and at work, and by having the most tepid, uneventful dreams in human history.

For example, I set my alarm clock for 7:04 every morning, having to slide the switch to "radio" every night before I go to bed. But I can't just set it now. I have to check it and recheck it, repeatedly putting my finger next to the switch to make sure that I did indeed move it over to "radio." I jump back and forth, bending over and staring at the

I used to dream about sex. Now I dream about mail.

alarm clock, all the while thinking in self-disgust, "What, do you think the wind is going to move the switch back to 'off'?"

You say, "That's compulsive behavior. People get medicated and institutionalized for stuff like that." I'm not worried about being medicated, I just think it's pitiful that I'm reduced to this. It's boring! With everybody talking about their dysfunctional behavior—being dopers, drunks, sex addicts, compulsive gamblers—what am I going to say? "Yeah, I double- and triple-check my clock radio." And this from someone who used to be a world-class party animal, for whom "getting down" was a nightly occurrence.

I've become addicted to wiping down the tiles in my shower stall every day to thwart grout mildew, too. The problem is I enjoy this wiping procedure *a little too much*. When sponging your shower tiles is a highlight of your day you're not exactly living on the edge. Of course, when I worry too long about it I tell myself, "Do this now and you save yourself a session with the Tilex later." So there are plusses—I did get a good deal on Tilex with a coupon recently.

Another excellent example of how boring I am happened just the other day here at the office. I received a publicity bra in the mail from a book publisher pushing a sex-filled novel. "Whew!" you say. "You got a bra in the mail! That's red-hot!" Not so many years ago I would have agreed. I would have snickered and horsed around with the bra, twirling it around my head. This time I just handed it to another editor, who had far more use for it than me. I've received plenty of pub-licity underwear and hats in the mail, and it's nothing to me anymore. I even lost a publicity bathrobe I once got from Stouffer's and didn't think twice about it. What pride is there in wearing a publicity bathrobe? Bathrobes have to be earned. That's my view today.

All this wouldn't be so bad if my subconscious wasn't boring as well. I know it is because of the dreams I've been having. I used to have Salvador Dali and M. C. Escher–like dreams, dreams that would rival anyone's for bizarreness. Just last night I dreamed I saw an item in the newspaper about Tim Conway. That was it! That was the most vivid detail of that dream. I remember it was concerning the young Tim Conway, so perhaps the dream was set in the '60s. Where others' '60s dreams might be about Vietnam, the Kennedys, or maybe an acid trip at a Janis Joplin concert at Fillmore West, mine was about a support-ing actor on *McHale's Navy*.

And where I used to dream about sex, now I dream about mail. I dreamed I was looking through the mail in our apartment building mailbox, and the more I paged through the mail, the more mail there was to page through. In other words, to my ultimate delight, *the mail kept replenishing itself*. All those years of my longing for more mail man-ifested itself in this dream, which drove me into such a frenzy that when I woke from it I felt like having a cigarette.

The dream I recently had about my wallet beats them all. When I went to bed that particular night I knew I had only two dollars in my wallet. I was concerned. I like to be a little more flush than that. But how boring are you when you dream you have *exactly* the same amount of money in your wallet as you have in real life, as I did? How boring are you when you *dream* about paying a cover charge to get into a bar, and you can't get into the bar because you don't have enough money in *real life*?

That covers all levels of being boring.

5/4/94

Buzzards Ripped My Flesh

Here's the true and very interesting story of our trip up to Northern Michigan involving the solar eclipse, turkey buzzards, and an overflowing toilet.

My wife Barbara and I drove up to Northern Michigan for a brief vacation this past week. We left Cleveland on the day of the full solar eclipse, and were on the road at its height. I kept peeking at it, although I knew I was taking a gamble with my eyesight.

MAN BLINDED ON DREAM VACATION

Toledo, May 10—Eric Broder of Cleveland, Ohio, gambled with his eyesight today during the solar eclipse and lost. Broder was blinded by the eclipse, his dream vacation turning into a nightmare.

What was I going to do—beat him off with my cereal spoon? No thanks. I was on my vacation.

Despite repeated warnings in the media to not look directly at the sun during the eclipse, Broder tempted fate and glanced at the sun while traveling with his wife Barbara on the Ohio Turnpike.

"He's a real loser," said Ohio State Trooper John Dietz, who came to Broder's aid. "All the papers told him not to look at the sun, and he did it anyway. It's ironic, because he wanted to see something and now he won't see anything. It's also too bad, because he's obviously a sex machine."

Added Barbara, "I told him not to look, too. But he was too smart to listen. He doesn't seem so smart now."

The eclipse didn't actually get me, as I have been able to see since May 10 (although bright yellow-and-black spots float in and out of my vision, and I'm hallucinating fairly heavily). And when we arrived at our place in Michigan I was certainly able to see the huge white splotches splattered over the side of the house. The splotches were clearly bird doo, but the work of giants.

At this point Marv the handyman drove up in his truck and told us that turkey buzzards had roosted on our house, and we saw them circling and soaring above us. Ay yi yi! I'd never seen such big birds. They were living on our roof and going to the men's and ladies' room on it and on our picnic table outside. The next morning as I was eating my Cheerios I saw one of the turkey buzzards land on the picnic table and stare at me in hatred. I felt like saying, "There's all kinds of deciduous woodlands out there for you to live in, and you choose our house? And go to the lavatory all over it? The hell with you." Of course I didn't say this out loud, because you never know what would make a sizable vulture of this kind go psycho and come smashing through a window into the house. What was I going to do—beat him off with my cereal spoon? No thanks. I was on my vacation.

Another interesting thing that happened during our vacation was that the toilet overflowed, and this became a watershed event for me, so to speak. I managed to stop the toilet from flooding the bathroom further, but I didn't know how to unblock the thing so it wouldn't overflow again. I had a cheap discount drug store plunger but it didn't work; so we called Marv, and he brought in a deluxe hardware store plunger and plunged it good.

To be honest with you, I had never plunged a toilet and didn't really know why you would, but my series of incisive questions to Marv during the plunging process taught me a lot about how toilets work. I've given up trying not to look stupid during moments like this. My new philosophy is, "Marv may see that you don't the first thing about toilets, but he'll politely answer your childish questions even if he does think you're an idiot." This philosophy works for anything, I've discovered. Marv wasn't born knowing how to plunge a toilet, you know. He had to learn stuff, too.

Our trip to Michigan also coincided with our first wedding anniversary, and as I believe in consulting the person to whom I'm going to give a gift, I asked Barbara what she wanted for an anniversary present. I figured I could get her something nice up north, some kind of stone jewelry, but all Barbara asked for was an auto compass. What kind of anniversary present was that? But that's what she said.

I kept bugging her to see what else she wanted, and then she said a horse. I had in mind a gift somewhere *between* a horse and a compass, and to be candid, pricewise a little closer to a compass. So I got her a 10-dollar compass, and we'll find something else later, back here in Cleveland.

5/25/94

The 42 Key Marital Phrases

When you've been married as long as I have—a little more than one year—you notice that communication between you and your spouse is pretty much reduced to several key sentences and phrases, uttered over and over, amounting to a kind of code language. That's why people who have been married for, say, 20 years, need only exchange a series of grunts to communicate fully.

Following is a list of the phrases heard most often in our marriage. For fun and to test your knowledge of normal marital relationships, see if you can guess who is speaking in these phrases, my wife or me:

> **People who have been married for 20 years need only exchange a series of grunts to communicate fully.**

"Don't fill your heart with hate. Then there won't be any room for the love."

"You are a real psychopath."

"Look, I put the lint from the dryer in my belly-button, and now it's belly-button lint."

"Let's go home, Barbara. *Let's go home.*"

"Don't stand by the window like that, people can see you."

"Don't you ever stop talking?"

"Ask for paper in plastic. Paper *in* plastic!"

"Let there be love."

"Don't you ever do that to me in public again."

(Singing) "On the road again, we're going on the road again, we're going on the road again, we're on the road again!"

"Get away from me, I'm warning you."

"Get out of the car."

"It looks like the sun is finally coming out, Barbara. *It looks like the sun is finally coming out.*"

"You're scaring me."

"Now you dance."

"Be a winner. It's a great feeling."

"You're a laundry asshole."

(Singing) "Lo-o-ve, soft as an easy chair . . . "

"I'm taping this."

"What happened to 'Judge not, lest ye be judged?'"

"I wasn't talking about *me* not judging."

"I'm a winner, baby. Dig? A *winner*."

"Don't you ever shut up?"

"What did I tell you about my ears?"

"Don't you *buy* no ugly *car*."

"Are you trying to kill me?"

"I have to go to the bathroom again."

"This is where you're getting out of the car."

"I'm *hongry*. This is by far the hongriest I've ever been."

"You have sick fantasies."

"I don't feel good."

"Why are you so filled with hate?"

"I don't like people touching my clothes."

(Singing) "To dre-e-am the im-*possible* dream, to fight the unfight-able fo-o-e, to . . . uh . . . "

"You are a sick puppy."

"First I was too hot, now I'm too cold."

"Why me, God?"

"Now you sing."

"What are you doing? What are you doing? What are you doing? What are you . . . *oww!*"

"Why do you insist on driving on Mayfield Road?"

"I know I sound like a broken record, but *I forgive you*."

"You're the one filled with hate."

"You are psycho."

6/22/94

The Dogs of Summer

Hollywood insiders are predicting a flat late-summer at the box office with an extremely uncertain crop of pictures being released in July and August. Among the higher-profile—and higher-risk—projects set to be premiered within the next two months:

Symphony of Fear (Starring Arnold Schwarzenegger, Julia Roberts, Meg Ryan, Macaulay Culkin, Gene Hackman, Whoopi Goldberg, John Goodman; directed by Sally Struthers.) Schwarzenegger has to keep conducting a symphony orchestra that will be blown up by Culkin's bomb if Arnold steps off the podium or the music stops; Hackman, Goldberg, and Goodman play the strife-ridden percussion section.

... a '90s updating of the 19th-century Charlotte Bronte novel, set in a summer camp in Maine, with an added twist: hero Rochester is a werewolf.

Buzz: Insiders say this all-star orchestra disaster pic, shockingly given to Struthers to direct, is fairly effective, but preview audience members asked for "bigger dinosaurs," a troubling sign.

Outlook: Could be "crescendo" b.o. with poignant breakout performance by Goodman as a sexually conflicted triangle player.

Jane Eyre (Starring Bridget Fonda, Pauly Shore, Cindy Williams; directed by Vicky Rubinoff.) A '90s updating of the 19th-century Charlotte Bronte novel, set in a summer camp in Maine, with an added twist: hero Rochester is a werewolf battling terrorists who plant bombs in the cabins, set to be detonated by the odor of suntan lotion. Director Rubinoff says, "I insisted on a feminist retelling of the Eyre story, making it very dark, very suggestive; but with plenty of summer fun, like volleyball."

Buzz: Word is that Shore is sensational as the werewolf Rochester in super-hot Beauty-and-the-Beast seduction scenes with Eyre (Fonda).

Outlook: Might do decent b.o. with literary-action-horror crowd.

First a Mountain (Starring Richard Gere, Cindy Crawford, Stream Gere, Jedidiah Gere, the voice of Edgar Buchanan; written, produced, and directed by Richard Gere.) Heavy spiritual flick based on the Donovan song "First There Is a Mountain," with Gere and Crawford as themselves, in endless conversations with Tibetan monks (played by Gere's preschool-aged children Jedidiah and Stream). Gere says, "I opened up the story a bit by driving the monks around in my Lexus convertible, so the audience can enjoy the sights of Malibu as we discuss the path to enlightenment." Highlight: the voice of the late *Petticoat Junction* star Edgar Buchanan uttering Zen proverbs, using edited tape loops from the corny '60s sitcom.

Buzz: Previews have not been encouraging, with a 98 percent walk-out rate after the first 10 minutes, but Gere tells us he's still working on the final edit. Said one preview audience member: "I may never see a movie again."

Outlook: Very shaky. Says one Hollywood wag: "Gere and Crawford could do this baby nude with automatic weapons, and it's still death."

Sing Along with Mitch (With Mitch Miller and the Mitch Miller Singers; directed by Mitch Miller.) Feature-length film version of the popular singalong TV show of the '50s and early '60s. "We will bring the action up to date with newer rock songs young people will enjoy singing along with, such as 'Bad Bad Leroy Brown' and 'Leaving on a Jet Plane,'" says Miller. "But of course we'll also sing 'Lazy Hazy Crazy Days of Summer,' 'Waitin' for the *Robert E. Lee*,' and 'Yellow Rose of Texas' . . . plus a special surprise for our hip-hop friends."

Buzz: Says one industry insider, "I really, really don't see how this can fly."

Outlook: With Miller and most members of his chorus in their 70s and even 80s, it's doubtful the film will reach desirable 26–44 age group demographic—and there haven't been singalong films since the 1930s. Upside: Miller did own stunts.

Knock Three Times on the Ceiling If You Want Me, Twice on the Pipes If the Answer Is No (Starring Tom Selleck, Diana Ross, Halle Berry; directed by Lou Boglio.) Riding on the success of the Tina Turner biopic *What's Love Got to do With It*, Selleck, Ross, and Berry star as Tony Orlando and Dawn in what first-time director and Dawn fan Boglio says is a "hopefully interesting story of a successful vocal trio who scores some hits, bickers a little, and then breaks up."

Buzz: Not too good, as Selleck and Berry completely disassociated themselves from the project during filming, deliberately screwing up their lip-synching to Orlando and Dawn's original recordings. Selleck is also seen rolling his eyes and surreptitiously giving the camera the finger in many scenes. Not encouraging.

Outlook: With unwieldy title and unenthusiastic cast, success of K.T.T.O.T.C.I.Y.W.M.,T.O.T.P.I.T.A.I.N. problematic.

Death of a Salesman

I'm constantly amazed by the account executives here at the office. They call people they *don't know* and quietly and effectively sell them advertising space in our newspaper. I couldn't do it. One of the account executives suggested that editorial and sales people trade jobs for a day. But I don't think I could do it, even for a day.

I was trying to think of how I'd handle making cold sales calls.

ME: Hello, is this the person who makes advertising decisions for the company?

Potential Advertiser (P.A.): Yes, indeed it is.

ME *(slurring nervously)*: I was wonnering if you'd be innerested in advertising in our paper.

P.A.: I'm afraid our budget won't allow for it right now.

ME *(gasping in embarrassment)*: I'm sorry! I'm sorry! *(quickly hanging up)*

Next call:

P.A.: What can I do for you?

ME: You wanna advertise in our paper?

P.A.: What paper is that?

ME: It's . . . uh . . . uh . . . it's called, uh . . . *(quickly hanging up in embarrassment)*

Next call:

ME: Do you wanna put an ad in the paper? I'll sign you up for two weeks.

P.A.: I don't think so.

ME: Why not?

P.A.: I'm no longer in business.

ME: I'll give you half price!

Next call:

ME: Hullo, I was wondering if you wanna put an ad in our paper. It's a good paper.

P.A.: Well, I might be interested.

ME: *Really!?* I mean, really. That's excellent. How much ads are you interested in? Uh, I mean . . .

P.A.: I should tell you I deal exclusively in trade when buying print advertising space.

> I'm constantly amazed by the account executives here at the office. They call people they *don't know* and quietly and effectively sell them advertising space in our newspaper.

ME: What would you want to trade?

P.A.: What I sell to my customers. The very finest in infant bicycle helmets.

ME *(confused)*: You'd give us infant bicycle helmets for an ad?

P.A.: *An* infant bicycle helmet.

ME : Er . . . I don't know if I can do if for just one helmet . . . don't you have any money?

P.A. *(insulted)*: This conversation is terminated. *(hangs up)*

Later. I'd have worked a little on my opening pitch:

ME: Hi, how you doing today!

P.A. *(suspicious)*: Fine, how are you?

ME: Hey, I'm super, thanks! Hey, I was wondering if you'd like to advertise in our paper! I can get you a super deal!

P.A.: I'm sorry, I'd like to, but I can't right now.

ME: Why not?

P.A.: I don't have the money.

ME *(panicked)*: I'll *lend* you the money!

I would, however, have gained some confidence as the day wore on.

ME: Hey, Sarah, how you doing.

P.A.: Fine, okay.

ME: That's fantastic. Sarah, I had a dream last night, and I want to tell you about my dream. It was a dream of your business and ours, walking hand-in-hand down the bright side of the road, together, towards a future of mutual success and prosperity. The vehicle to get us both there, Sarah, is advertising, and, believe me, Sarah, I can get you a fabulous rate. So what do you say, Sarah? May I take you by the hand and lead you down that road? May I?

P.A.: One of your other account executives called me already today.

ME: *Son of a bitch!*

The end of the day:

ME *(answering the phone)*: Hello, may I help you?

P.A.: Hi, I'd like to find out about your advertising rates.

ME: Let me transfer you to an account executive. I just do the listings.

8/3/94

Looking to Feed Somebody

So far it's been an uneventful summer. The biggest thing that happened was that one day at work the zipper on my pants broke, and I had to walk around the office with my fly open. I couldn't just stay at my desk and ride it out, because I'm a go-go executive who needs to move around to supervise others. So I told people to not look down there—which of course is like an engraved invitation to look down there. Humiliate yourself first, that's my motto. Then you'll be part of the *humiliation process*, instead of merely being the brunt of ridicule. This has netted excellent results for me on several occasions.

> I don't think sitting around in a petting zoo in a Cleveland suburb was the career path this goat wanted to take.

The other highlight of my summer, however, was my trip this past weekend to a South Euclid community fair. I went with my wife Barbara, her sister Kathleen, and Kathleen's two children, Megan and Charlie. I'm more comfortable when I'm accompanying a family to these things, as it makes me feel legitimate, instead of like some lone nut loitering by the corn dog booth, smoking non-filtered Pall Malls, and picking tobacco flecks off his tongue while eyeballing other fairgoers.

In any event, we walked through the fair, making our way to the petting zoo, the main attraction. There was a good assortment of animals there, unlike the fair Kathleen told us she went to earlier in the summer that had a petting zoo of a dog and a cat and what might have been a dead fox. This zoo had a chicken, a turkey, a parrot, a cow, a llama, a pig, a donkey, goats, sheep, a lizard, turtles, and a few animals I couldn't identify but that seemed to belong to the yak or alpaca family.

There was a small feed machine—much like a Spanish peanut or M&M machine—from which you could get a handful of generic animal chow for a quarter. I turned the crank, and out cascaded a party mix of grain, seeds, and brown nuggets. I took a handful of this chow and walked around, looking to feed somebody. I saw a disgruntled goat sitting under a tree and tried to feed him/her, but he/she wasn't interested. I don't think sitting around in a petting zoo in a Cleveland suburb was the career path this goat wanted to take. Another goat nearby, though, wasn't so particular about the party mix, and ate it right down. I have now fed goats in two different states, Ohio and New York.

Most of the other animals seemed in pretty good spirits. You can't keep a pig down, and the llama and his unidentifiable buddies in their corral seemed to be in excellent moods. The llama sucked the chow out of my palm with a *gnar, gnar, gnar* sound. I think it's amazing that a llama would eat food out a human's hand, whereas if the situation were reversed a human wouldn't eat out of a llama's hand. Not that llamas have hands, but still, they're walking around in who knows what. If you knew that a llama would wash its hooves—and I'm talking about Lava, or some strong antibacterial soap—then maybe you'd consider it. Or maybe you wouldn't. It's a matter of choice for each individual.

After the petting zoo we stopped off at the crime booth, presented by the South Euclid police. The crime dog McGruff was there, walking around with a paw to his mouth as if he were having gum pain. The booth itself displayed cuffs, billy clubs, pepper spray, and a megaphone used to talk somebody out of a house: "Come on out of there, Glenn!" or "Let's talk, Glenn!" or something of that nature. I wanted to ask the cops if I could do a "Come on out of there, Glenn!" thing on the megaphone but didn't have the nerve.

I did get a crime pencil that said Say No to Drugs, however, which I put in the side pocket of the passenger door of our car. I have that one palpable souvenir, plus my assorted animal memories, to commemorate our day.

8/10/94

Secrets of Swinging Singles

An article in the *Plain Dealer* about the difficulties of being single in a family town like Cleveland made me think back to my own single days and the problems I had in meeting women.

"The sex machine had problems meeting women?" you ask in surprise. Yes. In my 20s and early 30s I wasn't at the level of sophistication I am now. In those days I would go to bars by myself and sit and stare grimly at my beers. This is not exactly catnip to women. On occasion I would laboriously turn in my barstool and drunkenly squint at the women in the place, hoping to catch someone's eye. I never did.

If only I knew then what I know now.

If only I knew then that all people, men and women, respond to personality. Looks aren't all that important if you have personality. I should have taken the hint when the only time I seemed to be successful with women was when I would say things to them like "I'm not wearing any underwear."

> Despite overwhelming evidence to the contrary, I continued to think silence and smoldering looks were the way to go.

I was raised to be a gentleman, so I was loath to say things like "I'm not *wearing* any *under*wear" too often, but really, it all depends on how you say it. I said it brightly: "I'm not wearing any underwear!" When you say it this way you're not some leering, phlegm-hawking creep; you're a happy guy who wants to share good news. You've worked in your sexual subtext, too; you've mentioned "underwear." The word "underwear" gets people excited because, you know, we're talking about scanties and undies and such. That's sex talk. That's the height of titillation.

In those morose single days I didn't know these things. Despite overwhelming evidence to the contrary, I continued to think silence and smoldering looks were the way to go. Maybe that would work for hot studs like Erik Estrada or Randolph Mantooth (this was the '70s), but not for me. When people mistake your smoldering looks for gas or a psychotic episode, you're not getting anywhere.

Another thing I now realize is that I underestimated the power of dancing in this business. I seemed to do all right on those rare occasions when I overcame my fear of humiliating myself on the dance floor and went out there and "shook my booty" or "let my backbone slip" or what have you. I don't really know why dancing is sexually exciting to some people, but I have my theories. One is that you're hopping around and that gets different juices flowing from when you're sitting in a chair. "Are these sexual juices?" you ask. Maybe. That's for me to know and you to find out.

Another theory is that the beat of the music tends to give you "ideas." I'm not saying you can't get "ideas" while sitting in a chair, but the *thunka-thunka-thunka* puts you far more in mind of sex than sitting around watching TV or reading the *PD* Real Estate section. Anyway, that's the power of dancing, and if I were you, I'd get over any anxieties about looking like a geek or falling down on the dance floor because that's where the action is. Baby.

You say, "Beyond dancing, what are good methods to meet people, so I don't spend my autumn years alone in a poorly lit room with a tin of sardines, cracker packets I stole from a cafeteria, an unworking fire detector, and at the mercy of the state? Not that I'm desperate or have a glum view of the future."

Well, if I were "in the market" today, I'd turn on the aforementioned personality—but plenty. If I went to a public place today with the aim of meeting someone, I'd stand against a wall and grin and whistle and snap my fingers. I'd move my feet around and periodically dip. You know when women would begin approaching me? *In about two seconds.* Here is how it would go:

WOMEN: Hey, you look like you're having a good time.

ME *(dipping and grinning):* I'm havin' a decent time, ladies, and how you doin'?

WOMEN: What's your name, anyway?

ME *(pulling out a referee's whistle and blowing it):* Foul! You ladies want me to tell you my name before I get to hear yours. That's a five yard penalty.

WOMEN: I'm Tabitha and this is Brittainy. You've got a million dollar personality, you know that?

It's good I'm not out there in the singles scene today. Talk about having an unfair advantage.

9/14/94

Your Pal the Colon

On Fridays after work some of us here at the office go across the street to the Euclid Tavern to drink a few beers. Occasionally the art director Wendy's friend Ed, a medical student at Case Western Reserve University, joins us, and I take the opportunity to ask him perceptive and penetrating medical questions. After a half-dozen of these sessions with Ed, I feel I am now essentially ready to practice medicine.

What I propose to do here is pose a few common medical questions, then answer them with my newfound knowledge. For the benefit of the common layperson I've simplified some of the information I gleaned from Ed, as we doctors can get pretty technical.

I do not think that discussing medical matters with Ed while I'm drunk affects my credibility, if that's what you're worried about.

What is the purpose of the colon?

Ah, the colon, a subject close to my heart! Well, not literally *close* to my heart—the colon is several inches away from the heart, which is in the center of the body, or, more accurately, the center of the top part of the body. But here's a little secret for you: We doctors really consider it the center. Remember the TV show *Medical Center* with Chad Everett? That's where that comes from.

> You might say fiber transforms the colon into a *discotheque*, encouraging vigorous movement, with your bowel serving as a sidewalk on which security can throw out disco intruders.

In any event, the colon is part of the large intestine, which is connected to the small intestine. These long, curvy fellows do a great deal of work in your body, not the least of which is digesting your food. Did you know that if you pulled out your intestines and stretched them they'd reach 70 feet? Or was that 17 feet . . . I can't remember. I do remember that we talked about intestine-stretching at the Euclid Tavern, and that those gentlemen are plenty long and packed in there tightly for your convenience.

What the intestines do, really, is function as a *food processor*. The small intestine bombards your food with acids and juices that break it down into a liquid, which is then absorbed into the blood. The small intestine then passes to the large intestine the bulky leftovers, all wrapped up "to go," so to speak.

"Wait a minute . . . what about the stomach?" you say agitatedly. "Doesn't the stomach have anything to do with it?" Yes, indeed it does: The stomach is the first stop for that luscious meat loaf and fresh, crisp apple you've just eaten. The loaf and apple spend several hours in the stomach, sliding into the small intestine after they've been worked over by the stomach's digestive juices. *Then* your men the intestines do their work, and the colon's right there pitching in.

Here's a good way to remember what your intestines do: Picture yourself as a large office building. Your small intestine is the building's *security*, which escorts your waste through the halls and down the elevator, then shoves it into the *lobby* of your large intestine, who then throws it onto the *sidewalk* of your bowel. That's why you feel the way you do when your waste is about to be ejected—there's a commotion in the lobby while security is *kicking out* unauthorized personnel.

It's not disgusting. It's beautiful.

How does fiber work, and where do I get some?

Ah, fiber, another major player in our digestive process! This particular question is one of the first I asked Ed. What he told me, I think, is that fiber acts as an irritant to the colon and fluffs up your waste so it can easily be pushed out by the honked-off lower intestine. Contrary to how this sounds, it's beneficial to your body.

You might say fiber transforms the colon into a *discotheque*, encouraging vigorous movement, with your bowel again serving as a sidewalk on which security can throw out disco intruders (your waste). Water is involved too, in a beautiful, natural process.

You can get fiber in such foods as things in boxes that say "high in fiber," graham crackers being a particularly delicious example. I personally use a powdered dietary fiber supplement, which I spoon into a glass of water and drink down. You can find these supplements in the Colon and Anal Needs department of your local pharmacy. Or look for the shelves of stomach soothers Pepto-Bismol or Alka-Seltzer, as these potions are usually situated nearby, the stomach and colon being "kissing cousins," as we in the medical profession say.

10/5/94

Vexing Questions

These questions have been bothering me for several weeks, and in some cases, several years. They're not trivia questions, like the one that kept me tossing and turning in bed the other night when I couldn't remember the name of the actor who played TV's Dobie Gillis. I did remember that the guy had a brother who was also an actor, but all I could come up with was Dean Stockwell. I then came up with the name "Dwayne Stockwell," which sounded completely ridiculous and propelled me out of bed to look it up before I went insane. I discovered it was Dwayne Hickman, whose brother is Darryl Hickman, who I always got confused with Dean Stockwell as both were child actors, which explains why I came up with Dean Stockwell's name in the first place. The whole Hickman-Stockwell affair was Kafkaesque, actually.

Snack war in Pennsylvania Dutch country! It must have been ugly.

The Dwayne Hickman problem was something I could solve through direct action. The following questions are things I can't do anything about.

Why is that Head and Shoulders TV ad with the model and photographer so stupid, and why is it on so much? I hate Tony, the photographer who says "Absolutely!" to the model's simpering "Better than last time, Tony?" referring to an earlier session when she had dandruff and it was showing up in the photo proofs. I hate the way he says "Absolutely!" I hate his hair, which reminds me of the bad-poet, ferret-faced dead *thirtysomething* character Gary's, and I hate him circling her dandruff on the photo proofs with a grease pencil. I hate everything about him.

I hate the model wiggling her eyebrows during the post-dandruff session, too. Would Kate Moss wiggle her eyebrows while modeling? Vendela? Isabella Rossellini? No way. They wouldn't last five minutes in the modeling profession if they wiggled their eyebrows while being photographed! What is she, Groucho Marx? That eyebrow wiggle says, "Look at me, I'm a model, and I don't have dandruff either." That's not even close to being right.

Why do some TV weather forecasters pretend that they're responsible for the weather? Obviously they know they don't control the weather, but they still act genuinely concerned when anchors say things like "You didn't give us a very nice day today, Brad!" Everyone knows it's a foolish charade, yet they go through it anyway. Why bother? What are we, pre-schoolers? Sometimes the forecasters talk about viewers calling the station to complain to them about the weather. Here's what I'd tell people who call in: "What the hell am I supposed to do about it, you simple m-----f-----?" Maybe I'd get fired, but better to die on your feet than live on your knees.

Why are most of the delicious food products that I enjoy unavailable to me or discontinued? Now I can't find Snyder's of Berlin Sourdough Pretzels except for at a few locations. They used to be everywhere, always shelved near the Snyder's of Hanover Sourdough Pretzels, with both companies taking pains to point out that they are unaffiliated with each other. I'd go to the grocery store and get a big kick out of seeing them together, twins that hate each other's guts. I'd think to myself, "There's Snyder's of Berlin and Snyder's of Hanover. I wonder which Snyder I'll go with this time." (I'd go with Berlin, of course. I'd just do the wondering bit as a teaser.) Now Snyder's of Hanover is everywhere, and Snyder's of Berlin is disappearing, leading one to think there was a monumental Snyder's power struggle with Hanover coming out on top. Snack war in Pennsylvania Dutch country! It must have been ugly.

But this goes right along with the other discontinued or unavailable items that I loved, like Patio Frozen Cocktail Tacos (my little buddies, containing their smudge of mystery meat: I don't care what's in the meat, I'll eat it! Bring them back!); Tip-Top bread (roll it up into a ball or fold it and squeeze the peanut butter you slathered on out until it's paper thin, tear the brown crust off and suck on it); and Dan Dee Hard Pretzels (plenty o' salt, crunchy and slightly overbaked; bite the nibs off first). All my favorites, and all gone.

As my brother-in-law Steve once said, speaking on the same subject, "Anything I've ever cared for they've done away with." Amen to that.

10/19/94

The World's Oldest Dad

Seeing all my young nieces and nephews from various sides of the family once again brings to the fore my fears about having children at an advanced age. Let me get one thing out of the way before I go any further: I do realize I would not be the one actually having the baby. I mention this because every time I bring up this anxiety to people they say, "What do you care? You wouldn't be the one having the baby."

I think this kind of remark is the height of insensitivity. Although I would not be the one physically giving birth to the child, I would certainly be involved. When my wife Barbara drives us in the car, for example, I am involved in the motoring process as a passenger, gasping at close calls and giving the finger to other drivers. We're a team. If Barbara said, "I'm going to have a baby now," I wouldn't just raise a hand and say, "I don't want to hear about it. That's not my business." I would say, "Well, Barbara, how may I be of help at this time? Shall I plug in the heating pad?" So enough of the insensitivity already.

> When my wife Barbara drives us in the car, I am involved in the motoring process as a passenger, gasping at close calls and giving the finger to other drivers.

My fears of having a baby at an advanced age also don't include things like 2 A.M. feedings, or being woken up by crying. How is that worse than staring at the bedroom ceiling at 2 A.M., as I often do now? You might as well cart an infant around the room as lie there trying to think of all the actors' names in *Mission: Impossible* or *Room 222*. And I'm certainly not queasy about changing diapers, considering my medical knowledge of the workings of our friend the colon and the entire gastrointestinal system. When you're a scientist like me you have an analytical attitude toward such matters.

No, my fears are focused on the child's developmental years, adolescence and beyond. At the rate I'm going, I'll be in my fifties by the time the child gets in nursery school. I'm looking forward to the nursery school superintendent asking me, "Will you be accompanying your granddaughter to school every day?" And my daughter smacking herself on the forehead and saying, "I *knew* this would happen. This guy's older than Moses."

When my child is in elementary school and bringing home his or her little friends, what will they make of me? "Is *that* your daddy?" they'll say. Their daddies will be working out in the yard in their plaid shirts and jeans, and I'll be lying in front of the TV in my underwear and black socks and slippers. Their daddies will be taking them to Chuck E. Cheese while I'll be watching TV documentaries I've seen a hundred times about the last days of Hitler and the JFK assassination. And I'll attempt to talk my child out of wanting to go to places like Cedar Point or Disney World, selling food as a substitute. "How about some of my great scrambled eggs? Hah? How about some nice tuna salad?"

When my child is in his or her teens and rebelling, I'll be ill equipped to handle it. "I'm walking out, man, I am tired of this *bulls---!*" I'm not sure how I'll respond. As an old guy with eyes glued to the set I'll probably say something like, "Fine, fine, but first look at this. They're closing in on Oswald." The whole thing will make the James Dean-Jim Backus relationship in *Rebel Without a Cause* look like a tea party.

And of course I'll be on Social Security with a child in college. All my daughter's friends will be talking about how I broke my hip helping her move her stuff into the dorm. "He's still in the infirmary," they'll whisper. "They're afraid to move him. She has to take him lime Jell-O every night." I'll be the only father sitting in a chair covered with a wool blanket at commencement.

Grandchildren? That's a good one.

11/2/94

Path of the Grocery People

My wife Barbara and I have a definite route we take once we're inside the grocery store on our weekly trip there. First we go to the fruit, which always seems to be on an outer aisle. There I select my four Red Delicious apples, which I test for crispness by pushing in the skin with my fingernail. If it gives too easily, the apple is mushy and thus rejected. If I have to struggle to break the skin, the apple is crisp enough that if I were wearing dentures, my teeth would come out while biting it. That's the acid test.

From the fruit we walk over to the onions and potatoes—"from the heartland." I particularly admire the large Idaho baking potatoes, vegetables that would wear overalls and drive tractors if they could. They're working vegetables. Bake those babies for an hour at 500, slather on the margarine and salt, and that's it. Add some carrot and celery sticks, and you don't have to apologize to anyone. You'll live to 95 while the tofu and sesame eaters are long in the grave. Too bad, suckers! I ate potatoes while you frittered your lives away on "health."

> Do you know how hard it is to stretch and prod a piece of bread back into shape once it's bent? There's no guarantee it won't tear, either.

We cruise along the dairy case and take a left into the breakfast aisle. Now that I buy ground coffee, I can select among Maxwell House, Chase and Sanborn, Hills Brothers, Chock Full O'Nuts, and 8 O'Clock Coffee. This is the absolute height of adulthood, choosing coffee. Sometimes I pretend Mrs. Olsen, the Folgers woman, is standing with me in the coffee aisle. She'd say in her Swedish accent, "Why not try Folgers? It's mountain grown, you know." And I'd reply, "Listen, Mrs. Olsen, I drank Folgers Crystals for years, but I've got a coffeemaker now, and I'm not going to tie myself down to one brand. So stop hassling me." When she turns away with tears in her eyes, I put my arm around her and say, "I'm sorry. I might end up back in the Folgers camp yet. But I need to 'date around' right now." Eyes glistening, she says, "Ja, ja, but it's mountain grown," and I laugh, "You don't give up, do you, Mrs. O?" and give her an affectionate chuck on the chin. She wasn't really Swedish anyway.

Another favorite section of the grocery store is the bread racks. I always buy Roman Meal bread, which is grainy yet soft. I have to watch the bread like a hawk, however, unless I want it smushed. I place it well away from other items in the cart so it isn't mashed by detergent bottles or bags of sugar. Sometimes, however, if I'm not on top of things, it will be crushed by the other groceries in the trunk of the car while we're taking a curve on the ride home. A few weeks ago this happened, turning a beautiful new loaf into a V-shaped monstrosity. I held it in my arms after I got out of the car, crying, "my boy, my boy." Last week I had to yell to Barbara, "Grab the bread!" before the Roman Meal was crushed against the edge of the moving check-out conveyor. Do you know how hard it is to stretch and prod a piece of bread back into shape once it's bent? There's no guarantee it won't tear, either.

From the bread we like to go to the sauces, which is a touch of exotica for us. We like looking at all the various steak, Worcestershire, and barbecue sauces, and different mustards. These sauces and mustards make you feel British. Nip that sauce round 'ere for me banger, mate. And another stout, Reg. Some of the bigger grocery stores have extensive sauce and gourmet sections, and when I'm surrounded by imported gourmet foods I fantasize. European travel. First class flights on British Airways to London. The finest hotels and restaurants. Whitewashed walls and cobblestone streets. Would you care for some biscuits, sir? Ow, you've got a 'ealthy appetite, if I may say so, sir . . . You speak French like a Parisian, monsieur . . . Hey, can I have a piece of cheese? Mais oui, monsieur. It's great until I open my eyes and see the Seaway ketchup, and then I'm back in the grocery store.

12/14/94

How We Put Out a Newspaper

When people come up to me and ask, "Isn't it difficult to put out a newspaper every single week?" I have to laugh. *Of course* it's difficult. People who aren't in newspapers—"outies," as we in the business call them—have absolutely no idea what goes on here. Whatever you may believe about the journalism business, the reality is far more mundane. Permit me to illustrate.

The process of putting out a weekly begins weeks ahead of time, before the issue "comes out," as we in the business say. Stories are assigned to writers, who are given "due dates" by the editors, which simply indicates the "date" that the story is "due." If a writer has a problem with a story, he or she calls the editor, and says, "Due plus two," which is journalism code for "I'm going to be late." The editor then responds, "Due plus two: copy" which means the writer will never work in this town again.

Once the story comes in, it goes through a process we call "reading it." Reading it involves

> When a mistake, or a "typo," is found, a large bell is rung by the editor, salsa music is piped in over the office loudspeakers, and the other editors run over.

making sure that there are no mistakes or misspelled words in the story. When a mistake, or a "typo," is found, a large bell is rung by the editor. As soon as the bell is sounded, salsa music is piped in over the office loudspeakers, and the other editors run over to the typo-finding editor's desk and begin to dance, like on that Mexican game show featuring the live geese televised Saturday nights on the cable network Telemundo. The editor then has to correct the typo or be penalized 25 points.

(Some editors here have abused the typo bell, ringing it just to start the music and see the other editors dance. Consequently "false alarms" are now penalized 100 points.)

Once the story is read, the editor's name is "checked off" on the folder that contains the article. *Only one editor at a time may read a story.* If it is discovered that two editors are reading the same story concurrently, the story is then discarded, and the writer will never work in this town again. This may seem harsh, but it is for the protection of all.

The story then goes to "production" where it is "laid out." The art director assigns "art," which are simply the photographs used to illustrate the article. (It is always best when the art has something to do with the story.) Once the photographs come into the office, they are given to the managing editor—in this case, me—who laboriously draws an exact replica of the photograph on art paper, which is then used in the finished newspaper. This photograph copying takes many hours, and in some cases, days. Some people inexperienced in the business have asked me, "Why not use the original photograph in the paper instead of copying it?"—a question to which I invariably respond, "Sure, that'd be the 'easy' thing to do."

During production, the editors stand over the production people and help them with suggestions for how to improve the finished product. In the longer articles that we put on the front of the paper—what we in the business call "the cover"—it is usually necessary to place breaks in the story. We call these breaks "puppies and kittens." This comes from the centuries-old practice of putting clip-art drawings of puppies and kittens in long stories not only to provide relief to the reader's eyes after inches of text but to lighten the mood when stories concern murder, war, various molestations, death-dealing natural disasters, etc. When an editor calls for "puppies and kittens," he or she can also mean mood-lightening clip-art drawings of holly, Santa Claus, doughnuts, tots and toddlers, bunnies, and so on and so forth.

Once these processes are completed, the paper is "put to bed." An often-bitter argument that occurs at a newspaper before it is put to bed is over which editor gets to change the issue number and date on the cover. This has forced many a publication, including ours, to hire a functionary to dress up in a dog suit and portray "Ishy, the Issue-Changing Dog," designed expressly to perform that task. When people ask me why we need a person in a dog suit to change the issue number and date, I tell them, "You obviously have never worked at a newspaper."

1/25/95

A Day in the Life

7:01 A.M.—Got up. Dreamed again about missing an entire semester of classes at school, but this time some other guy, an unholy combination of Daniel Day-Lewis and Ted Danson, was involved. There was something about a hippo or a rhino in the schoolyard, too. Why can't I have good, normal American dreams!

7:26 A.M.—Drank my joe and read the paper. Mark Price is out 6–8 weeks. That's just my luck. Maybe a Cleveland team will win a championship when I'm 50 years in my grave. Then I can wave my little pennant in my coffin. What a joke.

7:40 A.M.—Worked out on The Chairman and did my sit ups. I think I'm destroying my back muscles while ostensibly attempting to strengthen them. I'll find out when I bend over one day and *sproing*. Hunchback time.

7:50 A.M.—Took a shower and the soap broke in half as I lathered. This is really the limit.

7:50 A.M.—Took a shower and the soap broke in half as I lathered. This is really the limit.

8:05 A.M.—Had a coughing fit. My coughs are productive, but I don't know what to do with what they produce. I got over my virus in one day, but the mucus remains. Do people still get tuberculosis? What if I have to spend the rest of my life in a sanitarium, covered with a wool blanket and wheeled around by male nurses like in *One Flew Over the Cuckoo's Nest*! Well, maybe that wouldn't be so bad. As long as there's cable.

9–12 A.M.—Worked.

12 noon—Began talking about lunch with L., L., and W. Argued over whether to go to Club Isabella or Club Illusion. Hey! That's two "Club I"s within walking distance. Wrote that down, can use that.

12:15 P.M.—Had a grilled cheese for lunch. I think it went directly to my lungs.

12:16 P.M.—Had another coughing fit.

1–5 P.M.—Worked.

5–5:45 P.M.—Listened to Les Levine sports talk as I walked home, and the old questions kept coming up. Is Bill Belichick a quietly effective Chuck Noll type—or just an inflexible, stubborn martinet? Are we really going to go with Vinny? And what is this with Michael Dean

Perry? First I read he's shocked about being left on the unprotected list, then I read he asked to be put on it! What goes on here, anyway! I was so worked up over these issues I almost got run over crossing North Park.

5:45 P.M.—Got home and checked the message machine. The light was blinking! I pressed play and it was a message for "Dave." Not only was it a wrong number, the guy mumbled and I couldn't understand the message. My luck again.

6:30 P.M.—Prepared dinner. Tonight's menu: peanut butter and jelly sandwich, potato chips, flagon of 2 percent milk. When will I stop eating these childish foods? But God! There's nothing like a sip of cold 2 percent washing down a sweet wad of Jif Creamy, Smucker's strawberry jelly, and Roman Meal bread. Then a crunchy bite of potato chip for the perfect complement . . . who'd have thought peanuts, potatoes, and jelly could melt in your mouth like this? Heaven. And tomorrow night I'll mix up a box of Shurfine macaroni and cheese. What can I say, I love to cook.

6:45 P.M.—More coughing.

7 P.M.—Watched *The Simpsons*. All right! It's the one where Homer leads a strike at the nuclear power plant, and the dentist says to his child patient, "Why do you turn this office into a house of lies?"

8 P.M.—Watched a TV biography of Soupy Sales.

10 P.M.—Read *The Dick Van Dyke Show Book* for a while before going to bed. Why do these show-biz authors use so many exclamation points! This writer also uses dramatic sentences to end chapters, like "The name of the character was Rob Petrie." It reminded me of that other book I read, *The Walter Lantz Story*, about the guy who invented Woody Woodpecker. That author used, "And that character . . . was Oswald the Lucky Rabbit" to dramatically end the chapter. Ah, what do I expect. Tolstoy?

11:45 P.M.—Had a final coughing fit, and drifted off to sleep.

2/1/95

Death of a Garden Celebrity

This year I had a celebrity garden at the National Home and Garden Show at the I-X Center. You have no idea what pressures we garden celebrities face. When the advertising agency promoting the show asked me if I would like to have a celebrity garden I was excited, but as a garden celebrity I had certain duties I felt compelled to carry out.

One was to make an appearance at the garden itself and stand next to my publicity picture and assume the exact same pose as in the photo, as Lloyd Bridges did in *Airplane!* On our way out to the I-X Center last Saturday, however, I told my wife Barbara I was "nervous" about this. I didn't want to appear to be a preening, hoity-toity garden celebrity. I wanted to be a *people's* garden celebrity. Accessible! Down to earth!

"That over there, Bobby, is juniper. They make gin out of that. And over there is sweet woodruff . . . don't *touch* that, that's not a toy."

I envisioned a scenario where I would walk a family through the garden, pointing out pine trees and other things lying on the ground. "That over there, Bobby, is juniper. They make gin out of that. And over there is sweet woodruff . . . don't *touch* that, that's not a toy." I already knew what would be in the garden, so I could name the actual flowers and plants in my fantasies. But as we got closer to the I-X Center I got progressively more anxious. The traffic was heavy on I-71 and all seemed to be headed to the show.

This was our first trip to the I-X Center. That's one big mama, with one big parking lot. In fact, an I-X guy sang to us as we made the endless walk through the parking lot, "This is the way we walk to the main entrance, walk to the main entrance, walk to the main entrance." Barbara wanted to whack him one, but I thought it was funny. The walk to the main entrance was about as long as the walk from, say, the end of the Yellow Brick Road to the Emerald City. But you could hardly expect the world's largest international exposition center to have a parking lot the size of a Rite Aid's.

When we walked in, we saw that the crowd was shockingly big, thousands and thousands of people. The place was as busy as a state fair. We made our way over to the celebrity garden section, and I was trembling as I saw Don Webster's garden, then Carl Reese's, then Wilma Smith's, then Connie Dieken's, then Jack Marschall's. The celebrity photos, placed on easels by the gardens, were large and conspicuous, and presented somewhat in the manner of lobby art for vaudeville or burlesque shows starring Jackie Mason or Morey Amsterdam.

Consequently when I spied mine, I kept several yards away out of embarrassment. I was wearing kind of a ratty shirt in the picture, with a cheap Bic pen I had forgotten to remove sticking out of the pocket. It wasn't a bad picture, and nobody cares, after all, but I just didn't have the nerve to go stand by it.

There was no way I would meet and greet anyone there, as had been my plan, so I decided to go have a beer at one of the temporary bars set up at the show. I considered getting hammered and going back to the garden, but was this really a good idea? That wouldn't present me in the best light, lurching around in the garden, perhaps falling over and, face down on the stepping-stone pathway, groaning, "This is my . . . garden . . . this is . . . my . . . " Then Barbara leaving the facility in a rage without me, and me drunk and standing by my photo, trying to trade on my fame, begging strangers for a ride home. That's total degradation, hardly befitting a garden celebrity.

One beer did help, though, and we went back to the garden to give it a closer look. It was a good-looking garden. I saw it had won a prize. But what do I know? I've never owned a plant, or even a Chia Pet. I'm not at all certain my future as a garden celebrity is assured.

2/22/95

Baywatch: Symbols and Themes

The compact disc placed on my desk last week bore a Post-it note with a simple command: "Eric." No amplification or further instruction necessary. This was my assignment: review the *Baywatch* CD. No argument, no discussion. *Cover it.*

My desk is often the repository for the flotsam of record companies: the Fabio and Barney CDs, soundtracks to unsuccessful, off-brand animated films, Christmas reissues by washed-up acts like the Chipmunks. And now this, a collection of music by the participants in the TV show *Baywatch*.

I don't know much about *Baywatch*. I've only watched a few minutes of it while channel jumping. From what I can tell it's about swimsuit dopes and beach feebs who carry around little hydroplanes or surfboards, and watch over a bay. I suppose when someone's drowning they wait for the perfect wave, surf over, grab them, lash them to their boards and drag them to safety. I also saw a woman topple sideways out of a boat on the show, if that helps your understanding of the premise.

> My wife Barbara yelled angrily from the other room, "What *is* that?" I replied, "The *Baywatch* CD. Do you like it?" She said, in a masterpiece of understatement, "Not really."

The main appeal, however, are the swimsuits. The only other time I watched it, two women in hot swimsuits were heatedly discussing something in a cabana dressing room. They stood several feet apart so the camera could go from one to another, for full body shots. Then one stormed out of the room, which was your drama part.

But the crucial element to *Baywatch*—the straw that stirs the drink, if you will—is its star, David Hasselhoff. On the CD cover, his visage, seemingly all-knowing and set parallel to the sun, looms over the picture of the cast. I sensed a real correlation here to the Jack Lord empire of *Hawaii Five-O*. Mark my words. In 10 years David Hasselhoff will have parlayed this *Baywatch* business into all-encompassing power in the entertainment business, like Wayne Newton.

This is why I've chosen to primarily discuss Hasselhoff's contributions to the CD. His first song, a duet with post-disco "Gloria" yowler Laura Branigan and called "I Believe," begins with him singing "In a mo-ment of cri-sis you have to be-lieve in yourself." His voice is pret-ty much what you'd expect, quavery '70s macho. Branigan then re-sponds, "Though you may be fright-ened you know there is no-bo-dy else." (I'm trying to approximate the beat here.) Hasselhoff: "You're a sur-vi-vor you'll be a he-ro for sure . . ."

(At this point in my audio monitoring of the CD, my wife Barbara yelled angrily from the other room, "What *is* that?" I replied, "The *Baywatch* CD. Do you like it?" She said, in a masterpiece of under-statement, "Not really.")

The next Hasselhoff song is called "Lifeline." The theme to his work began to become apparent with this song: "Hold on tight/I know it's your life in my hands." As is the theme to *Baywatch* itself, Hasselhoff's work deals with rescue. Not just rescue in the water. Rescue in life, and in love.

Out of respect to the Beach Boys, I skipped their contribution, "Summer of Love," moving on to "Ooh La La" by David Hallyday, with its "We're gonna make it, get hotter yet" lyrics and porno flick background music sound. Then, eagerly skipping the rest of the cuts, I went to Hasselhoff's final song, and the climax—the summing up—of the CD itself, "Current of Love."

In "Current of Love" Hasselhoff takes the rescue theme and runs with it. "Like a ship that's tossed out on the ocean/We get caught up swimming in emotions." The set-up. Then: "Keep your eye out, search for the horizon/Lots of struggle, full of compromisin'." Hasselhoff fully links the land/water images with relationships, and rhymes them, too: *ocean, emotions, horizon, compromisin'*.

Finally, the payoff: "Reach out when you're caught in the current of love/You've got to reach out, 'til you're safe on dry land." Hasselhoff, as he does on the show, has grabbed a victim from the crashing waves, lashed her to his board, and dragged her to dry land. But these aren't literally the crashing waves of the bay Hasselhoff watches. They're the waves of emotions, and when you're under them you're—

Oh, the hell with this.

3/22/95

Film Festival Losers

Some of the films that didn't make this year's Cleveland International Film Festival:

The Sheep (Russia; Vladimir Koussetvsky, director): A tale of a simple village shepherd whose flock's interior monologues constitute the bulk of the film's 239-minute running time. The camera follows the animals as they walk through a meadow, focusing on each individual sheep's overdubbed thoughts about life, the new Russia, and their harsh criticism of the shepherd, a symbol of Russia's current leadership. ("Where is he leading us? Does even he know? I think not.") Said one film festival judge: "After you listen to about four sheep, the novelty wears off very, very quickly." Commented another: "If you're gonna have sheep think out loud, you gotta make 'em sound peppier than this."

> Said one film festival judge: "If you're gonna have sheep think out loud, you gotta make 'em sound peppier than this."

Serving Dish (Sweden; Ola Brugman, director): Brugman frames the momentous events of Sweden's Vasa Dynasty (1521–1654) by showing the meticulous hand painting of a huge serving dish, done by a family through several generations. We watch the highly detailed work done by this family of artisans, interrupted on occasion by neighbors rushing into the family's home, relating news about various wars with Denmark and Poland. A judge said that "watching someone paint a dish for two hours is death," and "during those long, long stretches when there was no news, just dish painting, I really wanted to cry."

Disappearances (United States; Ronny Fulmer, director): Feature-length animated film employing trick photography: first you see an object, then you don't. "Fulmer takes a shot of a box, stops the film, moves the box out of the picture, continues filming, and we're supposed to think it disappeared. Then he does it with pop cans, shoes, waste baskets, and other stuff," said a judge. "It's absolutely pathetic."

Bingo, The Bravest Dog in the Whole World (United States; 1958; Andy Warhol, director): An early film by Warhol, starring the very young Lou Reed as a boy whose life is totally wrapped up in his dog Bingo. An extremely conventional drama centering on Reed breaking his ankle in the woods, with Bingo ultimately dragging him to safety and into the arms of his widowed father (Allen Ginsberg), the film was so ridiculed by Warhol's friends and associates that he isolated himself in his apartment for six months. A codicil to Warhol's will dictated that the film not be shown in public until 200 years after his death. A judge said, "This is Warhol's dirty little secret. If this thing ever got out . . . "

Ramona (Australia; Susan Lockland, director): Documentary about a woman who believes she is the anointed messenger of intergalactic creatures and delivers her message of peace to embarrassed onlookers at Sydney and Melbourne city parks. "You sit through 100 minutes of this woman's incomprehensible babbling, and then at the end she says she's just kidding around," said a judge. "No, no, no."

The Brady Bunch Goes to Sex Hell (United States; the artist formerly known as Henry Hole, director): Sexual deconstruction of American icons, the Brady Bunch, wherein the female members of the family wear masks representing their male counterpart, and vice versa: Carol wears a Mike mask; Greg wears a Cindy mask, and so on. The family then takes an automobile trip to "Sex Hell," a fictional town in Indiana where their masks are torn off and they're beaten to death by rodent people. "You'd think this would be good," said a judge. "But it wasn't."

Festival! (Brazil; Juan Leon, director): Director Leon brings us the festivals and carnivals of Rio, focusing on the common people, their colorful costumes, and the exuberant music of Brazil. Using a hand-held camera, Leon strives for immediacy in conveying the fun and color of this special time. "Would someone tell Leon that he can't dance and film at the same time?" complained a judge. "I thought I was gonna throw up."

Lights of the World (Great Britain; Beatrice and Graham Mobley, directors): Documentary on the various shapes of light bulbs the world over. "The Mobleys put together quite an impressive collection of light bulbs," remarked a judge. "Unfortunately, who gives a rat's ass?"

3/29/95

Partying Down with Tots

My wife Barbara and I had a tea party last Saturday night for our nieces and nephew, Jane, Megan, and Charlie. I wasn't nervous, as these are well-behaved tots—but they are tots nonetheless, so you have to watch them like a hawk. And my niece Jane unnerves me when I reproach her for something and she looks at me and says, "What did you say?" I repeat it, and she says again, "*What did you say?*" Jane hears fine at all other times, so I have no choice but to take this as some kind of a threat.

Preparing for their arrival, I put away everything that could be knocked over, scattered, shaken out, or smashed. Barbara put out chips and French onion dip, prompting an argument over whether this was suitable fare for children. I contended that this fell into the hors d'oeuvres category—on the level of pate or brie and crack-

You might as well toss your dip if it's filled with chip breakage from a previous use.

ers—and would ultimately lead to post-parents'-cocktail-party drink draining in the formative years. Not to mention the possibility of French onion dip smeared all over the furniture and chip fragments in the dip container as a result of poor scooping methods. You might as well toss your dip if it's filled with chip breakage from a previous use.

When my sister Emily brought Jane over and Barbara's sister Kathleen arrived with Megan and Charlie I saw these fears were unfounded. The children dipped like normal people and were soon eating hot dogs and drinking their tea (fruit juice), anyway. I argued with Barbara over whether she had cooked the dogs long enough. Does the word *trichinosis* ring a bell? I was assured by Barbara and Kathleen that hot dogs are already "fully cooked," implying that, as with the dip, I was being anal on this matter. Fine, I won't try to help children.

After dinner we watched Jane, Megan, and Charlie play. The only negative of this period was the simultaneous sound of the *Lion King* tape being played and Charlie running the Dustbuster. When you're not used to it, the aural combination of Elton John singing and a hand-held vac vrooming can get under your skin. Charlie also stood by the VCR, staring at it and longing to press the buttons, which I frankly could not permit because of the delicate balance I had worked out between the TV and VCR. You can have all kinds of toys available for kids, and they still go for your Dustbuster and VCR. But I felt the same way in the early '60s about my parents' hi-fi and magnificent Sylvania console TV. These were the height of glamour with their buttons and knobs.

The Lion King video itself was typical Disney, '90s style. Why do some of these lions talk like they read self-help books and watch *Montel Williams*? Aladdin acted like a refugee from a Beverly Hills mall, so this should be no big surprise. Well, you don't get anywhere in this world criticizing Disney.

For contrast I put on a Little Rascals tape. Kids may like Disney, but they like the Little Rascals, too. In the one we watched the gang had a mule-driven taxi service. There's nothing like mule-driven cars or duck-driven boats! In this, a passenger would put a nickel in a slot marked "Radio," and Stymie sang through a funnel into the back seat. The gang drove over to rich kid Dickie's house and pulled him out of his sickbed to give him a ride (Stymie: "This boy's got a lot of dough and craves excitement!"). The tiny Spanky also rode in the taxi, along with a little girl and a monkey who was wearing a wool beret with a ball on top and a nice-looking sweater. I'm sorry, but *that's* entertainment.

When it came time for the children to go, Barbara held Charlie while I pressed his stomach and squeaked with my lips, my lone uncle trick. Some uncles pull coins from behind their ears, but I squeak. Charlie looked at me as I did this with a bemused half-smile. I was reminded of the scene in *Annie Hall* with the child Woody Allen's uncle Joey Nichols saying to him "I'm Joey Nichols! Joey Nichols! If you can't remember think of Joey Five Cents!" then sticking a nickel to his forehead for emphasis, and the young Woody walking away in embarrassment. I just hope Charlie wasn't thinking what Woody was.

4/5/95

Jobs I Lucked Out On

When I get sick of doing this job, it always makes me feel better to think back on the jobs I lucked out on and didn't get.

One was a job at Northwest Orient airlines, which I applied for in the late '70s. I thought not only "Orient" but even "Northwest" sounded glamorous, and I liked being in planes. I applied for a ticket sales job, thinking I could work my way up to being a "flyboy." However, since I wasn't a pilot or navigator, that would obviously translate to becoming a steward.

It dawned on me that if all you do is spend time in planes as a steward you might get tired of it. Twenty years in-flight and I'd become cynical about the whole flying and service experience. At some point I'd probably begin nipping at the tiny airline liquor bottles.

You know people who don't take "no" for an answer? I take "no" for an answer and always have. Most times I walk away relieved.

ME: How about some peanuts? (*Tosses a bag at the passenger.*)

PASSENGER: I'm not sure I want any. (*Handing the bag back.*)

ME: Take 'em or don't take 'em, I don't give a s---.

If passengers complained about the food, I'd snarl, "What are you gonna do, walk out?" While demonstrating emergency exit procedures and how to inflate life jackets, I'd make remarks like, "Yeah, let the charade begin," or "Like this is gonna make any difference." Because of union protection, I wouldn't get fired but would end up riding in the baggage hold along with the cats and dogs in their carriers. That would be that career.

Another job I applied for was at an insurance company, going so far as to take an aptitude test. The test showed I had no aptitude at all, which is good. You know people who don't take "no" for an answer? I take "no" for an answer and always have. Most times I walk away relieved.

If I had gotten the job, I believe that after several years I'd have acquired a bad insurance attitude.

ME (*to phone prospect*): How about some insurance. I got auto, I got home, I got a special on fire.

PROSPECT: I really can't afford it. I just got laid off, I've got car and medical payments and—

ME: Yeah, I know, I know, spare me the song and dance. Cheap bastard. (*Hangs up. To a co-worker*): Hey, Dave, it's buck-a-shot happy hour at the Lion's Den. I'll tell Buttface we're going on a call, and we can shake our booties on over there.

One job I actually held, but only lasted 45 minutes at, was advertising copywriting. My first assignment was to write a brochure for Thistledown race track. After several minutes of staring at the materials I was given, I walked into the boss's office and told him I had to leave. I would have been asked to leave anyway as soon as he saw what I would have come up with.

"If you like horses and gambling your money away, then Thistledown is for you. Thistledown has plenty of horses racing around, and 'you can bet on that.' Bring plenty of money. Maybe you can double or triple it and 'that ain't hay.' Look in the phone book for the address and the phone number if you want more information."

Maybe the boss would have been dumb and given me another chance, and I would have become competent enough at copywriting to stay employed. But it seems to me that after several years I'd just be going through the motions with that, too.

ME (*during client presentation*): Then we show the horse racing with the jockey on top of him, the jockey waves at the camera, we cut to the logo and boom, that's it.

CLIENT: That doesn't seem very imaginative.

ME: No, it doesn't, but I don't feel like working on it anymore.

No, I've got a good job.

4/19/95

Secrets of Fine Writers

Have you seen that TV commercial depicting the "publishing house" Gramercy Press wooing a "writer" over a telescreen? This writer had long, shaggy hair, wore a thick sweater, and spoke in a soft British accent. As a writer in the real world, I'm here to tell you that there's far more to writing than wearing fat sweaters, puffing a pipe, and murmuring like Jeremy Irons or Ralph Fiennes.

But this is typical of the idea people have about writers and writing. The truth is, writing is a cut-throat profession where, if you're any good, you leave dozens of bodies in your wake. And if you follow the so-called "rules of writing," you'll find yourself holding a one-way ticket to Nowheresville, living in a cheap motel with paper bath mats and an air conditioner that doesn't even have a HI-LO setting.

> **Writing is a cut-throat profession where, if you're any good, you leave dozens of bodies in your wake.**

I suppose the notion about writing I find most amusing is "Write what you know." I have several novels-in-progress, and *not one* is about anything I know. For example, one of these novels is a western. Here's the opening paragraph.

Brad Summers looked at his watch. The digital display said 10. The stagecoach bringing his girlfriend Courtney to Dodge City was an hour late. Brad peered down the railroad track. Where were those horses anyway! He decided to go over to the bank machine and take out $500. He'd need it for the Civil War coming up.

Did I live in the Old West? No. Have I done any research on the subject? Certainly not. But you're going to read on, aren't you? That's because you're being carried away on the writer's imagination.

Here's another example, from the medical thriller I'm working on.

Suddenly the kidney jumped out of Tony Lloyd's body and leaped onto the floor of the airplane. With its tiny arms the organ grabbed the leg of Nurse Brittany Rodriguez. "I'll tackle her!" it threatened. The medical personnel froze as the kidney then ran up to the front of the plane and wrested the controls from the pilot.

What do I know about kidneys? Nothing. But I know if a kidney jumped out of a body it's better that it does it on an airplane, where hundreds of people can be put at risk. That's called plotting, and that's called imagination. It's the writer's most important tool.

Another cliché about writing I find laughable is that writers write "every day." I don't know about other people, but I write only when I feel like it. We writers have what is called a "muse." It inspires us to do our work. If your muse isn't around, you're totally wasting your time trying to write. Writing isn't like mowing a lawn or scraping a garage overhang; the words must be carefully harvested out of your inner being, like grapes.

One time I made the mistake of trying to force it. I sat down and summoned forth my muse, which was nowhere to be found. I was uninspired, and my writing showed it. It happened as I was writing my medical thriller. Sans muse, this is what I came up with:

Suddenly the kidney fell on the surgical room floor. Nurse Brittany Rodriguez picked it up and put it back in Tony Lloyd's body. "Thank you," said Tony. "You're very welcome," replied Brittany pleasantly.

There's no greatness in this writing; no suspense, no conflict. There's no airplane! My muse is the one that told me to put the kidney in the air, give it legs and arms, and the ability to threaten the lives of hundreds of innocent passengers. I am but a medium; I accomplish art by channeling this muse onto paper.

Naturally when my muse is inspiring me, I cannot be disturbed. That's why, when my co-workers bother me with trifles like phone calls or asking about lunch, I have to say to them through clenched teeth, "Can't . . . you . . . see . . . I . . . am . . . composing?" On occasion I've had to jump up from my chair, whip off my cape, and cane them about the head and shoulders. However, I hope this article has helped them, and you, gain a small understanding of what it is we writers do.

6/21/95

Is the Cat Dizzy Crazy?

I think the cat Dizzy is mentally ill.

I've been reading the *Globe* mini mag, *How to Talk to Your Cat*, which I picked up for 99¢ at the checkout counter at Heinen's. Some of the stuff in the book I don't buy, like the author's brother teaching his cats "to go potty on the bathroom toilet . . . Now if he could train his cats to FLUSH the toilet after each use, we'd have a truly *purr-fect* situation!"

What if she's enraged by inanimate additions to our home, like, say, a new bookshelf, or groceries?

Now I've always believed the litter box to be an excellent facility for a cat, and I certainly like the fact that I have my own toilet. If you took the author's logic to its extreme, dog owners would end up going to the bathroom on tree lawns. No, I think animals and people should have exclusive—and *separate*—toilet facilities.

Regardless, there are many interesting points in the book to consider. In the section "Mental Health," the author asks "Why does a previously pleasant pet suddenly turn into the devil cat from hell?" This is the core of the problem with Dizzy.

For example, during her morning rubdown Dizzy is at first extremely pleasant. However, after a few minutes she begins to get cranky, then bitterly resentful, and then openly enraged. She gets what the book terms "aggressive ears . . . indicated by a slight rotation. The ears look like the wings of an airplane, ready for flight." Once those ears rotate you know she's ready to commit violence. But why would anyone rotate their ears like airplane wings while they're getting a massage or a rubdown? She's the one that wanted the rubdown in the first place! No one's putting a gun to her head! It doesn't make sense.

One possible answer the book proposes is that the cat may have a medical condition, but Dizzy is healthy as an ox. She saunters around the apartment like royalty, eats the finest in chow, and sleeps like a baby. So it's not that. Another explanation involves territory and dominance. If a new pet or household member is introduced, it may trigger offensive behavior in the cat.

We certainly haven't introduced a new household member or pet, but I'm wondering if Dizzy is so crazy she's perpetually honked off by even brief, temporary additions to our home, like my niece Jane E. Frazier, who on occasion comes to visit and, shrieking, chases Dizzy around the living room. What if she's enraged by inanimate additions, like, say, a new bookshelf, or groceries? What if when she sees a can of bean soup or box of Ritz crackers, she's thinking, "There ain't room enough here for the both of us"? And punishes us later for bringing these things into her home?

Another factor the book doesn't bring up—and which I hope is not involved—is that she may be irritated by my personifying her, which I've done to cats for years. By this I mean I ascribe human characteristics to her in a variety of situations, and often these characteristics aren't flattering. When I say stuff in her voice—which I imagine to be a squeaking Brooklynese, similar to Bugs Bunny—I make her out to be fairly stupid and shallow.

For instance, when I'm watching a video while she's in the room, I say in her voice, "I don't care for this picture, this ain't a wholesome picture. There's no cats in this picture. I wanna see a picture with cats in it." When I do this, I glance over at her, and she's usually giving me a dirty look. She also gives me dirty looks when I'm cussing in her voice, as in "Giddadahere, yuh doity bastard. Shuddup and gimme sometin' to eat, yuh prick yuh. I hate yer guts, yuh lousy schmuck" etc., etc.

I don't know why I imagine Dizzy talks like a Bowery Boy or Joe Pesci in *Goodfellas*, but maybe I shouldn't go on this way around her (which, I should admit, I do all the time). She might be very sensitive. Her behavior might be her way of telling us, "Don't put me down. Don't make me out to be a fool, 'cause I'll tear you up. I'll kill you."

Ah, I'll bet she's just mentally ill.

6/28/95

The Joy of Gloating

The greatest thing about the Indians doing so well is this new, unaccustomed feeling of superiority I have.

Following Cleveland sports has been so discouraging for so long I was surprised that it only took a half-season of baseball for me to feel this way. As I watch the Indians play other teams, I'm filled with a sense of power, but a power tempered with pity and condescension. That's the best part. The Indians are so clearly several cuts above most other teams in the league, I can, for the first time, feel sorry for other teams rather than the Indians (i.e., myself).

> I can't tell you how much more satisfying this is than the usual envy, fear, and hatred I've harbored for other teams during my lifetime.

For example, in several games the Indians were losing in the final inning, then beat their opponents in their last at-bat, which is heartbreaking if you're on the losing end. I find myself sending out sympathetic vibes to the other team: "Now don't you dwell on it. We're winners, you're losers, and that's simply the way of the world." I can't tell you how much more satisfying this is than the usual envy, fear, and hatred I've harbored for other teams during my lifetime. It's like I'm suddenly a wise, just ruler who can afford to be merciful. And that this would profoundly irritate fans of other teams makes it even better.

The only problem is, I have no one to actually lord it over in this matter. My friends are here and feel the same way I do. I don't know any Chicago White Sox fans—fans of the team we've really screwed by being this good—but I enjoy daydreaming about it.

MYSELF, INDIANS FAN: I'm sorry to hear that the Sox aren't doing well this year. Perhaps next year things will go a little more smoothly. I was also sorry to hear they fired your manager because the Indians beat you.

WHITE SOX FAN: The Indians didn't look too good when we swept you in Chicago a few weeks later.

MYSELF (*chuckling indulgently*): Ah, yes, that series—the fellows' minds weren't really on the game, I'm afraid. Let's hope we don't do that in the playoffs, *but you wouldn't know about the playoffs, would you?*

WHITE SOX FAN (*angrily*): We knew about playoffs when the Bulls waxed the Cavaliers on their way to three world championships.

MYSELF: It's a truism that we often take refuge in the past when we see nothing in the present or, for that matter, the future. Perhaps you might enjoy getting involved with neighborhood sports like, say, lacrosse or soccer.

WHITE SOX FAN (*sputters in ineffectual rage, then drops dead*).

My brother lives in New York City but is as big a fan of the Indians as I am, so I can't get on him about the Yankees. (When I once asked him about "your team," the Knicks, he said coldly, "Don't call them my team.") But it's enough to know that there are millions of Yankees fans whom I now have the capacity to annoy.

MYSELF: I'm sorry to hear that the Yankees aren't doing well this year. I'm sure the addition of high-priced drug addicts to your line-up and the shrewdness of George Steinbrenner will vault your team back into contention.

YANKEES FAN: You better hope we don't see you in the playoffs.

MYSELF: I am fearful of that. The Yanks certainly seem to have the capability of beating the Indians between snorts of crack cocaine.

YANKEES FAN: The Yankees beat the Indians plenty in their time.

MYSELF (*chortling hatefully*): Ah, the past. Such a comfortable, and comforting, place to live when the here-and-now is so dismal and depressing.

YANKEES FAN (*sputters in ineffectual rage, then drops dead*).

I suppose sooner or later the other shoe will drop—we are talking Cleveland sports, after all—but in the meantime I'm going live up here in this rare air where I can look down on everyone else. There's really no other good reason to follow sports.

7/26/95

A Poet, But I Know It

Amy Bracken Sparks, an editor here at the newspaper, also happens to be, by all accounts, one of the best poets in this city. You ask, "Does she walk around the office saying things like, 'I know not when/I lost my pen'?" No, and frankly that's a rather childish view of what a poet is. Amy's a little more sophisticated than that.

Enough about her. It may surprise you to know that I write poetry too. I realize that some readers of this column consider me "shallow" and "lite," but since childhood I've often been visited by the poetic muse.

In my youth I mostly wrote and read what we term "pastoral poetry." One of my favorite pastoral poems went like this:

The horns were loose
On the moose.

This is pastoral, obviously, because it's set outside, and it evokes what we poets call a "feeling"; that is, it makes you think about horns being loose on a moose. Why are the horns loose? Do they slip down on the moose's head when he bends to eats grass? Do they rattle when he runs? The poem provides many questions, but few answers. (This poem had special meaning for me, too, during that difficult period in 1987 when I was sure a small antler was growing out of my ear.)

> The poem evokes a particular feeling in me, as my older brother would beat hell out of me after I recited it in his presence many, many times.

Here's another pastoral poem of my youth, one that I wrote myself:

See the birds in the air
Dropping turds everywhere.

Again, the poem evokes a particular feeling in me, as my older brother would beat hell out of me after I recited it in his presence many, many times. It also falls into the category of "naturalism," with its unequivocal identification of bird doo-doo as "turds" (which may sound coarse and vulgar, but precise naming of stuff is important in poetry).

As the years went on my own poetry became more honed and refined. I was able to evoke feelings and actions in just a few words. A recent poem I wrote, entitled "Elevator," demonstrates this:

Up
Down
Up
Down

The words "up down" not only describe what an elevator does, but in the way I've stacked them, form a kind of elevator shaft. It's what we call in the business a "full service poem." Another example is "Bank Machine," which I wrote in a frenzy after using one:

Key in your PIN
Choose Transaction
Press Enter if Correct
Another Transaction?
Please take Card and Receipt

I've shrewdly designed this work to permit the reader to key in whatever amount he or she chooses, making it, too, a full service poem.

Not all poetry, however, has to be full service. The influence of Japanese haiku may be seen in the following work, which I composed after eating an entire stak-pak of Premium Saltines.

Saltines baked salty
Scrape salt with teeth okey-doke
Bite down and swallow

Haiku is traditionally three lines containing five, then seven, then five syllables. This explains the presence of the word "okey-doke" in the second line, which fulfills the seven-syllable rule, though the word itself is not, in the strictest sense, necessary to the meaning of the poem. But then again, isn't eating saltines okey-doke?

There you have the essence of poetry.

8/8/95

Plusses and Minuses of Turning 40

My wife and I drove up to Michigan on my fortieth birthday. As we drove, Barbara asked me how it felt to be 40.

"I don't know," I said. "It's a very strange feeling. Who am I? Where have I been? Where am I going?" These are the kinds of profound questions that came to me as I pondered being 40.

But, as usual, Barbara went on automatic pilot as soon as I began my "Who am I?" riff, which, to be honest, I've gone through many, many times before with her. She said "uh-huh, uh-huh" at the appropriate moments, but she wasn't listening. I think I got the "Who am I?" bit out of some 1972 ABC *Movie of the Week*. My parents warned me then that watching that crap would give me brain damage, and it did.

> **My parents warned me then that watching that crap would give me brain damage, and it did.**

However, turning 40 does give one pause, particularly, again, in the child-rearing arena. Up in Michigan I watched an elderly man in a restaurant stare dully into space while his toddler grandson went bananas around their table, and I thought, "That's it. That's my future." Too arthritic to grab the little booger, and too old to care! And this led to other fantasies, such as the one where I'd lose control of my car—by that time I'd have an old guy car like a Monte Carlo or a Ninety-Eight—while trying to park it at the day care center, and drive right into the building. That's elderly parenting. Tick, tick, tick.

Another troubling aspect to me about turning 40 is my *financial planning*. The problem is I have neither finances nor planning. I have lots of credit card debt and hardly own anything, except for my books and CDs. I do have a fan that makes a loud clacking noise, but I don't think I could get more than three bucks for it. I also have a long-obsolete CED videodisc player, which is broken, and nearly a hundred discs, such as *Golddiggers of 1935*. If I got 50 bucks for the whole shmear I'd feel fortunate. This is not a lot to hang your hat on.

Plus now I'm forced to begin to think about insurance, with my various fears about ending up dead, in a wheelchair, coma, nursing home, plastic bubble, respirator, dialysis machine, insane asylum, drug rehab, Turkish prison, etc. Now that I'm 40 this stuff looms directly on the horizon. I saw an ad on cable the other night offering children life insurance for $1 a month, but I'll bet I'll have to pay more. And I'm not looking forward to finding out how much.

But, on the positive side, as I age I can feel a newfound maturity. I believe I'm getting less selfish and more flexible as time goes on. For example, I bought a plastic goose coffee cup at Kmart last summer, a very handsome item with a dynamic picture of flying Canada geese on it. It holds a lot of coffee, too—it's nearly in the flagon category. When our friends Kirk and Gina came up to Michigan, Kirk tried to take over the goose cup. A couple of years ago, this would have upset me. But this time I decided to make sure I got up in the morning *before* Kirk, so I could get dibs on the goose cup and drink out of it first. This is the hallmark of maturity and grown-up behavior.

Another thing that happened while Kirk and Gina were visiting was that their dog, Zooey, got temporarily lost in the woods. Again, in the old days this would have upset me, but with my new maturity I now realize, Hey, it's *not my dog*. The incident with Zooey fighting three teenaged ducks and their mother might have bothered me too, but now I just walk away. I can't control how dogs and ducks behave, and being 40 I see this.

Even one of my greatest anxieties, bath tubs backing up and toilets overflowing (I have bad dreams about it), came about during our vacation, and I handled it all right. What's worse than filthy water backing up into your home through tubs and toilets? Nothing, in my opinion. But it happened. I would stare at the dirty water in the tub, driving Barbara crazy. "You think staring at it's gonna help?" she cried. But I obsessed about it only for a few hours, whereas a couple of years ago the obsession would have been a full-day affair. I'm getting there.

9/13/95

The Indoors Fall TV Preview

Highlights from the new fall season on TV, including sample dialogue:

Pals (Wednesdays, NBC), also *Buddies* (CBS), *Amigos* (ABC), *Chums* (USA), *Homeys* (Fox) Dariel Hunt, who played a sullen department store clerk in an episode of the smash hit *Friends*, stars in this comedy about a close-knit group of single young professionals struggling, living, and loving together in Chicago.

LIZBETH (Hunt): Aw, I got a date tonight with some guy my mom set me up with. I think he's a gynecologist.

MURIELA (her friend): And this is a bad thing because . . . ?

Howard (Fridays, NBC) Comedy featuring the Seinfeld-ish humor of Howard Liddell, who made four partially successful appearances in East Coast comedy clubs.

HOWARD: If a woman orders soup on a dinner date, you know she's thinking sex. You're getting sex that night.

BEN (his best friend): Conversely, if a woman orders salad, you know she's not thinking sex.

HOWARD: Soup, sex; salad, no sex.

Majority Whip (Tuesdays, Fox) Zany comedy about a Senate majority leader (Ted Nugent) who's into sadomasochism and the efforts of his staff to cover up.

SENATOR HOILES: I've been a naughty, naughty boy today. I should be trussed up like a Christmas goose, gagged with duct tape, and whipped within an inch of my life right on the Capitol steps.

CLAIRE (an aide): I don't think that's such a hot idea, Senator.

Gastrointestinal Center (Tuesdays, NBC) The dramatic inner workings of a gastrointestinal unit of a big city hospital, featuring prominent stars as guest patients each week.

DR. WALKER: We need to scope this colon—*stat!*

GUEST STAR OPRAH WINFREY: You're not going up *there*, with *that!*

DR. WALKER: Hold 'er down, boys!

> **DR. WALKER: We need to scope this colon—stat!**
>
> **GUEST STAR OPRAH WINFREY: You're not going up *there*, with *that!***

Without a Clue (Thursdays, ABC) High school comedy concerning a popular girl who shows her friends and schoolmates that promiscuity doesn't necessarily equate with popularity and vice versa.

BRAD: Let's have a boinkfest, Heather.

HEATHER: As if, pantload.

Mega Bytes (Saturdays, Fox) A gang of computer nerds battle authorities in this comedy.

STEVEN: I've programmed it so that it makes a pooping noise every time he turns on the monitor.

OTHER NERDS: Heh heh! Heh heh! Heh heh!

The Accountants (Wednesdays, CBS) Sizzling drama concerning the torrid relationships within an Indianapolis accounting firm.

ANGELA: Would you mind faxing that financial report over to Powell Liggett and Harper?

TONY: Certainly, when I get a free moment.

Virginia (Sundays, ABC) Comedy featuring the gentle, family-oriented humor of Utah mother of six Virginia Hummell, who made a mildly successful appearance in a Provo comedy club in 1993.

BOBBY (Virginia's 10-year-old son): Mom, what happens in an X-rated movie?

VIRGINIA (*embarrassed*): Nothing that I'm aware of.

New York Expose Confidential (Saturdays, NBC) Hard-hitting, explosive drama set in the offices of a New York City tabloid, featuring realistic glimpses at the inner workings of a newspaper.

MACGUIRE (the editor): I need that photo, and I need it now. Do what you have to do.

BELLAROSA (the photographer): What I want to know is, do I pay for developing the roll myself? If I do, can I just give you the receipt? Or should I give it directly to bookkeeping? What's the time frame on reimbursement on this? And how am I going to get down there?

MACGUIRE: Just *get it done*, Bellarosa!

9/20/95

No More Mr. Nice Guy

On the recent PBS documentary, *Rock & Roll*, punker Johnny Rotten sneered, "Anyone can be *nice*."

This was like a cold slap in my face. I've spent most of my life trying to be nice. If not nice, agreeable. I agree with everyone, all the time. Where has it gotten me? Am I rich? No. Am I famous, like Johnny Rotten? No. I'm the leading citizen of Agreeable Land, the place where nothing happens. Where I get pushed around. Where I don't make any cash.

Well, I'm done being nice and agreeable. From now on I'm going to be a dirty bastard.

I've started being one already, as we speak. Here at the newspaper, my office mate, Lisa, takes sticks of *my* Beemans gum out of *my* top desk drawer, gum I paid for. Guess what? *She ain't gonna do that no more.* I've hidden my Beemans. Yeah! She wants gum, she can go over to Medic like I do and buy it herself. The next time Lisa asks me for gum, I'll point out the window towards Medic and say, "You go on over there, woman. I ain't supplying you with free gum no more." I'm letting the grammar go, too, by the way. From now on I'm talking like a biker. I'm gonna put "at" at the end of every question. Like, "Where's that review at?" or "Where's my fine-point pen at?" Using superfluous prepositions shows you are ready, willing, and able to stomp some booty.

I used to go around this office chatting up my co-workers. Old Mr. Conviviality, spreading his sunshine. Well, I just signed a card for Tom, a sales executive here who's celebrating his 30th birthday, by writing, "In your 30s life becomes progressively more difficult." Is that "convivial" enough for you? Is Tom gonna have a "nice" day after reading this? No. But this is the message of one tough hombre who won't be trifled with. I ain't no simpering daffodil who writes "Happy Birthday! Good luck!" on every card that's handed to me. I'm a rotten nasty sonofabitch and nobody's sweetheart!

I'll tell you what else. Up to now, when publicity people called me on the phone to pitch their events for the listings, I've been a pushover. "Sure, send it along," I'd mewl. "We'll take a look at it." The next time I get a call from someone trying to do this, I'm gonna say, "You got a

> **Well, I'm done being nice and agreeable. From now on I'm going to be a dirty bastard.**

fine chance of getting *that* crap in here." If they complain about this treatment, I'll taunt them: "Come on, crybaby! *Sell it to me!*" Only the strong survive in this world. You go toe-to-toe with me, you snap 'em back at me, and I'll reward you with a listing. This is how the big ones—the listings legends—operate. And it's got nothing to do with being "nice."

The same goes for my other management and executive duties. For example, I always line my own wastebasket. Does Donald Trump line his own wastebasket? No way. Leona Helmsley doesn't take time off from screaming at some chambermaid in one of her hotels to line her wastebasket. Guess who just stopped lining his wastebasket? You got it. From now on, I'm just filling it up *au naturel*. This is a statement. And the statement isn't "This is the wastebasket of a nice guy." It's "This is the wastebasket of a big-time executive with a massive personality who didn't get where he is today by worrying about lining wastebaskets and other niceties."

You don't get remembered for being nice. How many gravestones do you see engraved with the words "He/She was nice"? When I'm gone, people are gonna remember me. I'm the guy who hid the gum, was pessimistic on greeting cards, and challenged listings. My grave will say, "Here lies a real scumbag." And I'll own the cemetery it's in.

Just now I went over to the sales executive Casey and gave him the finger, and he gave me one right back. Well, no one said this was gonna be easy.

10/11/95

Tribe Psychosis

The recent Indians baseball playoff series against the Seattle Mariners induced in me a psychosis I'm not sure I want to experience again.

I waited 30 years to see the Indians in a playoff series, and I discovered that I couldn't handle it. There were several moments during games where I felt as if I'd black out, or pitch forward in death.

There were many such moments during the Indians' last home game. When Albert Belle dropped the fly ball that led to a Mariners run, I felt as if I were hallucinating. My vision sharpened suddenly into high focus, then blurred again as my pupils dilated and shrank in rapid succession, as they do when they witness something . . . unspeakably horrible. My eyeballs also went bananas at other Cleveland sports catastrophes, such as The Michael Jordan Shot and The Earnest Byner Fumble. Fortunately, this one was just a *faux* catastrophe.

> I waited 30 years to see the Indians in a playoff series, and I discovered that I couldn't handle it.

The same sort of thing happened later when Eric Plunk walked two batters with one out and the Indians clinging to a one-run lead. I was thinking, "You . . . they . . . he . . . it . . . ahhh . . . " Weird stuff like that. When Omar Vizquel doubled off the runner to end the inning, I didn't believe it. I was still thinking, "He . . . it . . . they . . . we . . . " It took several minutes before it sunk in that the threat was over.

The worst in that game, however, was the very last out, when Edgar Martinez flied out to deep center field. I watched Kenny Lofton head back towards the fence, then I saw childhood pass before my eyes. Look, there I am riding my pony, Bingo; there I am dropping off a swinging rope into the old reservoir. It wasn't my childhood, it was someone else's, but it was definitely passing before my eyes. That baby looked like extra bases to me for sure. Again, even after Lofton secured the ball I was experiencing these bucolic hallucinations for several minutes.

If the games themselves were stressful, anticipating them was even worse. I drove my wife Barbara crazy on the day after the infamous Jay Buhner home run that beat us in Game 3. We had been at a party the night before where I had been drinking many, many beers while watching the game with a bunch of people. If there are many beers available while I'm watching a playoff game that I'm pretty sure the Indians are going to lose, then I'm going to drink those beers. I'm not proud of this, but that's the plain fact.

So I sat there watching the game, sodden and muttering. We left the party as the game went into the tenth inning. I was determined not to watch anymore. I didn't feel good about the game and didn't want to know what happened, so I could go to bed with some hope. Then Barbara came up to me and said, "Bad news. The Mariners just went up by three." I felt my eyeballs go again and I cried, "Why did you have to tell me that?" She saw the look on my face and rushed away.

Saturday, in the car, I was feeling poorly from the many beers and the loss and filled the air with moans. I actually thought we had a good chance to win that night and perhaps secretly felt that my moaning and crying might give them extra luck. (Many fans believe that their personal moods are directly related to their team's chance of winning.) Barbara said, "Why can't you be a winner? You're so used to being a loser." I looked over at her. She was wincing and rubbing her forehead with her fingers. I was afraid I had given her a series of small strokes with my incessant whining and obsessing over the Indians. I decided to cheer up.

We went to a restaurant for dinner Saturday night, and I drank martinis, which is unusual for me, particularly if I drank the night before. We watched the game in the bar. It was a beautiful game, which we won 7–0. Fueled by vodka, I made suave jokes about the Slider injury to the woman sitting next to me at the bar. "Look, he's got the same look for pain as he does for happiness." She laughed, I laughed, the world laughed, and all was lollipops and rainbows. And I was worried! Little did I know that the next evening I'd be squirming like a dog again.

Up, down, up, down. During the World Series I'm going to take it easy. Uh-huh.

10/25/95

James Bond Indoors

The newest James Bond film, *GoldenEye*, starring Pierce Brosnan, is about to be released, providing yet another opportunity for those of us who grew up with Bond movies to indulge in our 007 fantasies. Unfortunately, as I get older and more painfully aware of my limitations, my illusions are somewhat tempered when it comes to Bond-like scenarios.

For example, if I got into a fight with one of the arch villain Blofeld's henchmen, one punch in the face and I'd go down crying. I might try to grab my opponent's ankle and pull him down, but that's about it. If there were more than one guy, I'd be finished. When I was younger I believed I could take care of four or five guys at once, but now I feel my best fighting strategy is sobbing, curling up into a ball, and threatening lawsuits. I don't think that's very intimidating to SPECTRE agents.

> **If I got into a fight with one of the arch villain Blofeld's henchmen, one punch in the face and I'd go down crying.**

Physically, I just don't have it. I can lift heavy things all right, carry boxes around and such, but one blow from Jaws and that'd be it for me. Straight to the morgue for old Jimmy B! I could be shot, strangled, decapitated, drowned, eaten by piranha, have my crotch laser beamed, all that—no problem. And I'd go quietly.

Say I walk into Blofeld's lair. He's got his white cat on his lap.

BLOFELD: So good to see you again, Mr. Bond. But I'm afraid to say you've become quite a nuisance to us.

INDOORS BOND: Hey, how ya doin'! Is that your cat? I love cats! What's her name? I—(*I'm shot instantly as I approach*).

When I was a kid I dreamed of driving an Aston Martin, 007's ride, with its machine guns, ejector seat, bulletproof shield, and quadruple cams or whatever it was that made it go 160 mph. But it turns out I don't like driving very much, and even if I were forced to, would probably go with our Nissan Sentra. My wife Barbara and I use the Sentra to drive to Marc's and Rini-Rego and places like that. However, the Sentra's got no pick-up and is slower than molasses, and could easily be caught and magnetized by a SPECTRE helicopter. And again, I'd be finished.

I really don't have James Bond's *savoir faire*, either. Of course, Bond's drink is a vodka martini, "shaken, not stirred." I can drink martinis, too, but I ain't cool like Bond when I'm on them. I tend to get sentimental, thinking about favorite sports heroes or my elementary school days. Or I get angry about imagined slights.

INDOORS BOND: Is that bartender ignoring me? Hey! *Hey!* What's he *doing* over there? I GUESS HE'S TOO BUSY TALKING TO HIS FRIENDS OVER THERE TO DO HIS JOB.

PUSSY GALORE: Keep your voice *down*, for God's sake.

Not that I'm always belligerent on drinks. Sometimes I imitate cartoon characters ("I don't think the Ranger's gonna like that, Yogi" or "I'll do the thinnin' around here, Baba Looey"), but that's not very 007-like, either. I've never seen James Bond talk like Huckleberry Hound in any of his movies. He's too busy swapping double entendres with his women co-stars. I, personally, can't think that fast.

TIFFANY CASE: My goodness, James, your pistol is so *thick* and *hard*. I'll bet it's very powerful.

INDOORS BOND: Yeah, but it's noisy. It makes me jump when it goes off.

TIFFANY CASE: James, would you light my cigar? I love *big, long* things that give me pleasure.

INDOORS BOND: I'm sorry, I think I left my Bic lighter on top of my toilet. Maybe I can find a book of matches in somebody's pocket somewhere.

TIFFANY CASE: Let's just go to your room, James. If we can't find your lighter maybe we can find . . . something else . . . *long and hard* . . . to give me pleasure.

INDOORS BOND: What do you mean, like beef sticks? I get charged for any missing food out of that room refrigerator, you know. That stuff's not free, okay? If you're willing to reimburse me I'd—

TIFFANY CASE: Just skip it, pantload.

11/8/95

Sundays Will Never Be the Same

I know the Browns leaving Cleveland is a drag, but instead of cursing the darkness, I've decided to light a few candles.

Sundays used to be Browns days for me, as they were for many others. To be honest about it, though, the past five years have been a lot less fun thanks to a head coach who thought you won games by boring the other team to death, and who seemed to consider fans to be somewhat feebleminded children who knew nothing about football. Hey, in a lot of people's minds the Browns were gone a while ago.

So now, at least for the time being, our fall Sundays are free. There are many places on earth that don't have professional football teams. People in these places have to do *something* on Sundays, right? But . . . what?

Well, for one thing, they can go to the Rock and Roll Hall of Fame. And this is where we have the advantage. *It's right here.* Some have to fly over entire continents to see the Rock Hall.

> **The past five years have been a lot less fun thanks to a head coach who thought you won games by boring the other team to death.**

We can just go down Carnegie or over a bridge, and a right or left turn down East 9th. Twenty minutes! No fancy-schmancy hotel charges! No hoity-toity restaurants! Take a spin around the place, learn all you want about Bobby Darin, and then go on home to a Schmidts' and a nice bowl of bean soup.

Besides, what were the chances of seeing Bob Dylan or Mick Jagger at a Browns game? They're a lot more likely to be at the Rock Hall. And if you see Jagger there, you can go up to him and say, "What can't you get no?" And he'll holler, "Satisfaction!" and high-five you. You can go up to Dylan and bleat, "How does it *fe-e-e-l* . . . to be in the Rock Hall?" I don't think Security will boot you out. Just tell them normally you'd have been at a Browns game. They'll understand.

Another thing I used to do on Sundays, and which I'm going to do again, is visit the art museum. I'm telling you, staring at some of those 17th-century domestic scenes is a lot more interesting than watching the Browns try to score in the red zone. You can imagine yourself in those English houses, clunking around in buckled shoes, wearing knickers and a huge bow around your neck. No Browns on TV? What the hell did *those* people do? Sew, play the harpsichord, paint flowers on bowls, and die at 37—that's about it. Today we're blessed with cable, SportsChannel, lite beer, microwave burritos . . . well, the list goes on and on.

I used to go to Sunday movie matinees all the time, too. I haven't been to a movie since 1993, and I'm missing all kinds of good stuff. I missed Demi Moore in *The Scarlet Letter*, for one. *Free Willy 2*. *Last of the Dogmen*. *Showgirls*. *Operation Dumbo Drop*. Get this: *I have not seen one Sylvester Stallone movie in ten years*. Ten years! No *Judge Dredd*. No *Cliffhanger*. "You're in for a treat," you say. Don't I know it.

On Saturdays my wife Barbara and I go shopping. Now on Sundays my wife Barbara and I can go shopping. I can spend even more time pondering deodorant choices at Marc's. Do I go Sure, or do I go Arrid? Can I afford the killer deodorant Mitchum? I bought Mitchum once several years ago, and I was dry as a bone. I thought to myself, "When my ship comes in, this is the roll-on I'm rolling with." I'm not quite wealthy enough to afford Mitchum yet, but with all this free time I'm looking at maybe I can get involved with a money-making scheme.

Hey! Maybe I can do phone sex on Sundays. I'll put an ad in the paper, and when people call I'll go, "Ooh, ooh. Sex, sex. I'm hot, I'm hot." At $3.50 a minute I can round up to the nearest minute, so even if sex callers just hear me do a few seconds of "Ooh, ooh, I'm hot" in my monotone, and then hang up angrily, I'll still get the $3.50. I probably won't make more than $14 in the whole scheme, but that's $14 I didn't have before.

See? There's lots of possibilities without the Browns.

11/15/95

Cleaning Fashion 1996

Many of you have wondered just exactly what type of outfit I wear while doing chores at home. Though I have never been *specifically* asked this by readers, either in writing or by telephone, I have a strong sense that this subject is being talked about in residences and workplaces throughout the community.

Therefore, I will do my best to give you a sense of a) what I wear; and b) what I do while I wear it. This should supply you a complete picture of how a winning household is maintained—fashionably.

I wear clothing, basically, that gives me total freedom of movement as I perform various tasks and functions around the house. While vacuuming, for example, a certain *joie de vivre* must be attained, and this can only be achieved by wearing shorts and a T-shirt. Pushing the vacuum should be accompanied by a brief step, consisting of a leg and arm thrust out to the side, giving the push a bit of body English. (More pressure is put on the vacuum, enabling it to suck better.) Heavy clothing such as denim jeans, leather vests or jackets, and ornately-buckled boots do not encourage this flinging out of the arm and leg, nor the requisite swiveling of the hip. Underpants may also be a hindrance while vacuuming, though this may be a matter of personal preference.

Underpants may also be a hindrance while vacuuming, though this may be a matter of personal preference.

The same outfit of T-shirt and shorts is required for the dusting process as well. The use of a feather duster necessitates holding out the opposite arm of the dusting arm, with the elbow bent at a 90 degree angle, the tips of the thumb and index finger lightly touching. Again, a heavy top of overcoat or sport jacket and tie prohibits effective application of this flamenco-type expression; and underpants, once more, are not altogether necessary.

For bathroom cleaning, the T-shirt and shorts ensemble is absolutely *de rigueur*. While scrubbing underneath the exterior of the toilet bowl, however, the positioning involved in lying on one's side on the bathroom floor, and the jiggling to and fro to reach the furthest regions of the bowl, may call for the wearing of sturdy undergarments. Underpants, however, are not essential for the action of transferring items *de toilette* from one fixture to another as the former fixture is being cleaned. A brief changing period, then, may be taken when going from the spraying and wiping of the sink and toilet bowl rim to the spraying and wiping of the exterior of the toilet bowl. Again—a matter of personal preference.

As for activities in the kitchen, some sort of thongs or sandals may be worn to avoid stepping barefoot on painful unpleasantries like hard food crumbs from pretzels or crackers, spilled coffee grounds, or similar items. Yet the kitchen is no place for capes, ponchos, or leather, studded pants set off by spurs on boots . . . no, our dependable old friend, the classic T-shirt and short outfit, is the way to go.

Regarding kitchen specifics: the loading of the dishwasher ought be accompanied by the aforementioned flamenco-type posture used in dusting (one arm out, elbow at 90 degrees, tips of fingers touching). Glasses and bowls shall be placed on the top rack; dishes and the occasional larger item on the bottom. *Note: The automatic dishwasher was not devised to be a handy receptacle or "hiding place" for every pot and pan one uses in the preparation of meals.*

The hand washing of pots, pans, and delicate utensils is ideally accompanied by a slight swiveling of the hips, though in not as exaggerated form as employed in vacuuming. While soaping pots and pans and rubbing them clean with a sponge, a low moaning sound may be emitted. Underpants? Your call.

1/17/96

Beating "Winter Blues"

Now that we're in the dog days of January, many of us are filled with the "winter blues," where we feel low and out of sorts. Certainly the cold has something to do with this, but, as Shakespeare said, "The fault, dear Brutus, is not in our stars, but in ourselves, that we are underlings."

Here are a few ways to *not* be underlings this winter.

Acquire a hobby or learn a craft. When the weather outside is "frightenin'," it's good to learn a craft like macramé, needlepoint, woodworking, or model-building to occupy your time indoors. There's nothing like an absorbing hobby to make the hours fly by! My wife Barbara and I spend time together in the winter building furniture, such as bookcases, highboys, bed frames, and cabinets, then applying a thin coat of varnish, and waiting for it to dry. We don't really do this, but you can.

> Some "experts" advise that you lay off the TV and spend time out of doors in the winter. Pish and tosh. You can't go out there; it's cold!

Or undertake some household projects. How about constructing a tax form holder from an old shoebox, and pasting little silver stars all over it? Or keeping track of all the doors in the house by placing numbered sticky notes on them? Or ripping all the labels off your clothes and making a montage to put on your refrigerator? There's no excuse to be bored in the winter when there are so many projects to do!

Watch TV. Some "experts" advise that you lay off the TV and spend time out of doors in the winter. Pish and tosh. You can't go out there; it's cold!

Stay inside and give the tube a workout. There are many excellent programs to choose from, such as *Baywatch Nights* and *Melrose Place*, not to mention superb reruns of *Hogan's Heroes* (remember Colonel Klink saying, "Ho-o-gan!" and clenching his fists when Hogan was getting into mischief at the stalag? You always wondered why Hogan was never taken out and shot!) and *The Big Valley* (remember Nick Barkley constantly leering at Audra Barkley? Hey, Nick! That's supposed to be your sister!). You can buy studded jeans or paste jewelry on Home Shopping Club, see a lion slaughter a gazelle on Discovery, or catch some of today's "now" music combos on MTV. There's really no end to it.

"57 Channels and Nothing On"? Hey, Bruce Springsteen, what TV are *you* watching?

Go shopping—and give yourself the gift of treating yourself right as you do. When Old Man Winter's got you under his icy thumb, it sure feels good to get yourself something special at your favorite store. Maybe you can't "buy" happiness . . . but you can certainly "buy it off"!

This past weekend, for example, my wife Barbara and I went to Randall Park Mall, and we had a wonderful time. We walked around the mall, laughing and singing, enjoying delicious treats along the way. The weather outside might have been crisp and cold, but the corn dog on-a-stick I ate inside the mall was mushy and hot. Squeezing the corn dog off its stick with my fist, I mashed it into a gob of ketchup, and down it went, like a sausage covered in tomato-ey cornmeal. For fun, I then held the de-dogged stick under Barbara's nose, and she almost fainted. I'll never forget it!

We may have been in a Cleveland mall in January, but it felt like we were at a state fair in Kansas in August. And that's super.

1/24/96

Valentine from a Prince

"As the sex machine, you probably don't need to do anything for your wife Barbara on Valentine's Day beyond just existing," you say. "That's enough for any woman fortunate enough to be married to you."

I agree with you in principle. But in the spirit of the day, I do have plans to make Valentine's Day something special for Barbara.

"Are you going to buy her flowers or take her out to dinner?" you ask. Certainly I would . . . if I didn't have any imagination. But our relationship is bigger than flowers, or dinner, or "being nice." Our relationship hinges on our *interaction* with each other.

> Well, there's nothing more stimulating to your mate than *surprise.*

When Barbara and I are together, I give fully of myself. In other words, I share all my opinions, thoughts, views, ideas, notions—everything, basically, that pops into my head. This is the essence of giving fully. You talk, and the other person listens, nods, and says "uh-huh."

But I've always been a giver. I can't help it. If you have the gift of gab, you have to share it. Even though Barbara pretends to have a "headache" from my "constant nattering," or threatens to "crash the car" to shut me up, or says I'm trying to "kill" her, my gift to her will continue and be unending. That's just the way I was brought up: to bring people to their knees with my kindness. This is what I do for Barbara.

And it's not like I don't have any other offers. Just the other day at Rite Aid, I held open the door for an attractive woman, who thanked me and exclaimed, "It's so cold out!" as she rushed inside.

How pathetically obvious can you be? This woman clearly desired me. She craved the Magnificence (as I am pleased to refer to it). But it's the same in every grocery or discount drug store I go to: women gazing at my green overcoat, brown shoes, and those sexy little bleach stains on the bottom of my jeans. Gazing. And desiring.

Do you know what I do? I snap my fingers at them. I'm not one of those packages of Corn King beef franks or cans of Alberto VO5 they see on the shelves. No, this is one item that has already been purchased and cannot be had for any price. As I told Barbara after this incident,

"That woman was flirting with me, but you've won this prize. You're the grand prize winner." And Barbara said, as always, "Uh-huh."

However, this Valentine's Day, I am going to attempt to spice up our relationship. "How do you do this?" you ask. "How do you improve on perfection?"

Well, there's nothing more stimulating to your mate than *surprise*. Some current books on relationships advise you to greet your spouse at the door swaddled in plastic wrap, for example. Certainly I could greet Barbara at the door wrapped in Handi Wrap, or aluminum foil, or even cheesecloth, but I'm not going to do that. And I'm not going to parade around in a thong singing Wayne Newton hits, or draw fat cherubs in red Magic Marker around my belly-button, as other men do. No, I'm going to give her an even greater gift.

What I'm going to do for Barbara on Valentine's Day is this: I'm going to continue to be who I am. I'll stop a moment and let you absorb the full impact of what I've just said.

In other words, the surprise I'm going to give Barbara is no surprise at all. When she comes home from work on Valentine's Day, I'm going to act as if the day were not Valentine's Day, but a regular day with the sex machine, which, after all, is what it is . . . but even more so, as it's Valentine's Day, the day of romance. Do you understand what I'm telling you?

The impact of Valentine's Day on our relationship will be far greater if I act as I always do—which is, as you yourself have said, perfection—with the added benefit of saving considerable money that would otherwise be spent on folderol like flowers and dinner. And this money can be used for more important things, like gassing up the Sentra for our weekend jaunts in the car where I bless Barbara with my continual sharing of thoughts and ideas, and she can say "uh-huh, uh-huh," which I know she enjoys as one of the plusses of life with the sex machine.

So, as you see, while I don't "need" to do anything for Barbara on Valentine's Day, I'm going to. That's just the kind of person I am.

2/14/96

Why I Talk to Food

The other day I was having lunch with Joe ("I heal sick minds") the psychologist, and he caught me talking to my ketchup.

What I mean by this is that Joe saw me take the ketchup bottle in my hand, look it right in the eye, and say, "Buddy, you and I are gonna happen together." Then I whacked it a few times on its side, and eventually its thick tomatoey goodness poured into a glob next to my fries. You've all seen that. You know what a beautiful sight rich, red ketchup next to a pile of fries is. And I was excited.

Now, I realize I shouldn't have done this in front of a mental health professional. Because Joe, in his smoothest, most comforting psychologist's voice, said, "You know, people who read your writing have no idea how f---ed up you really are."

But am I? Am I f---ed up? Who's to say what's f---ed up and what's not?

I happen to talk to some objects. When I'm very hungry, I talk to food. I've talked to burgers, cheese, onions, celery sticks, pickles, baked potatoes, bread, assorted condiments, and many other comestibles. My purpose in doing this is to make a meal fully interactive; to make the things I'm going to eat feel like they're part of a process, which, after all, they are. I'm going to eat them, and they're going into my stomach. We're working together to reach a common goal: to feed me.

> You've seen people communing with their drinks in bars. A lot of them are drunkenly staring into their drinks and thinking, "You're ... the only friend I got."

I do this with drinks as well. On Friday nights at Happy Hour I say to my Miller Lite, "Hello, my good man. I'm going to drink you now" and give it a pat on its head. This isn't so uncommon. You've seen people communing with their drinks in bars. A lot of them are drunkenly staring into their drinks and thinking, "You're . . . the only friend I got." Me, I don't talk to drinks when I'm all sentimental and mawkish. I'm positive and upbeat with drinks.

Before you say, "You're out of your goddam mind," wait a minute. I don't believe these things necessarily *understand* what I'm saying to them. What I'm doing is creating an event, a ritual, like they do in Far Eastern countries. These items I'm about to eat are going to help me.

They're going to make me feel good. Why shouldn't I give them every consideration? Why shouldn't I treat them nice?

How do I know that when I die and go someplace in the afterlife, food items aren't going to be running the show? You say, "Food items aren't going to be running the show." You gonna bet your afterlife on that? Not me. The afterlife is pretty damn eternal to be taking chances. If I get to the afterlife, and discover that say, a big potato is in charge— I admit I'd be surprised by this—I want that potato to say to me, "You treated all my brothers and sisters down there on earth with love and respect before you ate them. Now I will give *you* every consideration you gave them."

That's why I talk to animals, too. Of course I talk to the cat Dizzy, but I talk to dogs, squirrels, pigeons, crows, chipmunks, and everything else I see. Most of the remarks I make to animals are of the teasing variety, but a good-natured teasing. When I see a squirrel digging around on somebody's lawn, I yell, "I'll knock you on your buns!" It's real friendly stuff. They know I'm horsing around with them. They know I'm like Daniel Boone, only without a musket. And both my wife and I yell at squirrels when we see them venture out onto tree lawns and too close to the street, frightening them to scamper back to safety. If the afterlife is ruled by a kingdom of squirrels, I'm going to be covered.

Psychologists don't know everything.

3/13/96

Natural Stuff Explained

I was intrigued by the column "Questions" in a recent *Plain Dealer Sunday Magazine*. The column dealt with questions of science and nature, e.g., if bumblebees sting, how hot are planets, where birds go during blizzards. But how do we know that the guy who writes the column knows what he's talking about, and the so-called "experts" he trots out to answer some of the questions aren't just figments of his imagination?

I'll say it one more time: There's no reason to read some syndicated Q&A column when you can get all the information about the natural world you need right here. And I don't need to bring in "experts." It's all up here (pointing to my head).

> **Why is canned bean soup so thin these days? Why is one side of the pillow cooler than the other? You can get all the information about the natural world you need right here.**

Why are there time changes from one part of the country to another? There's only one reason that times are different in different parts of the U.S. . . . and you spell it with an $. The TV networks have mandated that their shows, in which they've invested millions, be shown five times, in the five time zones, to maximize their advertising income. They'll tell you these time changes have to do with the "revolution" of the "earth," but if you believe that little piece of sci-fi, I've got one very large bridge I'd like to sell you!

What happened to tuna fish? How come it's so flaky now? There's just one reason that tuna, which used to be chunked, is now flaked . . . and it rhymes with "shmollars." Now tuna companies, which used to can the *fillet* (or center) of the fish, now use the butt and shoulder portions. If you want the fillet, you're going to pay 30–40¢ more per can for the privilege. Sorry, Charlie!

Why do they play soft rock in some discount drug stores? Discount drug stores play soft rock favorites like Loggins and Messina's "House at Pooh Corner" and America's "Sister Golden Hair" for much the same reason that soothing music is played in mental health facilities: to mollify people prone to rages while watching sullen cashiers call store managers over to void transactions for customers ahead of them in line; lengthy price checks; express line cheaters, etc.

Why is canned bean soup so thin these days? You can look to one reason that canned bean soup, which used to be thick and rich, is now thin and runny: the bean soup cabal has decreed that the broth be thinned to get more beans into the soup, thanks to their cynical and collusive deal with bean companies. When it comes to the bean industry, you can bet the almighty dollar rules.

Is fake doo-doo and vomit manufactured after real models? Yes, but only after photos of these items. The policy of using photos came into force in 1952, when fake doo-doo and vomit designers walked out in protest at years of being forced to work from real models, placed in front of them in their studios by callous management. The walk-out, the news of which was suppressed by the media *until now*, also spawned the huge underground doo-doo and vomit photography movement.

What really killed off the dinosaurs? There are a lot of smart alecks who contend that dinosaurs died from changing temperatures, toxic gases, even a huge comet slamming into the earth and smushing them. Well . . . *I don't think so*. And who stands to profit from all these wild theories? That's right: our friends the paleontologists.

Why is one side of the pillow cooler than the other? This is easy. Pillows are designed to *absorb* heat, and while we lie in bed, our heads emit more heat than any other part of our bodies. Therefore, the part of the pillow our head is on is much hotter than the opposite side, which compensates for the head-generated heat by cooling down by as much as 36 degrees per second. But as soon as we put our head on the cool side, it warms up! However, I don't think Donald Trump or Bill Gates have this problem. You can get coolness on *both* sides of the pillow . . . *if* you've got what it take$.

Is global warming a myth? Yes, I wouldn't worry about it. It's a big money thing.

3/20/96

The NFL Owner's Manual

Since the Cleveland Browns don't have a new owner yet—or for that matter, a coach, players, or a stadium—please consider me as a candidate for the job. I would like to be an NFL owner. I think it would be a "hoot"—as well as looking awfully good on my resume.

For me to take over ownership of the club, however, there are certain preconditions we need to discuss. I've only got around $1,900 to my name, and this may not be enough to buy the team outright. Enough for a down payment, perhaps, but not to take full financial control immediately.

What I propose is that my taxes be abated. "Which taxes are those?" you ask. Well, any taxes I might accrue now or in the future, to be applied against the purchase price of the team. "What are you talking about?" you ask. Well, I want my taxes abated, that's all. Abated, and then applied. I'm not absolutely positive how this works, but I just want to buy the team and not pay taxes, all right? Is that such a crime?

> I know it's an unusual idea to tax babies, but there's a first time for everything. We're talking about a pro sports franchise here.

I realize that this still might not be enough to cover the possible $300 million-plus cost of the franchise. With this in mind I propose a countywide 17 percent tax on diapers and school lunches, to be taken directly from those who benefit most from these services. Every baby needs diapers and every child needs lunch, right? So we tax the crap out of 'em. I know it's an unusual idea to tax babies, but there's a first time for everything. We're talking about a pro sports franchise here.

The spoonful of sugar to help this medicine go down will be my TV campaign, Grow Up with the Browns, with the genial, elfin character Cleveland Brownie saying to the kids, "If you want football, you're gonna have to pay for it." Maybe Brownie should have some kind of a tax puppet with him. Taxy the Tax Rabbit? It doesn't matter. Kids go for puppets. You can name it whatever you want just as long as it's got big ears.

The proceeds from these taxes will go to a fund that I will name after me. Because I'm a good corporate citizen, I am willing to pay taxes on any income I disburse to myself from this fund, but I do ask that these taxes be abated, too. I'm willing to *pay back* the county for helping me out in my effort to buy the Browns, but only from my estate after my death. In other words, I don't want to pay any taxes until I'm dead. Hey, talk to my lawyer, I don't know how it works.

As to me as owner kicking in any dough to pay for a facility . . . *I don't think so.* You think I want to go to league meetings with all the other owners tittering at me? We've already got the sin and parking taxes in place to build the thing. If that's not enough, you plop a hefty tax on baked goods, cable TV, E-checks, milk, and those little bags of Dan-Dee Bar-B-Que Potato Chips. If this doesn't put us over the top I don't know what will.

I'm not looking for any co-owners, by the way. I'm taking full control. I've been watching assorted numbskull owners run their teams into the ground all around the league for years, and I know exactly what to do. And what *not* to do. I'm *not* going to pay big bucks for some hotshot running back or wide receiver who's only going to end up getting caught sniffing dope with a hooker in some hotel room. I'll pay players $75,000 per annum, tops.

No, I won't get any good players. No, the Browns won't win any football games. But that won't be a problem. With permanent seat licenses, club seats, loges, and $65 bleacher tickets, it's not going to matter.

5/1/96

Indoor Style Tips

This new book I received from HarperCollins, *Instant Style: 500 Professional Tips on Fashion, Beauty and Attitude*, has stuff in it I wouldn't have thought of in a hundred years.

A sampling: "Underwear should match your skin tone, not your clothing color." "Once in a while don't carry an evening bag to a dinner or a party. It's a young look that says: 'I don't have to check my hair or makeup.'"

"It's spring! Wear your old blazer with a short, sarong skirt."

"Pick out new sunglasses to feel instantly chic and today."

"White shoes says you're from 'out of town,' even during the summer."

"When you take a pen out of your purse, it becomes an accessory. It should be carefully chosen."

If you think you're too short, carry a tiny cane—stooping over to walk with it will make you appear taller.

"Don't wear perfume to the gym. It's a place where natural body scent is best." "Self-confidence is not looking at yourself in the mirror when you're in public." Plus there's 492 more.

Although one of the tips in *Instant Style* is, "We think giving unsolicited fashion or beauty advice is inappropriate," I can't let that stop me. And my fashion tips are unisex, unless otherwise indicated.

Scotch-tape a trail of toilet tissue to the bottom of your shoe for a look that says, "I just got back from going to the bathroom."

Wear a navy blue woolen cap, with a ball on top, to a formal dinner or party. It's very Michael Nesmith, and very today.

Bright sky blue pants, a red-striped shirt, and multi-colored athletic shoes will give you the appearance of a circus clown—and nothing makes others happier.

If you're a little heavy in the rear, dye your eyebrows.

If you're a little heavy up top, shave off your eyebrows.

Men: when wearing light-colored slacks, put a little orange food coloring by the crotch. It's a look that says, "My urine is vitamin rich."

T-shirt decorations come and go, but Ziggy and Snoopy are always classic.

If you wear eyeglasses, wrap masking tape around the right temple for a sassy "I won't get my glasses fixed" look. And when you bring out your sunglasses, have tape around the right temple for a devastating combination.

Wide, bright orange belts do have a slimming effect, but not without the big gold buckle!

A quick peek of toilet tissue from the breast pocket of your blouse or shirt says, "I'm ready to go to the bathroom."

If you think you're too short, carry a tiny cane—stooping over to walk with it will make you appear taller.

On your paisley shirt or blouse, with a laundry marker draw little blue woolen caps (with a ball on top) on the fat part of the paisley designs for an instant fashion update.

Always bring a huge plastic bag filled with candy bars and bubble gum to important business meetings—it shows you think young.

Wear a large plastic corncob pipe on a simple silver chain and clasp around your neck; it can be easily removed if others make fun of it.

Wearing a hooded sweatshirt and sunglasses is totally Unabomber, and totally current.

If you want to look like you're shrinking, wear clothes that are at the most eight sizes too large for you. If you wear them any bigger, you simply look ridiculous.

Self-confidence is wearing your underwear around your shoulders like a cape.

Ladies: Attach and loop a long string to an empty tuna fish can, leaving the label on, for a perfect small purse. Remember: Solid White is more Paris than Chunk Light—and Bumble Bee out-chics Star Kist every time.

Stripes, solids, and prints call attention to your ear lobes. If you must wear them, be sure to tape your ear lobes to the sides of your head.

For an instant unique look, put a Tina Turner wig on top of your hooded, sunglassed Unabomber outfit.

5/8/96

Fun in the Office

While in the workplace, it is, of course, vitally important that you perform your duties to your fullest capacity. But it is nearly as important to know when, and how, to "play."

There may be times during your workday when you find yourself with a spare minute or two, and this is the perfect opportunity to take time off for less serious activities. *As long as you are not bothering others,* there is nothing wrong with enjoying a light moment with yourself—or with your co-workers, if they too find themselves in a "lag."

Here are a few ways we here at the newspaper enjoy ourselves in our spare time.

The Time Expansion Game. One of my personal favorite workday games is Time Expansion. In this I talk about a certain subject—say, my choice of shirt that day—to a co-worker, then an hour or so later go back to that co-worker and say, "Remember when we were talking about my shirt? Those were the days, huh?" And I'd pretend to get misty with the recollection, and sing in a quavering voice, "Memories . . . memories . . . " Talk about mindbending fun!

> When I want to take a brief respite from work, I "talk" to myself, answering by moving my fingers in puppet fashion while speaking in a different voice.

Once, on our way to lunch, my co-worker and I had an argument about legalized gambling. After lunch—where the subject had been totally forgotten in the urgent business of eating food—I said to her, "Remember that time we argued about legalized gambling? We were so young then. We were passionate and we cared. Perhaps we cared *too* much." And my co-worker said, "Shut *up*," knowing full well that I had just scored point, game, and match!

Try Time Expansion at your office. You'll have the "time" of your life!

Imagining Happy Hour Themes. On Friday evenings here at the office, several of us head to the bar to drink beers at Happy Hour. To liven up this activity, we think up exciting "themes" for each Happy Hour.

For example, one week we had a "Hootenanny" theme. The next we had a "Rodeo" theme. The next, "Carnival in Rio." In following weeks:

"Under the Serengeti Skies," "The Canals of Venice," "Ski Lodge," "Arrivederci Roma," "Paris Cafe," "North to Alaska," and many others.

These themes are all total fiction. We never follow through on any of them. We just go down to the bar, drink beers, complain about work, and then ooze off our separate ways.

But it sure is a "hoot" to think 'em up!

Finger Puppets. At your desk, an amusing thing to do with your fingers while they're momentarily idle is to pretend you're operating a puppet. When I want to take a brief respite from work, I "talk" to myself, answering by moving my fingers in puppet fashion while speaking in a different voice. I thus have a short but very stimulating conversation with my hand before getting back to work.

ME: What's your name, little fella?

MY FINGERS: I'm Fingers the Puppet. Why don't you quit d---king around and get back to work?

ME: All right, all right! You're one tough little taskmaster, aren't you!

MY FINGERS: Go to hell.

Now there's one conversation you're in complete control of—when you want it to stop, just stop moving your fingers!

Listings Fantasy Land. Another activity I do while at my desk and without urgent business to transact is to type my name into this newspaper's listings file to make myself the star of various concerts, shows, and films.

So, for example, if the Art Museum is showing *A Streetcar Named Desire*, I go into the file where the information has been input and substitute my name for Marlon Brando's:

A Streetcar Named Desire. Vivien Leigh as Blanche DuBois and ERIC BRODER in his stunningly convincing performance as animalistic sex machine Stanley Kowalski in Tennessee Williams' poetic drama. With Kim Hunter and Karl Malden, 1951.

In this manner I've also starred in *Casablanca, High Noon, Malcolm X,* and *The Wizard of Oz*; was the featured artist in the Concert for the Rock and Roll Hall of Fame; and appeared on stage in the lead roles for touring productions of *The Music Man* and *Fiddler on the Roof.*

Of course I only leave my name in for a few seconds, then re-input the correct information. It's fine to enjoy yourself, but not irresponsibly.

6/5/96

Tacos and Aging

I am distressed by the signs of aging I am exhibiting.

My eyes have gone way south. I am one of the few people I know who has to wear glasses over contact lenses. There is no contact lens strong enough to correct my right eye. Maybe NASA could come up with something, but I doubt it.

When I'm not wearing my contact lenses or Coke-bottle glasses, I only see blurs of color. Once when I didn't have my lenses in I mistook a white plastic Heinen's bag for the cat Dizzy. "Dizzy, come here," I said and smacked my lips. But she didn't move. When I went over to try to pet her, I expected her to coyly trot away as she usually does, but she didn't, of course, because it wasn't her. I had to be right on top of the bag before I realized this. I petted it anyway, just to save face.

I also have pains in the worst places. Old guy stuff, in those regions that receive little to no daylight. I've tried to maintain some *savoir faire* about this, but how can you have a cosmopolitan attitude and insouciance about rectal complaints? You can't put a cast on it, like a broken arm. It's not a good conversation piece at parties. Nobody mistakes you for Denzel Washington or Tom Cruise when you're talking about your rectum. There are rectal anecdotes in *Modern Maturity*, not *Spin* or *Details*.

> Once when I didn't have my lenses in I mistook a white plastic Heinen's bag for the cat Dizzy. "Dizzy, come here," I said and smacked my lips. But she didn't move.

You ask, "What about the hair growing in the ears and nostrils?" Absolutely. The nostril hair has to be trimmed once a week, not to mention the eyebrows, which seem to be going crazy too. I not only have tufts growing out of my ear holes, but single hairs growing directly out of my ear lobes, which my wife Barbara tries to pluck while she's driving. "Stop it!" I say, squirming in the passenger seat. "You can't let that stay there," she says. She doesn't want to live with some stooped-over old carpet salesman whose last good year was 1957. That's what ear hair's all about.

My behavior is old guy behavior, too. I have to have things just so. I get upset at bedtime if I don't maintain my ritual of peeling off my shirt and shorts, opening the bedroom door, tossing them into the bedroom, quickly closing the bedroom door so the cat Dizzy won't run in, and making sure to face the bathroom at all times while performing this function. If I have my back to the bathroom it doesn't feel right. I have to be situated correctly and make all the proper movements so I can then enter the bathroom to smoke my three ciggies and freely perform my *toilette*.

Before I go to bed I'm also compelled to check the chains on the front and back doors by tugging down on the chain when it's in its slot, pop the side of the slot with my index finger several times to check its security, tug at the chain again, then turn the knob repeatedly for good measure. Barbara says sneeringly, "Make sure the doors are locked." I also check my alarm clock every night, pressing the "Time Alarm" button *at least 10 times* to ensure it's set at 7 A.M. In Poland they make realistic and depressing art films about stuff like this.

Food is becoming way too important to me. When I was younger I never could understand older people making such a big deal about food. Now all I think about is food and where I'm going to eat. On Saturday nights I like to go out to dinner *at the finest restaurants*, which to me is the height of glamour. I eat steak and drink booze, like Frank Sinatra, and indulge myself in sentimental martini talk. Barbara hates this, calling the Saturday restaurant thing "this obsession you have."

But even normal everyday food is affected by aging. The cocktail taco fiasco is a good example. For years I have been searching for frozen cocktail mini-tacos, a special treat of my childhood. As a full-grown man with my healthy appetite I could eat literally dozens of these cocktail tacos, and would certainly like to. But I can't find them any more.

During a recent trip to the grocery store Barbara spotted a TV dinner in the freezer case that featured mini-tacos. When I saw the box my heart leapt. At long last, here were my babies! But this was some kiddie dinner, with five lousy tacos. Five cocktail tacos is *nothing*. Five cocktail tacos is a complete joke to a full-grown man. And the corn niblets, brownie, and cheese dipping sauce—pure kid stuff—that accompanied them were taking up critical space that should have been used for 20 more tacos. It was heartbreaking.

The hippo in the sombrero on the package seemed to mock me: *Up yours, man. These are children's tacos.*

6/12/96

I Wanna Do TV News

I suppose my real dream has always been to be a local TV news anchor. Can you imagine? What an awesome job that would be.

There are certain things I'd have to change right away. My nose won't fly on TV. It's too round and the nostrils are somewhat obscured, giving the entire unit the appearance of being packed solid. So I might have to whack some of it off. But I'll make sure not to *whack off* too much. Hee hee! Ha ha ha!

(Oh, I almost forgot. Off-color material doesn't make it on TV news. You gotta have dignity if you're an anchor. If you get on TV and start making jokes like that, you're going to have real trouble with the dignity issue.)

I'll have to get a hairpiece, although sometimes my hairline does rally and come charging back. What's the anchor formula? *One inch from hairline to eyebrow.* I can't comb down; I have to get the wig. Who cares, I don't mind wearing a rug. The station pays for that, right? I'm not paying for that.

I also have to rehearse the way I talk. Mumbling and muttering won't cut it on big-city TV news. I mean, MUMBLING AND MUTTERING WON'T CUT IT ON BIG-CITY TV NEWS. Can you picture a news anchor giving a report and having his or her co-anchor say, "What?" You have to enunciate. So I've been rehearsing various common anchor phrases, saying them slowly . . . and . . . clearly.

> I've been practicing eyeball shifts from camera to camera, tapping my pen on the desk, paper-shuffling, eyebrow-raising, thoughtful lip-pursing, and the occasional saucy head-cock.

"Neighbors complained about a bad smell—and what authorities found will shock you."

"We'll be keeping an eye on the situation."

" . . . who showed no emotion as he was sentenced for the brutal beating death." "Uh . . . apparently we're having technical difficulties. We'll get that report to you later in the newscast."

"Jennifer, what's going on over there?"

"Brad, do police think this is an isolated incident?"

"Disturbing news from Berea."

Those are the only lines I've been rehearsing except for the segue into weather, e.g., "Steve, have you got good news in the forecast for us? We could use some," and the segue out, "We'll take it. Thanks, Steve." But I've also been practicing eyeball shifts from camera to camera, tapping my pen on the desk, swiveling to the remote monitor, paper-shuffling, eyebrow-raising, grinning, frowning, thoughtful lip-pursing, nodding, and the occasional saucy head-cock.

I've been working on the pantomime at the end of the broadcast, when the anchors are apparently having a conversation with the sound muted. I've been mouthing stuff in front of the mirror, laughing soundlessly, and repeating words like "rutabaga, rutabaga, artichoke, artichoke, elephant, elephant." I'm not going to get caught with my pants down and say out loud what I'm really thinking. I've heard of instances when the audio was inadvertently left on, and you'd hear the anchor say something indiscreet like, "Viewers are d—kheads. Let's go find some hookers and take drugs." That's a career-ender, and it's not going to happen to me.

But the very, very best part of being an anchor is taping promos. I've set up a table with a stack of notes on it, which I then grab and head out. *This is the anchor on his way to deliver a late-breaking story.* I've worked on my facial expression, with the mouth slightly ajar—I'm out of breath—and my eyes fixed on my goal. *Get to that news desk and inform the people.* The videographer will blur my image to simulate lightning-fast movement. I've tripped and toppled over a few times practicing this move, but in the finished promo no one will suspect that I've fallen down at all.

7/3/96

Ways I'd Rather Not Die

There was a story in the newspaper about a man who, while sitting in a boat, yawned—and a fish jumped from the water into his open mouth. He choked to death.

I find this to be a bummer on two levels. First, I hate eating fish, those slimy, smelly, disgusting things. I see fish lying in ice-chips behind glass at the grocery store, and I say to them, "Here's a news bulletin. You I'm not eating." I walk on by and proceed to the real meat.

For example, I wouldn't want to die wearing shorts at an amusement park on an extremely hot, humid day.

Secondly, this is the worst possible way to eat fish, even if you do like eating fish. You have no control over the process. The fish is dictating to you that you're eating it. It's saying, "So you want to eat fish, you bastard? Here I am." And, as a special added bonus to this wonderful experience, you wind up dead.

I suppose there are worse ways to die, however.

For example, I wouldn't want to die wearing shorts at an amusement park on an extremely hot, humid day. It'd be awful to lurch around, mortally ill, at the amusement park with my shorts climbing up my thighs, the smell of cotton candy and grilled sausages nauseating me, and eventually toppling onto a tattooed biker, who heaves me off in revulsion. Then have to lie in melted, off-brand ice cream until I die, right on the midway.

I don't want to go like Elvis. To be found lying dead next to the toilet, pants around my ankles, wallowing in feces and God knows what else, with all kinds of illicit narcotics in the medicine cabinet. That's not the glamorous final image I want to present. Or what if I'm flirting with an attractive woman at a bar or party and then start choking on my own vomit? You know she's not going to remember my charm and wit; she's only going to remember me choking on my own vomit. People tend to focus on the negative.

I don't want to die dancing, either, because I heard that when people die while dancing their butts continue to swivel minutes after they expire. Tragedy followed by tittering at the discotheque! I also didn't particularly enjoy the way Robert Shaw died in *Jaws*, kicking fruitlessly at a shark's head, then slipping into his mouth and being crunched down on like a pickle. I'd prefer not to be bitten by an alligator, either. Or, in another spin on animal participation, die alone in an efficiency apartment and then have my poodle eat me.

In the book *How We Die* I read about how after one guy died he arched his back and let out an ear-splitting howl. I'll go quietly, if you don't mind. If I have to say something, I'd like it to be somewhat sophisticated and not a bark from hell. Like, "So long, farewell, *auf Wiedersehen*, good-bye" (*The Sound of Music*). Or something flip: "So long, screwy. See you in St. Looey." Or the dignified "Well, it appears that I'm heading for the last round-up, and they're ringing down the final curtain. At this opportunity I'd like to thank all of you, and wish you the very best of luck in your endeavors." Then I'd go.

The best way, though, would be to just have everything stop. Here is my ultimate death scenario:

I'd be fabulously wealthy, mostly from the money given to me by my son, All-Star Cleveland Indians outfielder Eric Broder, Jr., who during my lifetime never gave me any lip, drove me around, and bought me my own loge at Jacobs Field.

One day I'd be home watching a great *Dick Van Dyke Show* episode, eating buttered popcorn, laughing at Rob Petrie . . . then that'd be it. I'd just nod off. No pain, no muss, no fuss, no barking like a dog or honking like a goose. No going to the bathroom!

I'd be grinning and giving the thumbs-up. And they could bury me that way.

7/24/96

Who Will Be My Lady?

People around town have been talking about the full-page personal ad a guy took out in this paper a few weeks back, and with all the talk, he's sure to get a response.

But this made me think about what I would say in a personal ad, were I single and looking. To set aside false modesty, I'm not sure the post office could handle all the replies that would be forthcoming.

Ladies: Dreams Do Come True

Hello, my name is Eric. I don't know yours yet. But I know you're out there somewhere, hiding!

I'm looking for a woman who is part angel, part devil, part pixie, part earth mother, part sporting goods store employee, part accordion-ist, part auto mechanic, part lover. I'm looking for 1/4 angel, 1/8 devil, 1/16 pixie, etc., until I get to the end of my list—and then I want 4/5 lover! If you're a lady who can do fractions, then you should definitely read on.

> I'm looking for a woman who is part angel, part devil, part pixie, part earth mother, part sporting goods store employee, part accordionist, part auto mechanic, part lover.

The woman I am looking for knows what she wants and how to get it. Does she need Prep-aration H or fast-actin' Tinactin? She knows where to go. Does she need Little Debbie cupcakes or Underwood deviled ham? How about frozen haddock or those packages of beef sticks that come doubled-up with cheese? Same answer. She pays cash, and only uses the express line if she has 12 items or less. Or 8 items—whatever the particular store's rules are. It doesn't matter. My lady is flexible.

She's not helpless, yet she's not afraid to be vulnerable either. She laughs easily, but doesn't like to poke at dead possums with a long stick. She likes puppies, whiskers on kittens, raccoons, ducks, Canada geese, squid, leeches, and won't hesitate to pick up a passing snail to help it to its destination. She's not allergic to bees and can't stand people who are. She's as comfortable in a bug- and rodent-infested outhouse as in a Beverly Hills mansion. That's my lady.

And what does my perfect mate look like? That's really not impor-tant to me. I look past the physical because I'm deeper than most men.

However, at the bare minimum, my lady must weigh between 108 and 108.6 lbs., have shoulder-length strawberry-blonde hair with raven highlights and a spit curl in front, a pert button nose veering just a half-millimeter to the left, fingernails not to exceed 1.45" in length, a waist not to exceed 28" in circumference, two ears of no more than 1.9" in height (and ladies—please make sure they match!), and an inny navel. Beyond these few requirements, I'm very open.

But enough about you. What about me? What can you expect if you answer this ad and we click?

You'll get a man who simply loves life. If do we end up together—and permanently—you'll see that from the moment I get up I embrace the day like no man you've ever known.

And milady will know it when her gentleman greets the day. All that loud phlegm-hawking and sinus-clearing you're hearing? Those sensual *aaaaacccch, aaaaacccch* sounds? Those are for you, my darling. I'm clearing my decks for action . . . for you! Hear those noises in the bathroom? That's for you, too. I'm getting rid of all the fluids and solids of the previous day so I can be with you . . . all cleaned out . . . *right now!*

That's not the only kind of music you'll hear in the morning. Do you like Alvin and the Chipmunks? Me too. The theme song from *Hawaii Five-O*? You got it. I'll play these for you every morning on my stereo, and we can face the day together with a smile on our lips and a song in our hearts. Love Count Chocula with a prune juice chaser? That's funny—so do I!

I'm a guy who loves to come home from work, lie down, and eat non-stop until it's time for bed. Do you admire a man who drinks lots of beer? What a coincidence! Do you dig a guy who enjoys making prank phone calls late at night? How about a guy who likes to deliver high-pitched squeals while you're driving him around in the car? I *do believe* you've found him!

Well, that's just a "taste" of me, and maybe it's too much for you to absorb right now. But if what you've read so far turns you on, why not answer this ad? Because that guy in those disturbing dreams you've been having . . . could very well be me.

8/14/96

The Indoors Academy Exam

Welcome to the pre-admission examination to the Indoors Academy. This examination tests your aptitude as an Indoors person, and assists the administration in determining if you will be admitted as a student.*

The Academy, which empowers young people to learn the ways of the Indoors through intensive instruction and a hefty tuition, is a totally non-accredited institution.

(TRUE/FALSE): Eating expired blue cheese dressing is tantamount to putting a loaded gun to your head.

An air conditioner is installed with the aide of:
A. Scotch tape
B. Crepe paper
C. Ribbons and bows
D. Duct tape

A plop of ketchup on your T-shirt front can be treated by:
A. Immediately blotting cold water on the stain
B. Blotting a mixture of lemon juice, vinegar, and Windex on the stain
C. Rubbing mustard on the stain
D. It cannot be treated or removed

What would happen if you accidentally dropped the hot dog you were eating down the toilet, then flushed?
A. The toilet would overflow
B. The bun would puff out and clog the pipe
C. Wiener particles would wash back
D. Nothing

Hangovers can be prevented by:
A. Taking a dose of Pepto-Bismol and two ibuprofen before retiring
B. Praying after your 12th beer
C. Remembering that you had a really good time

The trend toward eating low-fat foods is:
A. A fad that will be discredited in due course
B. Un-American
C. Perpetuated and financed by the low-fat cartel

Cleaning lint from the dryer lint screen should be done :
A. Humming and whistling, using the fabric softener sheet from the load
B. Silently, with a moistened fingertip
Name the saltine that, once the benchmark of quality and consistency, has clearly seen better days:
A. Zesta
B. Premium
C. Krispy
Betty has two Little Debbie chocolate cupcakes. Dan has one Hostess chocolate cupcake. Which of the two are in the better position for negotiation?
Your colon can be your:
A. Passport to riches
B. Ticket to popularity
C. Best friend if you treat it with respect and keep it clean and tidy
(TRUE/FALSE): Eating expired blue cheese dressing is tantamount to putting a loaded gun to your head.
Say you have a cat. Who scoops the litter box and disposes of the turds?
A. You
B. Someone other than you
Which vegetable will nutritionally offset potato chips when they accompany a Velveeta cheeseburger?
A. French fries
B. Carrot sticks
C. Kosher dills
D. Onion rings
Circle the funnier duck:
A. Donald Duck
B. Daffy Duck
ESSAY QUESTION:
Briefly compare and contrast the relative qualities of the discount drug stores Revco, Rite-Aid, and Marc's in terms of value, check-out, mood music, ambiance, etc.
    * Students with cash up front need not take this exam.

8/21/96

How to Get Yourself a Date

There are many fine strategies to help you find a date in Dr. Judy Kuriansky's book *The Complete Idiot's Guide to Dating*. However, although Dr. Judy is a nationally syndicated radio sex therapist and a clinical psychologist, I do consider some of her ideas to be, shall we say, rather unsophisticated.

For example, her chapter on opening lines contains a section entitled Charming Romantic Openers, which include such suggested lines as "Are you okay? That fall from heaven must have hurt," "Are your feet tired? You've been running through my mind all night," and "Quick, gimme a shot of insulin because you look so sweet I'm going into sugar shock."

Attractive strangers love to hear about illnesses kept under control with medication.

What are we, in first grade here? That heaven-and-insulin crap will get you nothing but a horse laugh and a quick trip to the showers. What you need to do is present yourself as a grown-up—with grown-up emotions, and grown-up *capabilities*, if you catch my meaning. Your opening lines have to show that you've been around . . . which implies that you've been around the bedroom, too. *Rrowf! Rrowf!* Hah? You see where I'm going with this? Hee hee!

For instance, the line "I have ulcerative colitis, but my rectal bleeding is kept under control with medication" is a fabulous icebreaker. Attractive strangers love to hear about illnesses kept under control with medication. Most people will reply, "Oh, really? What kind of medication?" and it's off to the races. *Then* you got heaven, my friend.

Other opening lines to show you're no first grader:

"I may work in a slaughterhouse, but baby, you're killin' *me*."

"I had to urinate a few minutes ago, but the sight of you stopped it in its tracks."

"Me . . . drunk."

"My pee-pee is tingling, pulsating, pounding, and dripping as well, if you don't mind me saying so."

"Listen, I can tell a person who wouldn't give me rabies if we had sex, and, believe me, you're one of them."

In Dr. Judy's flirting chapter, too, the section Nonverbal Ways to

Tell Him You're Interested includes such advice as " . . . lick your lips, trace the outline of a scoop-neck top, or run your hand down your leg."

That might have worked for Farrah Fawcett in bad '70s TV, but this is real life, Dr. Judy. Again—can we be grown-up here?

What you have to do is stick out your stomach, let your arms hang by your sides, and swivel those hips. And keep 'em swiveling. Then bare that tummy and finger that belly-button, making squeaking noises with your lips. Stick out that tongue and move it around. You're sending a message here, and you want it to come in loud and clear. If you don't get removed by Security then you will get a date.

Dr. Judy also espouses self-love as a necessary ingredient in attracting others. "Look in the mirror and say, 'I love you,' or 'I've got something to make you happy today,'" she advises.

First Dr. Judy pitches these ineffective, kid-stuff strategies to meet people—then she advocates something which can easily get out of hand. During my own dating years, many was the time I had looked in the mirror before going out and said, "I love you." But, inevitably, this led to "I love you, oh my darling, oh, darling, I love you, oh, dearest, sweetest darling" which *then* led to a lot of mirror kissing and other nonsense . . . to the point where soon I found I didn't need to go out at all! And I was right back where I started! These days all I say to the mirror is a neutral "how you doin'?" I just don't have the strength.

Now that my dating years are through, all I can do is pass on these tips. I'd be curious to hear from the fellas, though. In the days when I was trying to meet women, I didn't have a lot of luck getting dates with them because unfortunately most seemed to have leprosy, cancer, or other terminal diseases, they always had to wash their hair, or had boyfriends who were hit men. That stuff still going on in the singles scene?

9/11/96

The Sound of Mucus

Being a stoic, I don't generally like to talk about the way I feel when I'm sick. I suffer in silence, only fully describing my symptoms to others when they say hello or look at me.

However, the details of my recent bout with the bug that's been going around may be of value to the medical and lay community. I should add that I'm glad to talk about the course of my illness, and even answer any questions that you might have later—*as long as sharing my experiences will help others*. Readers looking for "cheap thrills" from gross descriptions of raging mucus are advised to look elsewhere.

With my own extensive medical training (Two years ago I drank beers with a medical student named Ed at the Euclid Tavern) it was obvious to me this past week that my raw, sore throat and aching joints portended trouble. Despite this, I went to work. We have a newspaper to put out, and the news doesn't come to a halt just because a person doesn't "feel good" or has a "sore throat." Not that I would find any pity in this office anyway. When I told a co-worker that my illness might well be "the last roundup," she replied, "Just stay out of my area," selfishly not wanting to be infected herself. I merely walked away in a dignified manner. Even sick as a pig, I retain my dignity.

That night I couldn't sleep, tossing and turning in a kind of delirium. I worried about surreal matters that, at the time, seemed extremely real. I worried about germs hiding in the bedroom walls, and I was determined that the next walls I "bought" would be germ-free. I agonized over what I was going to say to the clerk at the wall store. (The last time I was sick, I fretted endlessly about Jason Alexander's ability to perform his role in the recent TV version of *Bye Bye Birdie*, which I had watched that evening.) I woke up in total confusion, with my tongue coated and hanging out.

Not only that, there was big trouble when I tried to sing the first line of Leo Sayer's "You Make Me Feel Like Dancing" in my morning shower. The line, "You got a cute way of walking," came out in an unearthly screech, like the tires of Hell burning rubber. Out of the cor-

> **When I told a co-worker that my illness might well be "the last round-up," she replied, "Just stay out of my area."**

ner of my eye I saw the cat Dizzy rocket off in fright. She had nothing on me in that department. What if I had attempted to sing a Bee Gees song such as "Night Fever" or, God forbid, "You Should be Dancing"? My vocal chords would have jumped right out of my mouth, and I'd be lying dead on the floor. That's how bad it was. My ability to simulate '70s dance music was completely destroyed by this illness.

"But what about congestion," you say. "Tell us about the congestion." Oh, I had congestion—but plenty. I bought all kinds of cough and throat potions to tame that gentleman. One night I took an expectorant to loosen my mucus. It loosened it, all right. I coughed so hard in bed I threw my back out. I woke up coughing, bent, and dangling my paws in front of me like an injured dog. Every time I coughed I had to grab something to keep my back stiff so I wouldn't end up permanently shaped like an S.

That was a picnic compared to the next day. My back was feeling better, but in the early afternoon my eyes started to fill with mucus. This was a new one on me. I'd never had gobs of mucus covering my eyeballs before. It was like trying to see through milk, or cheesecloth. When my wife Barbara and I performed our usual Saturday night routine of going to a restaurant, I kind of enjoyed the novelty of not being able to see anything clearly. I pretended I was eating in an underwater restaurant. Dinner in Atlantis! I'm not sure Barbara enjoyed it, though, seeing strings of mucus slide around in my eyes and watching them drop off into my lap. I'm not convinced that's a big turn-on.

As we left, we ran into a friend who was eating with a couple of nationally known writers and we stopped to meet them. It's great to meet famous writers you've admired with mucus cascading across your eyes! To cover my embarrassment, I said to them, "I got mucus in my eyes." I didn't want them to think I was a lunatic or that my eyes normally looked like that.

That night as I slept the mucus hardened in my eyes like cement, and in the morning I had to chip it out of my eyelashes. But it didn't return, and my other symptoms finally eased up as well.

By the way, most of the people in our office had this bug, but no one suffered as much as me. As I said, I don't really like talking about it.

10/16/96

Blowing the Lid off Squirrels

Why doesn't anybody ever talk about squirrels? You never read anything about them. They're never on TV. You see squirrels every day, in both their dead and alive formats. So what's the big cover-up here?

Don't get me wrong. Not all my waking moments are consumed with thoughts of squirrels. But unlike many of you, I do have *some* thoughts of squirrels. They're not as invisible to me as they seem to be to you. They're *there*. How can you argue with that?

Every day I walk home from work, along busy Coventry Road. I see so many goddam squirrels . . . I can't even tell you. I see rear views of them digging in the ground, their tails sticking up in the air; front views of them on their hind legs, staring straight ahead; I see them holding nuts in their hands, cracking them with their teeth; I see them scrambling up trees and across streets. I don't think there's a squirrel activity I've missed seeing, except maybe for when they're being sexually intimate, or asleep.

> **I see far too many dead squirrels on the side of the road. How can animals so famous for their nervousness be so careless?**

But the most truly amazing thing to me about squirrels is that they all look exactly alike. What other rodent can make that claim—or for that matter, what other mammal? I'm not saying some aren't fatter than others, or that there may not be slight differences in tail thickness from one squirrel to the next. What I am saying is that in all my experience I have never seen animals who looked so much alike in terms of size, coloring, facial expression, or attitude.

Say as an experiment you line up six squirrels and give them names, e.g., Gary, Todd, Jane, Tiffany, Brittany, Alan. Then mix them up. Would you be able to tell Alan from Jane, Tiffany from Todd? No way. That's your ultimate tip-off that *there's no discernible difference from one squirrel to the next.* It's unfathomable!

Perhaps this is why nobody seems to care that there are so many dead ones lying in the streets. *Aah, what's one squirrel more or less. They're all the same. Just road pizza.*

Well, I care. As I walk I see squirrels rooting around on tree lawns, mere inches away from Coventry Road. I clap my hands to frighten them off, though I'm always afraid that my clapping might propel them right into the path of a car. But they always seem to run away from the street and up a tree. In my small way, this is how I assist them in my role as a pedestrian.

I see far too many dead squirrels on the side of the road. Some are pristine in death, looking they're napping or taking five; some are smushed big-time with their guts hanging out; some are flatter than a compact disc. How can animals so famous for their nervousness be so careless? Nobody wants to kill them. My friend Rick Montanari, who writes internationally published bloody thriller novels, told me he's upset when he hits them. "When I see one run in front of the car, I do my best to avoid him. But then when I look in the rear-view mirror I see him breakdancing in the middle of the street. Why can't they just stay on the curb?"

When my wife Barbara and I drive, we keep an eagle eye out for squirrels at risk, honking to warn them off. If, for example, we see a squirrel just lounging in the middle of the street, Barbara exclaims, "Look at this guy!" rolls down the window and shouts, "Excuse me!" and that gets him moving.

But usually we honk at squirrels who are racing across the street a good distance in front of us, as an admonition against future foolishness. To make this more entertaining I take on the role of the squirrels replying to our honks. I imagine the squirrels saying in a squeaky, insolent manner such things as "Shut up!" or "Mind your own business!" or "I made it across." Sometimes I'll pretend to be an arrogantly reckless squirrel, saying, "I know what I'm doing, I've been crossing streets all my life, I happen to have a sixth sense about these things, I don't need you to—" then SPLAT. That's a little scenario I've worked out in light of all the carnage I've seen.

I realize this sort of thing might cause you to consider my wife and me as potential poster children for the Get A Life foundation. We happen to like squirrels, that's all.

10/30/96

If You Had to Read This Column . . .

My nomination for the most inspiring new book of the year is *If 2 (500 New Questions for the Game of Life)*. Not only is it inspiring for the thought it provokes, but for the fact that people could put together such an E-Z concept and make money on it.

This little book consists entirely of such one-line questions as: If you had to describe the most memorable night of your life, what would you say? If you had to pick the worst driver you know, who would you pick? If you had to name the all-time best song, which would you pick? If you had to eliminate one emotion in your life, which would it be? If you had to name your greatest accomplishment in life, what would you say it was? and so on.

> **"If you were to be killed by an animal, what kind would it be?" A Tyrannosaurus, because then there wouldn't be any question about my manhood.**

I'll answer some of these questions from the book, and you see if your answers correspond with mine. They might not, but don't let that concern you. These are all purely personal responses.

If you were to be killed by an animal, what kind would it be?

A Tyrannosaurus, because then there wouldn't be any question about my manhood, as there would be if I were killed by a puppy or an otter.

If you could free yourself from one burden in your life, what would it be?

Paying taxes! Does anybody realize how much of a chunk of your money taxes take? Hell-lo!

If you were to eliminate one thing other people's children do, what would it be?

Jumping up to try to shake my hand. Hey, don't even bother, kid.

If you could change one thing about your typical day, what would it be?

Buttoning my shirt. You gotta move your fingers around, push the button through . . . and then you have to start all over on the next one! What a pain in the ass.

If you were to describe your favorite sexual fantasy, what would it be?

Well, I'd be in a nursing home pretending to be an old man, and a beautiful therapist would come in my room, and I'd tell her I'm really a young man pretending to be old, and she'd get real excited, and we'd get it on. Then we'd watch my '95 Indians' video, "Wahoo! What a Finish."

If you had the gift of magic for one day, what would you do?

I'd make everybody naked.

If you could have one television sitcom set as your real home, what would it be?

The Dick Van Dyke Show's. That bar separating the kitchen and the dining room is boss beyond belief. And Richie's room is a good distance from mine. Well, maybe Richie wouldn't even be around.

If you had to name a time when you helped a stranger the most, when was it?

Just last week in Revco, when some guy asked me where the facial tissues were. I jerked my head to the right and said, "Over there." It made me feel super the rest of the day!

If you could live in a past era just so you could wear the clothes in fashion at the time, when would it be?

The old West, but I'd put a spin on it—I'd wear six-inch disco platform shoes along with my cowboy hat, holster, and spurs. And I'd be known as "Big Eric."

If you could describe the thing done by someone at work that drives you the craziest, what would you say?

There's a person at this office who I hear sniff, like, twice a day. I could kill.

If you had to describe your worst experience with blood, what would you say?

When it was coming out of my thumb after I cut it with the lid of a tuna can. I had to hold the thumb over the toilet bowl for five minutes! And I'm saying, "You can stop bleeding any time now." Actually, it was kind of interesting. Who knew a thumb could hold so much blood?

If you could see inside of any single athlete's locker, whose would it be?

Michael Jordan's, because then I'd take his wallet.

If you had to name the single most erotic part of the human body, what would it be?

The ridge separating the two nostrils. Tickle that thing and you're in serious bidness.

If you could rid the earth of one thing, what would it be?

Stocking stuffer books.

11/6/96

A Very Nixon Holiday

This time of year always reminds me of my very special Thanksgiving of 1977.

I had woken early that Thanksgiving morning to prepare dinner for my entire family of seven. Although only 22 years old, and never having cooked anything in my life, I told my folks, "I want to do this for you. I'll make everything, from the turkey to the stuffing to the sweet potatoes to the squash. I'll bake a pumpkin pie, too."

My folks were a little surprised, as I had never shown any aptitude for cooking or, for that matter, helping out under any circumstances. But they acquiesced, thinking that perhaps this project would pull me out of my doldrums.

I hadn't been right since Richard Nixon's resignation three years earlier. I had put up a fence around myself no one could scale.

It wasn't so much Nixon I was thinking about as his daughter, Tricia, on whom I had a gigantic

> It wasn't so much Nixon I was thinking about as his daughter, Tricia, on whom I had a gigantic crush. She consumed my every waking minute.

crush. She consumed my every waking minute. When I was sitting in a classroom, for example, I'd pretend to be listening to the instructor. But what I was really thinking was "Tricia Nixon. Tri-i-i-icia Nixon. Tricia *Broder*." I envisioned her nuzzling me with her pert nose and drew pictures of it, her nose, in my notebook.

I knew she was married. So what? I harbored hopes of her husband croaking or getting caught boinking some babe, and then I'd move in like a spider. What a fool I was. What kind of chance did I have, some wiener dog out of Cleveland with no immediate prospects and a half-assed job as a shipper/receiver in a bookstore? Oh, I could just see Tricia telling Nixon, "Pop, I found this wonderful guy in Cleveland who works in a bookstore. He only makes $112 a week, but he's smart as a whip."

Nixon would say, "How did you meet him, Kitten?"

"He wrote me a sincere letter saying he loved me and that he wanted me to nuzzle him."

Nixon would shake his head. "I don't like it. I don't like it one bit."

Who could blame him? In my job all I did was check shipments against invoices when books came in and pack up books to send out. I was a good tape man and always remembered to pack the books spine out, but this wasn't like being a rising young lawyer or a state senator. And every night I went out and drank copious amounts of beer. If I were Richard Nixon I'd think, "This boy just doesn't seem to have it on the ball. I'd just as soon Kitten remain married to Ed [Edward Cox] if this is the alternative."

With Nixon in the White House, I had a chance. He'd be too busy to worry about any possible romance between Tricia and me. With Nixon out of the White House, I didn't have a prayer.

So I went into a three-year-long funk. During this period my mom would say, "Eric! Eric!" and I wouldn't respond, or I'd say, "I'm busy, Ma," which isn't too convincing when you're lying on a sofa staring straight up at the ceiling. But I was deep in thought.

Before the resignation, I fantasized about moving into the White House when Tricia and I got together. Not only would Tricia and I be lovebirds, but I could insinuate myself into her father's good graces and become a force in Washington myself. Although a Democrat, I was willing to give a little and become a Republican, if that meant I could hang in the Oval Office and have a real say in domestic and foreign policy. If that wasn't possible I was perfectly willing to work as a White House shipper/receiver, if that's what Dad (Nixon) wanted. I was easy.

Now, with Nixon's resignation, that whole idea was shot. What do you do when your dreams are shattered? I thought I could find some kind of peace, some kind of redemption, in cooking this Thanksgiving dinner for my family.

But when I woke up that day and looked at the turkey and all the other stuff, I didn't have a clue as to what to do with it. My mom ended up making everything. It was really good, too. And I sort of forgot about Tricia Nixon.

11/27/96

Obituaries

I'm like most people. I want a nice obit when I die. Page three is okay, but with a picture on the front page, above the fold, below the head "Legend Dies at 79."

CLEVELAND (From wire reports)—Eric Broder, legendary Cleveland writer and Nobel Prize winner, died at his home today of a heart attack while watching a rerun of *The Dick Van Dyke Show*. Death came instantly and painlessly for the beloved figure, said his wife, Brandy LaFlame, who was with him in the family room at the time of his death. Broder was 79.

Broder, winner of six Pulitzer Prizes for his humor writing as well as the Nobel Prize (in 2006), wrote until his death for first the *Cleveland Edition*, then the *Cleveland Free Times*, the alternative weekly that became a titan in the newspaper world, dwarfing in nationwide circulation competitors such as *The New York Times*, *The Christian Science Monitor*, and *The Wall Street Journal*, due mainly to Broder's behind-the-scenes maneuvering in marketing and promotions. Broder became a millionaire several times over thanks to his involvement with the *Free Times*.

Eric Broder, legendary Cleveland writer and Nobel Prize winner, died at his home today of a heart attack while watching a rerun of The Dick Van Dyke Show.

Broder's real fortune came, however, with his humor column, "The Great Indoors," the groundbreaking and phenomenally popular weekly feature syndicated worldwide to more than 6,500 publications. "The Great Indoors," a series of personal essays, touched a universal chord among its readers, as Broder mixed humor and pathos in what many considered to be the greatest writing of all time, better than Shakespeare even.

Broder won his first Pulitzer Prize in 2001, with the Pulitzer committee's comment that Broder's writing "might be the greatest of all times, anybody who doesn't like it has to be crazy." By the time of his sixth Pulitzer (in 2029) the Pulitzer committee stated, "We should have given it to him every year but we felt sorry for the other writers, who try hard, after all, but can't write as good as in 'The Great Indoors,' which is the greatest thing of all time, in our opinions."

"The Great Indoors" was made into a film starring Kevin Costner in 2002, becoming the highest-grossing movie in Hollywood history. In his acceptance speech for winning the Academy Award for best actor in that film, Costner remarked that "Without the advantage of a fabulous story and fantastic characterization—which is what 'The Great Indoors' and Eric Broder are all about—I wouldn't have won this award. So really this award is Eric's, who I know personally and admire above all others." Broder did win a special Oscar later that night, for "Greatness of Theme from an Original Source."

Broder published several books during his lifetime, all reaching the bestseller list. Among his better known titles are *The Great Indoors*, *Return to The Great Indoors*, *More Return to The Great Indoors*, and *The Best of The Great Indoors (vols. 1–8)*.

In his Nobel speech, Broder made his famous conciliatory gesture toward his early critics: "But you know all those people who wrote nasty letters to the editor about me to the *Edition* and *Free Times* criticizing my work, saying they didn't want to read about me going to the bathroom or about my cat? I forgive them, because they know not what they did." Broder was interrupted at this point in the speech by a 15-minute standing ovation, the audience transported by his generosity of spirit.

Broder lived in Cleveland his entire life, refusing to move to New York or Los Angeles, though both cities made numerous attempts to lure him. Regarding his loyalty to Cleveland, Broder once made the touching statement, "I wouldn't move out of Cleveland to some crappy p---hole filled with a bunch of weirdos. And you can take that to the bank."

Broder is survived by his wife and his four children, Eric Jr., Erica, Ericina, and Ericareeno.

Then again, things might not go so well.

From *The Plain Dealer*, May 11, 2003—Eric Broder, 48, who wrote the humor column "The Great Outdoors" for the *Cleveland Free Times* until his dismissal in 2000, was found dead in his one-bedroom apartment last night. Cause of death was undetermined. Broder had been unemployed since leaving the *Free Times*, and had caused various disturbances at local malls during the past years. The shirtless, shouting Broder was a familiar figure to several suburban police forces.

Broder is survived by a cat, Jinx, and a parakeet, Mr. Blabby.